SCOUT HANDBOOK

EIGHTH EDITION • SECOND PRINTING

Eighth Edition • Second Printing

750,000 February 1973

Total Printing Since 1910—27,010,000

This book, based on the experience of the
Boy Scouts of America in the United States
since its founding in 1910, was developed
under the auspices of
Norton Clapp, President
Alden G. Barber, Chief Scout Executive

Written by
Frederick L. Hines

Copyright 1972
BOY SCOUTS OF AMERICA
North Brunswick, New Jersey
Library of Congress Catalog Card Number: 11-15620
ISBN 0-8395-6500-3
No. 6500   Printed in the United States of America

CONTENTS

WHAT IS SCOUTING?

YOU IN SCOUTING

Your tent glows for a moment in a flash of lightning. You hear the patter of rain and the far-off rumble of thunder. The fury of the storm is over. It was rough for awhile, but your tent is still up. Your blankets are dry. You sleep.

You wake up to a bright sun warming your tent. The smell of breakfast drifts in. You look out the front and quickly wake your buddy to see a deer drinking at the pond.

The others in your patrol are already up. They are by the fire kidding the cooks. These are your best friends. You want to do things with them. And you do, because they are in your Scout patrol.

Other groups like yours are getting ready for breakfast, too. These are the other patrols in your Scout troop. They are all camping together at this overnight camp. Yet each patrol is separate. Each is part of the troop, but each does many things on its own.

Over there watching things is your Scoutmaster. He's a great guy. He gives hours of his time to you and the troop. And do you know why? Mostly because he knows Scouting is important to his city and nation. Besides, he is interested in boys.

You'll do lots of things on camping trips. But camping is only one part of Scouting. Another is learning and trying new things back in town. There are over 100 different merit badge subjects, each with a man who will help you. You will find many men who will work with you in Scouting.

Your homemade Geiger counter is slowly clicking. As you move across the rug in the scientist's office the counter starts clicking like mad. You found it! Found what? Why, the radioactive material your counselor hid. When you found it, you passed one of the tests for Atomic Energy merit badge.

Another Scout from your troop is showing an oceanographer the results of his plankton net experiment. He knew quite a bit about the sea before this meeting. He'll know a lot more when he leaves.

Want to meet an FBI agent? How about the fingerprint expert on your police force? You can when earning your Fingerprinting merit badge.

FINGERPRINT PATTERN

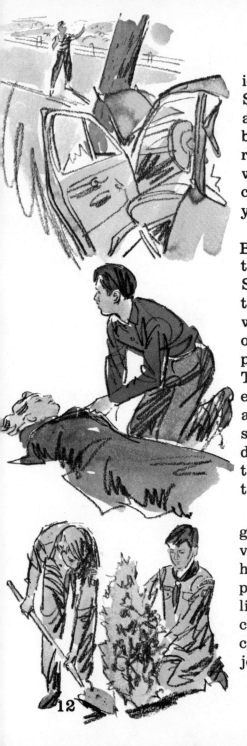

Scouting has a set of ideals to guide you. The Scout Oath or Promise and the Scout Law are based on the best experience of the ages. They will help you find success and happiness in your life.

The Scout motto is Be Prepared. Many of the things you learn in Scouting will help you to be prepared. They will help you to help others. A Scout is expected to do a Good Turn for somebody every day. This can be as simple as picking up something a person has dropped or as important as giving first aid to someone who is hurt.

Scouts often work together in helpful service to their neighborhood or town. They plant trees; clean up litter; and collect paper, cans, and bottles for recycling. They do vital jobs in time of disaster.

The badges of Scouting stand for many different things. Some tell the job you hold in your patrol or troop. Others say you have achieved skills. Still others tell of the activities you have been in. And others identify your troop, patrol, and council.

BADGES OF OFFICER

ADVANCEMENT

ACTIVITIES

IDENTIFICATION

13

Your uniform says you are a member of the largest boys' organization in the free world. You know you are a Scout whether you are in uniform or not, but when you wear it, others know it, too. They know what you are and what you and the uniform stand for. This can be very important when the time comes for you to serve in an emergency. Your uniform tells people you can be trusted to help where needed.

Your uniform is neat, yet tough. It will give good service during the years you are a Scout.

There are several combinations of parts of the uniform. Each troop decides which official combination its members will wear. You will wear the uniform chosen by your troop.

And fun — man, Scouting is a ball! You have fun at meetings, in games, outdoors, in advancement, and when helping others.

And best of all, Scouting and this fun is for you — no matter where you live. You can live in the big city, a small town, or in the country. It doesn't matter. You can get in on the fun of Scouting.

You probably already get *Boys' Life* magazine because in most troops it's part of the troop dues plan. So what do you get? Take a look.

BOYS' LIFE

Navaho Boy

BOY SCOUT

AN ANCI...

BASIC TOOLS

Think and Grin

Wolf Pup of the Tundra By THEODORE TAYLOR
Illustrated by WALTER RICHARDS

...yone could help me train Netsig, it would be the wise old Eski...

All of this in one magazine that keeps you waiting for the mailman each month of the year.

YOUR PATROL

Your patrol is a gang of good friends. It's fun being with them and doing the things they do. You work as a team to get things done. Your patrol has a name and an emblem that stands for that name. You wear the patrol emblem on your uniform and it is on your patrol flag. Most patrols have a patrol call. When your patrol wins a contest you shout out your call to let the troop know who you are.

Other patrols in the troop have their own names, emblems, and calls. The guys in these patrols are as proud of theirs as you are of yours. This is good because, when all patrols have spirit and do lots of things, you have a good troop.

19

Your patrol meets often. Here you learn and practice new skills. You plan activities and get ready for troop meetings. There are some patrols that only meet at troop meetings. But many others meet at the home of one of the Scouts in the patrol.

A patrol with a place of its own can fix it up. The corner of a garage or basement works fine. It becomes your own clubhouse. You make your own furniture and decorate it.

Even if you don't have your own patrol meeting place, you will have a corner of your own at the troop meeting. You can make your own decorations for this. You'll probably have to put them up before the meeting and take them down afterward.

You elect your own patrol leader by secret vote. The Scout you choose leads your patrol. He represents all of the members of the patrol in troop planning. Your Scoutmaster trains patrol leaders, so they will know how to be good leaders.

Patrols also have assistant patrol leaders picked by the patrol leader. The assistant's main job is to help his patrol leader.

There are many things that need doing in a patrol. On some you all pitch in and work as a team. On others the patrol leader names someone to handle the job. He might pick you to lead a game at a patrol meeting. You do the job at the meeting. Then your assignment is over — until the patrol leader gives you another job.

Patrols do lots of things outdoors. They go hiking and camping. These hikes and camps must be approved by your Scoutmaster ahead of time.

Some patrols go overnight camping by themselves. Your patrol can, too, if you have a patrol leader your Scoutmaster will approve as an overnight camping leader. If your patrol leader doesn't qualify, your patrol can still camp on its own. One of the dads can go along, or your patrol leader might ask for help from the troop leadership corps.

In your patrol you learn things to help you earn skill awards. Your patrol leader and other patrol members will help you. Sometimes you'll all learn together from a leadership corps Scout. You practice these skills in meetings, on hikes, and in camp.

Skill awards and merit badges are used to earn progress awards leading to the Eagle Award. For each progress award, you must also be active in your troop and patrol and show good Scouting spirit. For some you must also give leadership and carry out service to others.

Skill award tests may be passed to your patrol leader or some other leader he names.

YOUR TROOP

Your troop is made up of patrols. It has a regular indoor meeting place, but it often meets outside. Most troops meet every week. Some meet less often, but have patrol meetings in between.

Troop meetings have games, contests, simple ceremonies, and lots of fun. You'll probably learn a new Scouting skill at each meeting.

There are other kinds of troop meetings, too. These don't happen at the regular meeting place on the regular night. Maybe some night the troop will go to a fire station and you can start earning the Firemanship merit badge. Another time it might be swim fun at a local pool. The troop could go to a ball game or to city hall to see your government in action.

One Saturday your troop might visit a factory, a power plant, a museum, or zoo.

Troops don't just meet. Troops do things — exciting things you probably never thought of as Scouting.

Sports? You bet. In the spring and summer you'll play ball before the meeting starts. At other times of the year there will be basketball and volleyball. There's a Sports merit badge and lots of special-type sport badges like Archery, Rifle and Shotgun Shooting, Swimming, Canoeing, Rowing, Skiing, Water Skiing, Motorboating, Fishing, and Small-Boat Sailing.

Who decides what your troop is going to do? Who plans and carries out these things? Your patrol leader and all the other patrol leaders in the troop make up the troop leaders' council. This group, with help from the Scoutmaster, makes troop plans. Thus, through your own patrol leader you have a say in what the troop does.

Your senior patrol leader is a Scout elected by all the Scouts in the troop. He sees that things happen in troop meetings and activities. He is the chairman of the troop leaders' council. The senior patrol leader often goes to meetings of the troop committee to tell about troop plans. He may pick another Scout to be his assistant if he needs help.

A troop may also have junior assistant Scoutmasters. These Scouts are at least 16 years old and have real leadership ability. They are appointed by the Scoutmaster and work closely with him.

Your senior patrol leader may appoint Scouts to other troop jobs if the troop leaders' council thinks they are needed:

A scribe to keep troop records.
A quartermaster to supervise and maintain troop equipment.

A librarian responsible for the troop library.
A bugler to sound calls on ceremonies and outdoor activities.
Den chiefs to help Cub Scout dens.

If the troop doesn't have a leadership corps, the senior patrol leader may also appoint instructors to help teach skills.

The leadership corps is a group organized in some troops to help younger troop members and patrol leaders when asked. To have a leadership corps the troop must have at least three Scouts who are 14 or 15 years of age, are First Class or above, and show that they have what it takes to be leaders. Members may wear the green uniform and red beret regardless of the troop's uniform option choice.

Besides helping in the troop, the leadership corps may do special things of its own.

YOUR DISTRICT AND COUNCIL

Geographic areas are named districts in Scouting. A district could be one or more neighborhoods in a large city or several counties out in the country. Several districts make up a council. A council has a service center where your Scoutmaster can get books, badges, and other kinds of help. Your council has a staff of people who work full time helping volunteer Scouters make Scouting successful.

There are many other troops in your district and council. By joining together they can do things that none could do alone.

A camporee is a big weekend event where many troops camp together. Each troop shows off its camping ability. There are often contests between patrols of different troops.

Some councils also put on big shows called Scoutoramas, expositions, or circuses. Here troops show off their skills for the general public to see.

The biggest and best council activity each year is summer camp. Here you and the others in your patrol and troop camp together for a week or more. Water activities are big in most Scout camps.

In camp you have hours instead of minutes to learn Scouting skills. You have the equipment you need to do them. Best of all you learn from fellows who really know their stuff.

Did you say, "What is Scouting?" You've had a small peek at some of it. There's lots more. The way to find out is to jump in with both feet. Skim through the pages of this book. Decide what you want to do and start doing it.

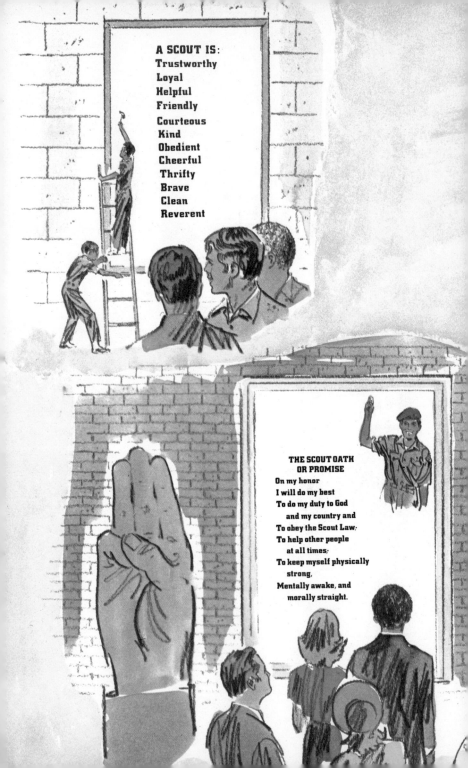

TO BE A SCOUT

You learned earlier the things you had to do to become a Scout (inside front cover). This chapter will help you to do them.

THE OUTDOOR CODE

As an American,
I will do my best to —
Be clean in my outdoor manners,
Be careful with fire,
Be considerate in the outdoors, and
Be conservation-minded.

THE SCOUT OATH OR PROMISE

On My Honor.—The signers of the Declaration of Independence pledged to each other "our lives, our fortunes, and our sacred honor." That puts honor in pretty high company, doesn't it? Honor is hard to describe. It is of the heart and mind of a person—something not easily seen. It is called integrity. A Scout once said that honor was the thing that made you act the same when no one was watching as you did when you knew you were being watched. In giving the Scout Oath you promise to act according to your own honor—not that of someone else.

I Will Do My Best.—These words change the Promise from an almost impossible job into something you can handle. It's still not easy, but since you are the only one who knows what your best is, only you can say whether you really do it. Are you doing your best? If not, then you are only mouthing words with no meaning.

To Do My Duty to God and My Country.—It's hard to describe duty to God for any one person. This duty is based on the person's own religious teachings. Duty to God is different for people of different faiths. However, for all people, it means living according to the teachings of their religion.

You do your duty to your country by being a good citizen, living by the laws and customs of our nation, and working to solve our country's problems. It will help if you learn about the men and events that have made America great. Their lives will inspire you to serve your nation as they did.

To Obey the Scout Law.—The twelve points of the Scout Law are the rules of the game—the game of Scouting and the game of life. These points are important directional signals for you—signals that can guide you when it's hard to decide what to do.

To Help Other People at All Times.—The help you give to someone is important to that person. But it is even more important to you. You become a better person when you help others.

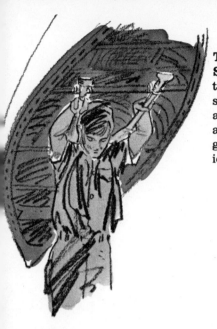

To Keep Myself Physically Strong.—Big muscles aren't the only sign of physical strength. A healthy body, able to stand up to disease, and carry on when the going gets tough is the kind of physical strength you need.

Mentally Awake.—Words describing this are "sharp," "alert," and "bright." When you are mentally awake you see, hear, smell, and even feel things that are missed by others. Did you ever notice that some days in school you remembered things a lot better than others? That's because you were mentally awake on those days. You should be that way every day.

Morally Straight.—You live and act and speak in ways that mark you as a boy who will grow up to be a man of good character. You are honest, clean in speech and actions, thoughtful of the rights of others, and faithful to your religious beliefs.

THE SCOUT LAW

A SCOUT IS:
Trustworthy
Loyal
Helpful
Friendly
Courteous
Kind
Obedient
Cheerful
Thrifty
Brave
Clean
Reverent

Trustworthy

A Scout tells the truth. He keeps his promises. Honesty is part of his code of conduct. People can depend on him.

For years Scouts have given the Scout sign and said, "Scout's honor." They knew then that what they said would be believed. This is great, but isn't it even better to have such a good reputation that you are believed without needing to say, "Scout's honor"?

Then people will say things like this:

"If he says so, it must be true."

"He'll be here. He said he would."

"Him cheat? He wouldn't even think of it."

"You can really count on him."

Think of the difference between that and:

"Don't listen to him. You can't believe him."

"Maybe he took it. He's stolen before."

"You'd better do it yourself. You can't count on him to do it."

Your reputation for being trustworthy will follow you through life, and is important to your future happiness. It will be important to your job, to borrowing money, to charging in stores, and even to the kind of people who will be your friends.

Loyal

A Scout is true to his family, Scout leaders, friends, school, and nation.

Being loyal is doing your best for all of these. It is being true to them —to support rather than knock down. This isn't always easy. There are times when you can't be loyal to two different people. Suppose your Scoutmaster asks you to do something at the same time your dad needs help from you at home. You can't be loyal to both. This problem is easy, because your Scoutmaster knows your family comes first.

But what if some friends take your sister's bike. They strip it and sell the parts. Where does your loyalty lie? This may be hard to decide. But if a Scout is trustworthy, the answer is clear.

Your decisions usually aren't that tough, but they are important because your answers will decide the kind of a person you really are.

When you get older, you'll find other places where loyalties conflict. It could be between your country and your religion. Maybe even between your country and other beliefs. Just remember to look at both sides. Listen carefully to the arguments and then do what you believe to be right. Then you will be loyal to yourself.

Helpful

A Scout is concerned about other people. He does things willingly for others without pay or reward.

The Scout slogan, Do a Good Turn Daily, spells out the Scout spirit of being helpful. The motto, Be Prepared, takes the idea a step farther. To be really helpful, you must know how. With first aid knowledge, you can help the injured. If you can cook, you can help when your mother is away. Know your town, and you can help strangers. Prepare yourself to be helpful. Then look for ways to help.

Scouts may work for pay, but they don't take money for being helpful. Think about the Scout in the

London fog described in "The Early Years" chapter. If he had taken pay for helping Mr. Boyce, Scouting might be different in the United States today.

Friendly

A Scout is a friend to all. He is a brother to other Scouts. He seeks to understand others. He respects those with ideas and customs other than his own.

The theme of the 1967 World Jamboree of Scouting was "For Friendship." Boys from all countries of the world with Scouting camped together for over a week. Here they lived up to the jamboree theme and to the 4th point of the Scout Law. Among the thousands of boys from all over the world were differences in race, religion, customs, age, and even political beliefs. Yet they all camped in friendship. There were no unfriendly incidents.

Friendliness is thinking about the other person. It is accepting him as he is, not as you think he should be. You know that each person is an individual with ideas and ways that are his own. To be a real friend you respect the other person's differences. Be interested in the other person. A friendless person is usually interested only in himself.

Courteous

A Scout is polite to everyone regardless of age or position. He knows good manners make it easier for people to get along together.

Courtesy is acting with respect for the feelings of others. It is doing thoughtful little things that make it easier for others. It is using words like "thanks," "please," "pardon me," "sorry," and "sir."

Think about how you react to someone who is rude to you. This is the same way they will feel about you if you are discourteous.

Courtesy means using good manners. These don't cost anything to learn and use yet they are a valuable asset to the person who uses them. They mark you as a person who cares. You never lower yourself when you are polite.

Start at home. Be courteous in your relations with all members of your family. Use good manners. The things you do at home will carry over into your public actions.

Kind

A Scout understands there is strength in being gentle. He treats

others as he wants to be treated. He does not hurt or kill harmless things without reason.

People do things for a bully because they are afraid of him. They will keep doing them only as long as the bully can enforce that fear. You do things for a person who is gentle because you want to. You will keep doing them even after he is gone.

"He treats others as he wants to be treated." Does this sound familiar? Maybe not the exact words, but the idea? It should, because this idea is basic to other points of the Scout Law. You find it in helpful, friendly, courteous, cheerful, and reverent. The way you treat others is part of each of these.

Kindness is more than just the way you treat others, though. A big part has to do with treatment of birds and animals. They are living creatures that can feel hunger and pain. Cruelty to people is bad, but they can at least fight back. Cruelty to helpless animals is inexcusable, since they can't defend themselves.

Live with nature and you'll learn to respect and love animals. Kindness to them will help you to know them better. With kindness comes trust and understanding.

Obedient

A Scout follows the rules of his family, school, and troop. He obeys the laws of his community and country. If he thinks these rules and laws are unfair, he tries to have them changed in an orderly manner rather than disobey them.

Rules and laws are the backbone of a civilized society. Obedience to them is vital or they become meaningless. Failure to obey causes death and destruction. Look at the highway accident rate. Many, many accidents are caused by disobedience of the law. Innocent people are killed and injured.

If a rule or law is bad, it should be changed. Laws made by man can be changed by man. Don't break laws you don't like. Disobedience to some leads to a breakdown of all.

Unfortunately, there are some who live outside the law. Thus, we need law enforcement to protect those who live within the law. Some don't like this, but if laws are to protect our lives and property, they must be enforced.

If your parents have rules for you to follow, you are lucky. It means they love and care for you. They make rules to protect you until the time when you can make your own decisions based on experience.

Cheerful

A Scout looks for the bright side of things. He cheerfully does tasks that come his way. He tries to make others happy.

We like to be with people who do things with a smile. They get things done because they think they can. The way they act rubs off on others.

Compare them with the grouches in the world who can spoil any activity. You know the kind. Nothing is right. "It's no fun." "The leaders don't know what they're doing." "The food is lousy." And on and on.

It's easy to be cheerful when things are great. The real test comes when things get rough. Can you smile when hiking in the pouring rain? How about the time you had to take care of your brother instead of going to a ball game with the gang? Everyone is faced with tasks he doesn't like. A cheerful spirit and a smile will make the job easier. It's a cinch that griping and complaining won't help.

Thrifty

A Scout works to pay his way and to help others. He saves for unforeseen needs. He protects and conserves natural resources. He carefully uses time and property.

There are many different kinds of work. There are simple jobs you do at home without thought of pay, and jobs outside the home like a paper route, yard care, door-to-door selling, and baby-sitting. You get paid for these and so become a little independent. With the money you get, you can decide some of the things you will do and buy. If the money you earn is used to help support your family, you are doing much more than working to be independent. It's a good idea to save a little, too. Then there will be money to buy bigger things later.

Thrift is more than working, wise spending, and saving. It is also taking care of things you already have. You grease and oil your bike so the parts wear longer. You use your clothing so it lasts. You paint things to prevent rust and rot. You protect things from the weather. A little care can save money—money you can use for other things.

Time is important, too. You know how boring it is to have nothing to do. So don't waste time just sitting around. Many a top athlete became expert because he used his spare time to practice. Lots of people have helped to educate themselves by reading in their spare time.

Thrift is also concern for and doing something about our natural resources. Read the explanation of the Outdoor Code and the Conservation skill award for an understanding of this.

Brave

A Scout can face danger even if he is afraid. He has the courage to stand for what he thinks is right even if others laugh at or threaten him.

Why can you face danger even if you are afraid? Because, as a Scout, you are prepared for danger. You have learned what to do in many dangerous situations. And you know that most dangers aren't as bad as they seem at the time. You can laugh at many of your fears later.

However, only a fool is never afraid. You face danger in spite of your fear because of your confidence in your ability to take care of yourself and others.

One of the real dangers you will face is that of giving in when others laugh at the things you stand for. Those who do give in lose their sense of values. To be popular they join in destroying property or start to smoke or use alcohol or drugs. All because they don't have the courage to say "No."

The greatest kind of bravery is to do what is right when others call you a coward or chicken for doing it.

Clean

A Scout keeps his body and mind fit and clean. He goes around with those who believe in living by these same ideals. He helps keep his home and community clean.

Your body and clothes get dirty in hard work or play. You can be proud of this kind of dirt. Soap and water will clean it off when the job or game is over.

In America today, personal cleanliness is an important part of being accepted by your fellow man. The kind of clothing you wear and the cut of your hair are not as important as their cleanliness.

Another kind of dirt shows up when a person swears, tells dirty stories, or travels around with those who do. You know this is wrong because you usually try to hide it from people you respect.

It's hard to get rid of this kind of dirt. It doesn't wash off.

The easiest way to be clean and stay clean is to not get dirty in the first place. This is true of both the dirt you can see and the other kind that can get into your heart and mind and shows up in the way you talk and act.

You will be judged in part by the friends you have. It has been said that if you travel with thieves, you will be considered a thief. "Unfair," you say? Maybe so. But we tend to make friends with people who are like ourselves.

You should also help with the cleanliness of your home. There are two ways you can do this: Don't mess it up and clean up the messes. It isn't fair to expect your mother to clean up after you.

The same thing goes for your town and countryside. Do your share in keeping a clean America.

Reverent

A Scout is reverent toward God. He is faithful in his religious duties. He respects the beliefs of others.

Reverence toward God is a whole lot more than going to church. It is shown in the way you act every day. You take care of your body. You live by the moral code and worship God in the way taught by your own religion.

There are many different religious beliefs in the world. Some are like your own. Others are very different. The men who founded the United States of America believed in the right of all men to worship God in their own way. This is a great heritage they have given us. Scouts can strengthen it by their actions.

A great teaching of most religions is known by us as "the golden rule." It says that you should treat others the same way you would want them to treat you. This is so simple that you can use this rule to easily measure yourself in your daily actions.

People who worship God in a way different from you can be very religious. Their ways mean a great deal to them. To laugh at or show disrespect for the beliefs of others is to make a mockery of all religions, including your own.

THE SCOUT MOTTO

You are prepared if you know what to do in an emergency. The skill award and merit badge programs will help you to be prepared, but you may be faced with emergencies that call for even more than you learned in skill awards and merit badges. Here are a few of these:

Building on Fire.—GET THE PEOPLE OUT. Yell, hammer on the door, ring the doorbell. Have someone call the fire department. Or, do it yourself after rousing the people in the building.

Person on Fire.—If a person's clothing is on fire, lay him flat on the ground. Roll him to smother the flames. At the same time, beat at the flames with your hands, protected by cloth. Cover him with a blanket, rug, coat, or similar piece of cloth if you have it. This cuts off the air supply and kills the flames. Give first aid for burns after the fire is out.

Electric Wire Contact in Home.—If someone is in contact with a live wire, pull the plug or shut off the power at the main switch. Don't touch the wire or the victim until the wire is dead. If the wire is not on a plug or you don't know where the main switch is, pull the live wire from the victim with a DRY cloth or DRY stick. Give rescue breathing, if needed. Get help.

53

Electric Accident Outdoors.— If a person is touching a powerline, don't try the rescue yourself. It is very dangerous. Call the electric company, police, or fire department for help.

Ice Rescue. — If someone has broken through ice, reach him while still in contact with solid ice or land. Throw a line, slide a ladder or board out to him, or make a human chain.

There are many other emergencies you might face. The best way to be prepared for them is to think about what you might do before they happen. You go into a crowded auditorium, for example. Before the program starts, think about exactly what you would do if a fire broke out. Then you'd be prepared if it happened. If you have a plan, you are prepared.

THE SCOUT SLOGAN
Do a Good Turn Daily

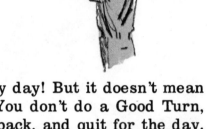

Daily means every day! But it doesn't mean just one each day. You don't do a Good Turn, pat yourself on the back, and quit for the day. You should always be looking for ways to help others.

The Good Turn is something special. It isn't something others expect you to do. Don't call it a Good Turn when you do a job that your parents have asked you to do at home. But, when you say "Hey, Mom, let me sweep the floor," it's a Good Turn, unless it happens to be one of your regular home jobs.

There are big Good Turns like working in an emergency such as a tornado or flood. There are little Good Turns like helping someone find an address. It's not the size of the Good Turn that counts. It's getting in the habit of helping others. It's looking for chances to be helpful.

The best part of the Good Turn is that it helps you, too. You feel better because you helped. Each time you do a Good Turn you become a little more of a man.

THE SCOUT BADGE

Your Scout badge signifies membership in a great national organization. It says you have joined millions of other members who are living by the ideals of Scouting. All of them wear the badges of Scouting.

Notice the badge at the bottom and compare it with your Scout badge. The similarity of shape is no accident. The bottom badge is the World Badge of Scouting. All Scouting badges in countries around the world, use the basic shape of the World Badge. So, your Scout badge says you have also joined a worldwide brotherhood.

WEARING BADGES

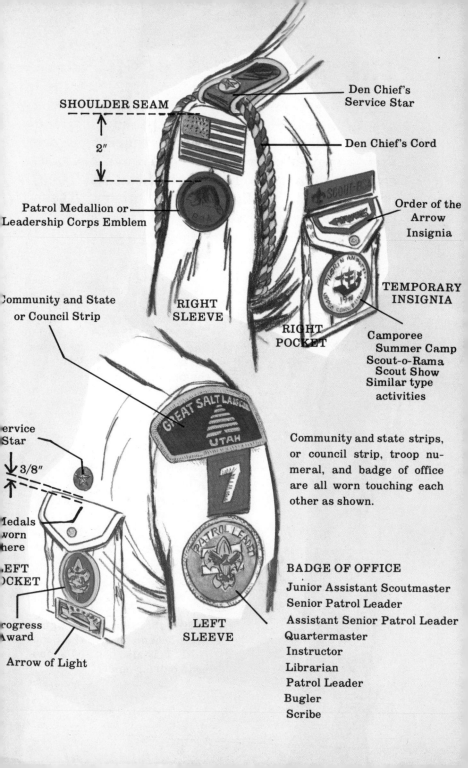

SHOULDER SEAM

2"

Den Chief's
Service Star

Den Chief's Cord

Patrol Medallion or
Leadership Corps Emblem

Order of the
Arrow
Insignia

TEMPORARY
INSIGNIA

Community and State
or Council Strip

RIGHT
SLEEVE

RIGHT
POCKET

Camporee
Summer Camp
Scout-o-Rama
Scout Show
Similar type
activities

Service
Star

3/8"

Community and state strips,
or council strip, troop nu-
meral, and badge of office
are all worn touching each
other as shown.

Medals
worn
here

LEFT
POCKET

BADGE OF OFFICE

Junior Assistant Scoutmaster
Senior Patrol Leader
Assistant Senior Patrol Leader
Quartermaster
Instructor
Librarian
Patrol Leader
Bugler
Scribe

Progress
Award

Arrow of Light

LEFT
SLEEVE

THE SIGNS OF A SCOUT

There are many ways for you to show you are a Scout. The sign, salute, handclasp, and uniform all do this. Even more important are things that are harder to see. Things like honesty, cleanliness, courtesy, kindness, and being prepared and willing to help others. These things mark you as a Scout.

The Scout Sign.—The three fingers stand for the three parts of the Scout Oath. The thumb and little finger represent the ties of friendship in Scouting.

Giving the Sign.—The sign is given when you give the Scout Oath. It is also used by a leader to call for quiet.

The Scout Salute.—The fingers are in the same position as in the Scout sign. The salute is used to show respect and courtesy. You use it to show respect for the flag of the United States of America.

The Scout Handclasp.—It is made like a right handshake of greeting except Scouts use the left hand. The little finger is not separated from the other fingers. The handclasp for Scouts in the United States is the same as for Scouting in all the other countries of the world.

World Scouting.—The Boy Scouts of America is a member of an organization which represents Scouting around the world. A part of your registration fee goes to support the Boy Scout World Bureau office in Switzerland. This office helps develop and coordinate International Scouting. The Bureau also arranges World Jamborees.

61

THE OUTDOOR CODE

THE OUTDOOR CODE

As an American,
I will do my best to —
Be clean in my outdoor manners,
Be careful with fire,
Be considerate in the outdoors,
and
Be conservation-minded.

You will spend many days and nights enjoying the outdoors as you hike and camp in the wonderland that is America. As a Scout, you have a greater responsibility to the outdoors than most people because you will be spending more time there than most. Failure to live up to the Outdoor Code, aside from the harm that would be done, could cause you and Scouts everywhere to lose the right to use the outdoors.

What does the Outdoor Code mean to you?

Be Clean in My Outdoor Manners

Treat the outdoors as a heritage to be improved for our greater enjoyment. Keep your trash and garbage out of America's waters, fields, woods, and roadways.

Trash and Garbage.—Put it in a trash can, if there is one near your camp. If not, burn what will burn. Bring the rest home with you. Never bury garbage. When hiking, put papers like candy wrappers in your pocket and then in a wastebasket at home.

Litter Attracts Litter.—Clean up littered yards, vacant lots, streets, and campsites even if you didn't cause the litter. Clean places stay clean longer. Dirty ones quickly get dirtier.

Be Careful with Fire

Prevent wildfire. Build all fires in safe places. Be sure they are out before leaving. See the material on fire building in the Cooking skill award chapter.

Never Leave an Unattended Fire.—Even in the safest place outdoors, a gust of wind can send sparks beyond your area of protection.

Cold Out.—When leaving, be sure your fire is cold out. Use lots of water. Stir soaked ashes with a stick. Sprinkle on more water. Then cautiously test with your bare hand.

Be Considerate in the Outdoors

Treat all property with respect. The use of the outdoors is a privilege you can lose by abuse.

You Are a Guest.—Wherever you hike or camp you are the guest of a landowner. All land is owned by either a private person or all citizens through their government. Act like a guest who wants to be invited back.

Deadwood.—Don't cut live trees for fires or camp making. Deadwood is better.

Prevent Erosion.—Don't dig unless you must. If you do dig, save the sod, if there is any. Put it back in place before leaving.

Hacking Trees.—Trees often die from disease that gets in through cuts. Their beauty is spoiled by meaningless initials. Don't use your knife or ax on a live tree.

Protect Wildlife.—You are the guest of the birds and animals, too. Help rather than hurt them. Then they'll be there for you to enjoy now and in the future.

Be Conservation–Minded

Learn how to practice good conservation of soil, water, forests, minerals, grassland, and wildlife. Urge others to do the same. Use sportsmanlike methods in all outdoor activities.

What does it really mean to "be conservation-minded"? The following three things are the keys.

Natural Resources.—Wise use of these is vital to your future and that of the world.

Interdependence.—Learn the relationship of all things to one another. Know that harm to one thing can cause changes that do harm to all.

Action.—Don't just sit there. Get out and do something about it.

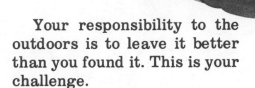

Your responsibility to the outdoors is to leave it better than you found it. This is your challenge.

ADVANCEMENT

There are three different kinds of advancement awards you can earn after becoming a Scout — skill awards, merit badges, and progress awards. The things you do for each award are fun and will be useful to you now and when you grow up.

SKILL AWARDS

Each skill award will help you become good in things that are related. In Cooking, for example, you learn to cook. But you also learn to use woods tools, build a fire, and clean up. The 12 skill awards are Camping, Citizenship, Communications, Community Living, Conservation, Cooking, Environment, Family Living, First Aid, Hiking, Physical Fitness, and Swimming. You can work for more than one at a time.

Learn

To earn a skill award you first learn and practice the things needed to become good at it. Your patrol leader or other boy leaders in the troop will help you learn. You can practice alone or with others. There will often be troop and patrol activities to help you.

Show Your Stuff

When ready, tell your patrol leader. He will test you or send you to another Scout or leader who will do it. You will pass some tests just by doing well in an activity. You might make a good ground bed on an overnight camp — not to pass a test but to get a good night's sleep. Your patrol leader could pass you on this part of the Camping skill award right there.

Get the Badge

When you have done everything for an award, take your record book to your patrol leader. He will sign it. Take it to your Scoutmaster, and he will give you the belt loop you have earned. You don't have to wait for a ceremony.

MERIT BADGES

You learn about hobbies, future jobs, and advanced Scoutcraft as you earn merit badges. There are over 100. Any Scout may earn merit badges. You don't need to have a progress award to be eligible. Requirements are shown in another section of this book.

Pick a Subject

Talk to your Scoutmaster about your interests. Read the requirements of badges you think might interest you. Pick one to earn. Find out from your Scoutmaster who the counselor is for that badge. These counselors are men with special knowledge in their merit badge subjects and are interested in helping boys.

Call the Counselor

Get a signed merit badge application from your Scoutmaster. Phone the merit badge counselor and tell him you want to earn the badge. He may ask you to come and see him so he can tell you what he expects.

Some counselors will do this over the phone. When you know what he expects, start to learn and do the things required. It will help if you can buy or borrow a merit badge pamphlet on the subject. Many public libraries have them.

Show Your Stuff

When you are ready, call the counselor again to make an appointment. When you go to see him, bring along the things you have made to meet the requirements. If they are too big to move, have an adult tell in writing what you have done. The counselor will spend time with you to make sure that you know your stuff and have done the things required.

Most counselors like to meet with Scouts more than once. Some will pass you on your first visit A lot depends on how well prepared you are.

Get the Badge

When the counselor is satisfied, he will sign your application. Give this to your Scoutmaster, and he will get your badge for you.

PROGRESS AWARDS

You get these awards by earning skill awards and merit badges listed for each award. The progress awards are Tenderfoot, Second Class, First Class, Star, Life, and Eagle.

There is more to each progress award than just earning badges. You must also be active in your troop and patrol and satisfy your leaders that you do your best to live up to the ideals of Scouting. You must carry out a personal growth agreement for each award. This agreement is made with your Scoutmaster. For Star, Life, and Eagle you must also take part in service to others and give leadership in your troop.

Progress Review

Check with your Scoutmaster when you have done everything. He will tell you when your progress review will take place. This review is by troop leaders who will talk with you about what you have done. A purpose of your progress review is to make sure that you have done all the things you were supposed to do. Another is to find out what kind of a Scout you are and to try to help you be better.

The troop leaders' council, which may have a committee member sitting in as an adviser, will review you for Tenderfoot, Second Class, and First Class. The troop committee will review you for Star, Life, and Eagle.

Get the Badge

When the progress review members are satisfied, they will sign the application for the award. You should be given your badge at a ceremony at a troop meeting very soon.

An Eagle application must also be approved by your Scout council and the national office of the Boy Scouts of America.

Get the Certificate

Many troops hold courts of honor about four times a year. These are usually parents' night programs that include a ceremony for recognition of Scout advancement. Progress awards and merit badge certificates are presented there.

ACTIVE IN TROOP AND PATROL

A requirement for each progress award says you must actively participate in troop and patrol activities for a period of time. You might wonder why you have to wait when you've done everything else for the award. You aren't really just waiting. The purpose of this requirement is to make sure there is enough time between awards for you to prove yourself.

You have to be active in troop and patrol meetings and activities. It would be easy to do this for a few weeks in a few meetings. But it's the long haul that counts. You must be active in troop and patrol service projects and outdoor activities, plus the meetings.

This is also a time for you to help in your patrol and troop. Some Scouts are so busy earning badges for themselves, they never get around to helping others. And part of being a Scout is helping other Scouts. It's not just doing everything for yourself.

So, you see, the time requirement isn't something to just slow down your progress. It is a test to make sure your advancement means something. Advancement isn't just doing skills. It's growing physically, mentally, and morally.

SCOUT SPIRIT

You show your Scout spirit in the way you act and the things you say. It isn't something you do once in awhile to pass a test. It is living every day according to the Scout Oath and Law.

From the time you become a Scout, you will be expected to show improvement in the way you make Scout spirit a part of all you do. Your leaders don't expect you to be perfect. But they do think you should grow in your understanding of Scout spirit — and the way you live up to these ideals.

This requirement for each progress award will be signed by your Scoutmaster as one of the last things done for earning the award. He won't sign it just because you are an active Scout, but because you have truly shown Scout spirit— have shown it in the things you have done in Scouting — and have shown it in your daily living.

SERVICE TO OTHERS

It has been said that service is the rent we pay for our space on earth. Service is an important part of Scouting. There are many words about service in the Scout Oath, the Law, and the slogan.

"To help other people at all times."

"He willingly involves himself in doing things for others without pay or reward."

"A Scout works to pay his way and to help others."

"Do a Good Turn Daily."

Service in Scouting ranges from the simple Good Turn all the way to big national projects like the safety good turn, conservation, and get out the vote campaigns. For Star and Life you must give 6 hours of service for each award. You can do this on your own or with your patrol or troop. The service must be approved by your Scoutmaster before you start.

Eagle Service Project

The service requirement for Eagle is different. Here you must plan, develop, and give leadership to a service project helpful to your religious institution, school, or community.

What is the difference between the service for Star and Life, and that for Eagle? In the first you can be a follower. For Eagle you must be a leader. It is possible that some of the service you did for Star and Life was in a project planned and led by a Scout working for Eagle.

Original?

Does the project for Eagle have to be original — something you dream up that has never been done before? The answer is "No, but it could be." You may pick an Eagle project that has been done before, but you must accept responsibility

for planning, direction, and even its success. The project must be approved by your Scoutmaster and troop committee before you start.

Size?

How big a project is required? It must be something really needed and of value when finished. It should certainly involve more hours in planning and carrying out than your Star or Life service. A look at a few projects other fellows have done for their Eagle will help you to understand.

- Made trays to fasten to wheelchair for disabled veterans in a VA hospital.

- Collected used books and distributed them to people in town who wanted and needed but couldn't afford them.
- Put a sturdy footbridge across a brook to make a safe shortcut for children between their homes and school.
- Collected and repaired used toys and gave them to a home for handicapped children.
- Organized and ran a bicycle safety campaign. This involved a written safety test, equipment safety checking, and a skill contest in a bike rodeo.
- Surveyed the remains of an old Spanish mission and prepared an accurate map relating it to the present church.
- Checked the condition of all street signs in a town and reported those that were missing, turned wrong, or couldn't be read.
- Built a "tot lot" in a big city neighborhood and set up a schedule for Scouts to run it.
- Set up a community study center for kids who have no place at home to do schoolwork.

Most of these projects needed many other Scouts to make them successful. The Eagle candidates planned, lined up manpower, and gave leadership to the work.

PERSONAL GROWTH
AGREEMENT CONFERENCE

One of the aims of Scouting is to help you grow. You can see yourself getting taller and heavier without much trouble. But you are also growing in other ways that are harder to see. Your actions and thoughts are growing and changing, too. These are the things that make up your personality and character and will help determine the kind of a man you will be.

Your Scoutmaster is interested in and wants to know about you. Only then can he help you to have fun in Scouting. Only then can he know how you can help your troop and patrol.

Every troop is different from every other troop. Why? Because each troop is made up of lots of different fellows. A troop isn't a mass of nameless, faceless people all forced into a common pattern. Each Scout gives a little of himself. Thus, each troop takes on some of the character of all the guys in it.

That's why your Scoutmaster wants to know you better.

He wants to see what you have to bring to the troop. Soon after joining you will have your first personal growth agreement conference with him. Here you and your Scoutmaster will sit down for a talk. Tell him about yourself. First about your family. Tell him about your father and mother and what they do. Describe your brothers and sisters and tell about the things you like to do with them. If you have a pet, tell about it, too.

Your Scoutmaster will probably ask about the things you like to do. Sports? Which ones? Music? Do you play a musical instrument? Do you like to read? Were you in the Cubs? What things did you do there that you liked? Was it making things, being in skits, playing games, earning activity badges in Webelos? How about school? What do you like best?

Your Scoutmaster will also want to know what things you do well. If you like sports, do you think you are pretty good at any? Think of all the things you do, and then think of the one you do best.

Setting a Goal

You have already thought about the things you do well. These are your strong points — your strengths. These are the things to build on as you grow. Your Scoutmaster will ask you to set a goal for yourself in which you will use one of your strengths. This goal could be something you will do with your family, in your troop, school, religious institution, community, or even alone. Whatever your goal will be, it will be something you decide on yourself. Because, you see, it will be up to you to meet that goal. You will do it to become a Tenderfoot Scout.

How do you decide what your goal will be? Let's pretend a little. Suppose you are good at sports — baseball, for example. Your goal might be to organize some ball games for the troop. You might even plan to be the umpire since you know all the rules.

Maybe you like to do handicraft like woodworking. Your goal could be to build an investiture set for inducting new boys into the troop or repairing chairs or benches for a neighborhood day-care center.

Or music is your strength. You might set a goal of entertaining the troop with your guitar at several troop campfires. Maybe you play the trumpet. How about becoming the troop bugler.

These are just a few examples. Get the idea? You use the thing you are best at to help. And you don't just let it happen. You decide ahead of time what you are going to do, set it as a goal, and then do it.

There will be many chances for you to meet with your Scoutmaster to see how you are doing and to set new goals. Part of each progress award is a personal growth agreement conference. Each will be kind of like the one described here. Of course, as you become older and have more experience, you will want to set bigger goals. But each time the goal will be your own.

At each personal conference your Scoutmaster will also talk over with you your progress in Scouting. He will help you to look ahead at earning your next progress award. He might help you to decide what skill awards and merit badges you will want to earn next.

THE MEANING OF THE BADGE

Every progress award badge you earn and wear will have some of the following parts. You should know the meaning of them.

The Shape.—This was taken from the north point of the compass. It is often called a trefoil or fleur-de-lis (flower of the lily or iris). This shape can be found in designs going back over 2,000 years. With small changes, it is the shape used for the Scout badge in countries around the world.

The Three Points.—These stand for the three main parts of the Scout Oath. These are duty to God and country, duty to other people, and duty to self.

The Stars.—These represent the ideals of truth and knowledge. The stars on the badge in their similarity to the stars in the sky remind you of the outdoors in Scouting.

The Eagle and Shield.—This is the emblem of the United States of America. It stands for freedom and readiness to defend that freedom.

The Scroll.—The motto Be Prepared appears on the scroll. The ends of the scroll are turned up like the corners of a Scout's mouth in a smile.

The Knot.—This is a reminder that you have promised to do a Good Turn to someone every day.

PROGRESS AWARD REQUIREMENTS

These may be earned by a boy who has qualified as a Scout. (See inside front cover.)

To Be a Tenderfoot Scout You Must

1. Be active in your troop and patrol for at least 2 months.
2. Scout spirit: Repeat from memory the Scout Oath or Promise and Law. Demonstrate that you have practiced these ideas in everyday life.
3. Earn Citizenship and one other skill award.
4. Earn any one merit badge.
5. Take part in a personal growth agreement conference.
(Memorization of the Scout Law in requirement 2 refers to the bold type on pages 39 to 51—not just key words as on page 38. Citizenship in the Community and First Aid merit badges are required for First Class. First Aid skill award is a requirement for First Aid merit badge, so it too is required for First Class.)

To Be a Second Class Scout You Must

1. Be active in your troop and patrol for at least 3 months as a Tenderfoot Scout.
2. Show Scout spirit.
3. Earn three more skill awards.
4. Earn two more merit badges.*
5. Take part in a personal growth agreement conference.

*Citizenship in the Community and First Aid merit badges are required for First Class.

To Be a First Class Scout You Must

1. Be active in your troop and patrol for at least 3 months as a Second Class Scout.
2. Show Scout spirit.
3. Earn three more skill awards.
4. Earn two more merit badges. (This is a total of five of which two, Citizenship in the Community and First Aid, are required.)

5. Take part in a personal growth agreement conference.

To Be a Star Scout You Must

1. Be active in your troop and patrol for at least 4 months as a First Class Scout.
2. Show Scout spirit.
3. Earn a total of nine merit badges, including four from the required list for Eagle.
4. While a First Class Scout, take part in service projects totaling at least 6 hours of work. These projects must be approved by your Scoutmaster.
5. While a First Class Scout, serve actively in one of the following positions (or carry out a Scoutmaster assigned leadership project to help the troop): patrol leader, junior assistant Scoutmaster, scribe, den chief, quartermaster, librarian, member of the leadership corps, senior patrol leader, assistant senior patrol leader, or instructor.
6. Take part in a personal growth agreement conference.

To Be a Life Scout You Must

1. Be active in your troop and patrol for at least 6 months as a Star Scout.

2. Show Scout spirit.

3. Earn a total of 15 merit badges including 7 from the required list for Eagle.

4. While a Star Scout, take part in service projects totaling at least 6 hours of work. These must be approved by your Scoutmaster.

5. While a Star Scout serve in one of the leadership positions listed in Requirement 5 for Star Scout (or carry out a Scoutmaster assigned leadership project to help the troop).

6. Take part in a personal growth agreement conference.

To Be an Eagle Scout You Must

1. Be active in your troop and patrol for at

least 6 months as a Life Scout.

2. Show Scout spirit.

3. Earn a total of 24 merit badges including the following: First Aid, Citizenship in the Community, Citizenship in the Nation, Citizenship in the World, Communications, Safety, Emergency Preparedness or Lifesaving, Environmental Science, Personal Management, and Personal Fitness or Swimming or Sports.

4. While a Life Scout, serve actively in one of the positions listed in Requirement 5 for Star Scout.

5. While a Life Scout, plan, develop, and give leadership to others in a service project helpful to your religious institution, school, or town. This project must be approved by your Scoutmaster and troop committee before you start.

6. Take part in a personal growth agreement conference.

Requirements for Eagle Palms

After becoming an Eagle Scout, you may earn a palm for every 5 additional merit badges beyond the 24 required. There will be a personal growth agreement conference before each palm is awarded. Being active in your troop and patrol for at least 3 months and demonstrating Scout spirit is required between the award of each palm.

The Bronze Palm represents 5 merit badges; the Gold Palm, 10 merit badges; and the Silver Palm, 15 merit badges. Palms may be worn in any combination to show the number of merit badges you have beyond Eagle.

SKILL AWARDS

Your citizenship in the United States of America is very precious. It is also a great responsibility. Men and women of the past made possible the rights you have. It is up to you to understand them and pass them to those who will follow you.

CITIZENSHIP

REQUIREMENTS AND PAGE REFERENCES

1. a. Describe the U.S. flag. Give a short history of it.   96-99
   b. Demonstrate and explain why you should respect your country's flag by displaying, folding, and saluting it the right way. Tell which special days you should fly it in your state.   100-105
2. Explain the meaning and reason for the:
   a. Pledge of Allegiance   106-107
   b. national anthem   108-109
3. Explain the rights and responsibilities of a citizen of the United States.   110-111
4. Do one of the following:
   a. Visit a community leader. Learn from him the duties of his job or office. Tell your patrol what you learned.   112-113
   b. Learn something about a famous U.S. person of your choosing. Give a short report of what he did to gain this recognition. 114-115
   c. Make a list of 10 things, places, or sayings that have some relationship to the history of the United States. Explain their meaning.   116-119
5. Seek an understanding of drug abuse. As a real demonstration of citizenship, help your friends to do the same. Explain five steps you can take to reach this understanding.   341-343

YOUR FLAG

Your flag is a symbol of a growing, changing, dynamic nation. It is the flag of the people — all the people in the United States. It is a flag of glory from the past and, like our country, it has a great future.

Men have defended your flag with their blood and their lives because it stands for all that is good about your country. Others have defiled the flag as a symbol of things about the United States they don't like. In each case it wasn't the flag that was defended or attacked, but rather the Nation, itself.

No country has ever given its citizens a better chance. In spite of this, there are those who have grave doubts about our country. The United States is great. A penalty of greatness is in not being as great as some think you should be. Greatness lies partly in being able to change when change is needed. The United States of America can and has changed over the years. Maybe the changes haven't been as fast as some would like, but there have been changes, nevertheless.

The United States of today isn't the United

The **Queen Anne flag** of England was the earliest flag leading to our present one. Its union combined the crosses of St. George and St. Andrew. It was flown in our country from 1707 to the Revolution.

The **Grand Union flag** first flew in early 1776 over Washington's headquarters. The war had begun a year earlier. The flag had the same union as the Queen Anne flag. The field was broken into 7 red and 6 white stripes.

Old Glory was the first official flag of the United States of America. It was created by a resolution of the Continental Congress passed on June 14, 1777. Flag Day, June 14 each year, celebrates this event. Old Glory had the stripes of the Grand Union flag. The union of crosses was replaced by a circle of 13 stars on a blue field.

The 15 Star and Stripe Flag was the Star-Spangled Banner of our national anthem. New stars and new stripes were added to the flag for each State admitted. It was seen the flag would become an awkward size under this plan. So Congress passed the flag law of 1818 described earlier. It said there should always be 13 stripes.

States of 1800 or 1900 or even 1950. The country your flag will represent in the year 2000 will be different, too, and it will take good citizens to see that the changes are right.

There have been flags over America for generations. Among the first were those of:

Spain in the Southwest and Florida

France in the Mississippi and Great Lakes regions

England along much of the east coast

The Netherlands in New York

Sweden in a colony in Delaware

Russia in Alaska and down the west coast

Mexico in ex-Spanish territory after 1822

The Kingdom of Hawaii before it became a protectorate

The Republic of Texas before it became a state

During the years before we became an independent nation in 1776, the colonies flew many different flags of their own. Among the better known were the pine tree and the rattlesnake flags.

Another flag that flew over part of our nation was the stars and bars of the Confederate States of America. These states left the United States during the Civil War. Their flag flew until they came back into the United States.

The flag has changed with the changes in the history of America. Our present flag is the result of a law passed by Congress in 1818. This law set the number of stripes at 13. It said there should be a star on the blue field for each state. The most recent change added the 50th star for Hawaii.

FLAG CODE

You honor the flag and the Nation for which it stands by paying it proper respect. To do this, Scouts follow the flag code set by Congress. Following is an interpretation of the parts of this code you should know. For a complete flag code, write to your Congressman in Washington, D.C. In the following, whenever the words "the flag" are used they mean the flag of the United States of America.

Two Scouts team up to raise and lower the flag. One holds the folded flag while the other fastens it to the rope. The Scout who fastened it raises it. He holds the ropes near the pole. The flag is raised briskly (fast). The Scout holding the flag steps back and salutes when the flag leaves his hands. The procedure is reversed when the flag comes down. The flag is lowered ceremoniously (slow).

A bugle is often used at flag ceremonies.

(1) During a flag raising, only "To the Colors" is played. Scouts salute during the playing.

(2) During a flag lowering, Scouts stand at parade rest during the playing of "Retreat."

They come to attention and salute when the flag comes down as the bugler sounds "To the Colors."

The flag is flown at half-mast in times of national mourning. It is first raised to the top of the pole. Then it is lowered halfway down. Before lowering for the day it should be raised to the top.

It is the custom to display the flag only from sunrise to sunset. However, it may be displayed at night if lighted to produce a patriotic effect. The flag flies day and night in a few places authorized by Congress or Presidential proclamation. In a few others it has been approved by long-established custom.

The flag should not be displayed in days when the weather is bad. It should be flown on all days when the weather permits, especially on National and State holidays.

These include New Year's Day, Inauguration

Day, Lincoln's Birthday, Washington's Birthday, Armed Forces Day, Easter Sunday, Mother's Day, Memorial Day, Flag Day, Independence Day, Labor Day, Constitution Day, Columbus Day, Veterans Day, Thanksgiving Day, Christmas Day, and the birthday of your state.

The flag should never touch anything beneath it such as ground, floor, or water.

Never use the flag as drapery.

Flags of two or more nations are flown from separate staffs of the same height. These flags should all be about the same size. International usage forbids flying a flag of one nation above another in time of peace.

If the flag gets dirty, clean it. If torn, repair it. When beyond repair it should be destroyed in a dignified way, preferably by burning.

Never dip the flag to any person or thing.

The flag should never be used for advertising purposes. Advertising signs should not be fastened to a staff or halyard (rope) with the flag.

SALUTE THE FLAG

Use the Scout salute when in uniform (with or without the cap or hat). In civilian clothes, stand at attention. Hold your right hand over your heart.

When the flag is carried past you in a parade or procession, salute when it comes directly opposite you.

Salute when the flag is raised or lowered.

Salute when giving the Pledge of Allegiance and during the playing of the national anthem.

DISPLAYING THE FLAG

Grouped Flags. — When flags (other than those of other nations) are grouped, the flag shall be in the center and higher.

Over Middle of Street. — The union (stars) shall be to the north on an east and west street and to the east on a north and south street.

Place of Honor.—The flag shall be flown in the place of honor. This is to the right of the person or group displaying the flag.

Displayed Flat.—The flag may be displayed flat on a wall behind or to a speaker's right. The union is placed toward the place of honor.

Crossed With Another Flag.—The flag is in the place of honor. Its staff is in front of that of the other flag.

Parade.—If alone, the place of honor for the flag is at the right front. In a line of flags, the flag is centered in front.

104

With Another Flag.—On the same pole with another flag (not of another nation), the flag is flown at the top.

Distress Signal.—The only time the flag is flown upside down is as a signal for help.

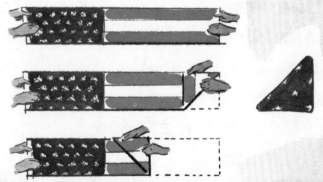

Folding.—Two Scouts work together. Fold it twice the long way so the blue shows on both sides. Fold in triangular folds from the end. When finished, it will be a triangle with blue showing all around.

THE PLEDGE OF ALLEGIANCE

I pledge allegiance
to the flag
of the United States of America
and to the Republic
for which it stands,
one Nation under God,
indivisible,
with liberty
and justice for all.

When you pledge allegiance to your flag you promise loyalty and devotion to your nation. And you promise it to a country you describe in these words of the pledge:

"the Republic for which it stands"—A republic is a kind of government in which the people elect others to represent them in governing. The United States of America is a Republic.

"one Nation"—Our country is made up of 50 individual States. Each has certain rights. Yet these States join together to make one nation.

"under God"—Our nation was formed by leaders who believed deeply in the guidance of God. The phrase was added to the Pledge of Allegiance in 1954.

"indivisible"—The 50 States will not be divided. They will continue as one single nation.

"with liberty and justice for all"—This is the great goal of America toward which we should all work. Under our form of Government, all men shall be free. All men shall have equal justice through the courts and in relations with their fellowman.

OUR NATIONAL ANTHEM

During the War of 1812, the British attacked U.S. Fort McHenry near Baltimore. An American lawyer, Francis Scott Key, watched the bombing. He worried about whether our soldiers could withstand the attack. The bombardment lasted all night. In the early morning Key wrote:

"Oh say can you see, by the dawn's early light,
What so proudly we hailed at the twilight's last gleaming,
Whose broad stripes and bright stars through the perilous fight,
O'er the ramparts we watched, were so gallantly streaming?
And the rocket's red glare, the bombs bursting in air,
Gave proof through the night that our flag was still there,

O say does that star-spangled banner yet wave
O'er the land of the free and the home of the brave?"

At 8 o'clock the bombing stopped. As the smoke cleared, Key could see the flag still flying and wrote:

"O thus be it ever when freemen shall stand
Between their loved homes and the war's desolation!
Blest with vict'ry and peace may the heaven rescued land
Praise the Power that hath made and preserved us a
    nation!
Then conquer we must, when our cause it is just,
    And this be our motto—'In God is our trust.'
        And the star-spangled banner in triumph shall wave
        O'er the land of the free and the home of the brave."

You have sung the words of our national anthem many times. But have you really listened to the words you were singing? Read them carefully, sentence by sentence. Only then will the real meaning come through.

YOUR RIGHTS

Citizens of the United States have rights guaranteed by law, the Constitution, and its amendments. Some of the most important of these rights are:

Freedom of choice of your religion.

Freedom of speech.

Freedom to peaceable assembly.

To own property.

To live where you choose.

To move when you want.

To equal education.

To choose public officials in free elections.

To bear arms.

To be free from having soldiers housed in your home without the owner's permission.

A prompt trial if accused of a crime.

Legal counsel of your choice.

Trial by jury of your peers (other citizens).

Protection against being forced to testify against yourself.

Protection against illegal search and seizure.

These rights may be qualified by law. You have freedom of speech, but not to lie about someone. You can own property, but must pay taxes. You can vote, but only if a registered voter. And, you can bear arms according to state and local laws.

Some of these rights may seem unimportant to you. Study what happens in countries without these protections. Then you'll value all of your rights.

YOUR RESPONSIBILITIES

The other side to having rights is having responsibilities. Citizens owe it to themselves and their fellowmen to share in the responsibilities of citizenship. Some of these are to:

Obey the laws of the land.

Respect the rights of others.

Respect property.

Serve on juries, if called.

Vote in elections.

Serve and defend your country.

Assist agencies of law enforcement.

Practice the principles of good citizenship.

Keep informed on issues of government.

Pay taxes.

Serve in government, if qualified.

Help correct, under law, those things with which you disagree.

COMMUNITY LEADER VISIT

What makes a community? Or even a nation? It's people. People with ideas and those who can make ideas work. People who can lead by getting others to do things and those who do them. There are these kinds of people in your town. They are your community leaders. Some are in positions in town government. But others are leaders in organizations that influence community life. Here are some examples of community leaders:

Mayor or city manager
City councilmen
School board members
Municipal judge
City attorney
School superintendent
Church leaders
Head of Federal agency
Block Club leaders
Members of municipal committees
Municipal department heads
Service club presidents
Ethnic group leaders
Volunteer agency directors like the
Red Cross or Scout council.
United Way of America officials

Visit one of these men or women. It will help you to understand your town. Community leaders are busy people, so make an appointment beforehand. Explain why you want the meeting.

Then keep the appointment. Be on time. Find out the things you want to know quickly. Make notes so you can report to your patrol later.

FAMOUS MEN

Mount Rushmore

Famous people are those who have influenced history. They have made a difference in the life you live.

There are many famous people. Here are a few. Do you know why each is famous? There are others who are famous for what they did locally. These people have caused changes in your town or region.

Learn about these people. Look them up in an encyclopedia. Then you'll better understand the greatness of the United States of America.

Whitney Young, Jr.   Albert Einstein   Walter Reed   Samuel Clemens

Thomas Edison   Dwight D.   Robert E. Lee   Martin Luther
              Eisenhower   King, Jr.

Benjamin Franklin   Henry Ford   Matthew Henson

   John D.   Walter Reuther   Samuel   Chief Plenty Coups
Rockefeller   Gompers

  Alexander   Daniel Boone   Padre Junipero Serra
Graham Bell

THINGS, PLACES, AND SAYINGS

The history of the United States is alive with places, things, and sayings. You will use and hear some of them personally. Others will live only in your mind. Here are a few to stimulate your thinking. How many can you name? Do you know why they are famous? What is their importance to our history?

Spacecraft on the moon

USS *Arizona* monument at Pearl Harbor

Wagon train

Pony express

Liberty Bell

Statue of Liberty

Old Ironsides

Wright airplane

Spirit of St. Louis

The Alamo

Minuteman statue

Driving the "golden spike"

Famous sayings also have a place in history. Here are a few. Find out the background of the men who said them and why.

"Give me liberty or give me death."
    Patrick Henry

"The world must be made safe for democracy."
    Woodrow Wilson

"Damn the torpedoes, full speed ahead."
    David Farragut

"Injustice anywhere is a threat to justice everywhere."
    Martin Luther King, Jr.

"I have not yet begun to fight."
    John Paul Jones

"The only thing we have to fear is fear itself."
    Franklin D. Roosevelt

"Speak softly and carry a big stick."
    Theodore Roosevelt

"The basis of our political system is the right of the people to make and to alter their constitutions of government."
    George Washington

"The ballot is stronger than the bullet."
    Abraham Lincoln

"There never was a good war or a bad peace."
    Benjamin Franklin

If you know first aid, you will use it for the rest of your life. With it you can care for yourself and others in times of accidents or emergencies. First aid brings together the ideals of the Scout motto—Be Prepared—and the Scout slogan—Do a Good Turn Daily.

FIRST AID

REQUIREMENTS AND PAGE REFERENCES

WHAT IS FIRST AID ?

First aid is immediate help right after an injury. First aid isn't playing doctor. It's doing the things that must be done before expert help arrives. How will you act in an emergency? Would you know what to do? If you do, you'll be cool and calm, because you know you can help. Your confidence will show and it will help the injured as you ease their pain and worry.

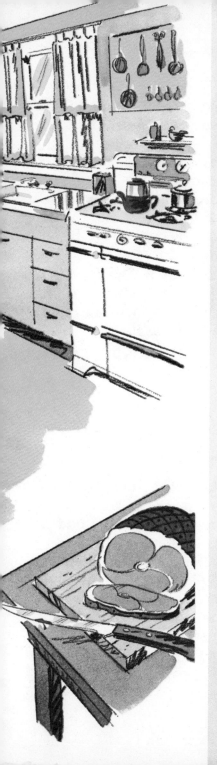

Get Help. — Know how to get expert help fast. One of the first things you do is to send for help. The way you do it is not the same in every town. Maybe you have a rescue squad, a hospital ambulance service, a police or sheriff's office. Make a note of your best way. Write the emergency number near your phone.

Carry an "emergency dime" with you at all times. Tape one on the lid of your first aid kit. You may have to use a pay phone. When you are away from home, dial O on the phone. Tell the operator what the emergency is and exactly where help is needed. If you can, wait. The operator may have other questions.

Don't Move the Injured. — It is dangerous to move the victim of a serious accident. Don't do it unless you have to get him out of a burning building, off a highway, or out of another danger spot. Bring expert help to the injured. Don't take the injured to the help.

Check an unconscious person for a neck, wrist, or ankle tag. The tag might show the victim requires special treatment.

SHOCK

Every accident brings shock. It's a quick loss of strength caused by pain, fear, and sometimes loss of blood.

A shock victim is very weak. His face gets pale. His skin is cold and clammy. He shivers from chills. He seems dazed and may vomit. In extreme cases he may pass out. Shock may come with the accident or soon after. It may even come a few hours later.

SHOCK IS DEADLY SERIOUS. DON'T WAIT FOR THE SYMPTOMS TO SHOW. Assume that shock will always be present in an injury. Treat for it and you may prevent it.

FAINTING

Fainting is a "blacking out" caused by not enough blood going to the brain. This can be caused by fright, bad news, breathing bad air, or standing at attention too long.

If a person faints before you can help him, loosen his collar. Raise his feet. Keep him lying down even after he has come to.

If the person does not come to right away, treat for shock. Get expert help.

If you feel faint, sit on a chair. Bend forward with your head between your knees.

Treatment for Shock or Fainting

What To Do.—For either shock or fainting, keep the patient lying down. In cool weather cover him to keep him warm. If it is hot, don't. The idea is to keep him warm. If the patient is conscious, let him sip a little water. If unconscious, don't force water between his lips. It may choke him. Raise his head and shoulders if he has a head injury or has trouble breathing. Raise his feet if he has no head injury or trouble breathing. Make him comfortable.

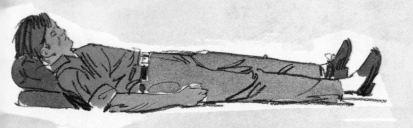

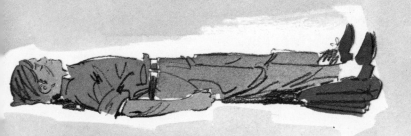

Severe Bleeding

Spurting blood must be stopped or the patient will quickly bleed to death. Spurting blood comes from a cut artery.

Apply Pressure.—If you don't have a cloth to press on the wound, grab it with your bare hand and press down hard. Your hand must be right on the cut to stop the bleeding.

Help control bleeding by raising the cut arm or leg above body level.

HURRY CASES

These accidents call for quick action to save life. This is a must for severe bleeding, stopped breathing, or internal poisoning. Bleeding must be stopped—right now! Breathing must be started—right now! Poison must be made harmless—right now! Get going—right now! That second—right now—may save a life!

HOW TO MAKE A CRAVAT BANDAGE

A cravat for holding a bandage can be made by folding a triangular bandage or neckerchief.

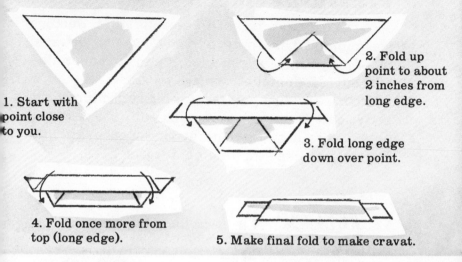

1. Start with point close to you.

2. Fold up point to about 2 inches from long edge.

3. Fold long edge down over point.

4. Fold once more from top (long edge).

5. Make final fold to make cravat.

Put on a Pad.—Quickly use your free hand to get a pad of cloth of some kind. Use anything. Don't worry about whether it's sterile. Your problem is to stop the bleeding. Let go of the wound just long enough to put on the pad.

Tie the Pad.—Wrap something around the pad to keep it in place. Use a neckerchief, tie, or belt. Tie it snugly with a square knot. If the pad gets blood soaked, don't take it off. Just put another on top of the first. Tie it on. Get medical help.

127

Pressure Points

A tourniquet is so dangerous that doctors recommend that only experts use it. Arterial bleeding from an arm or leg can be controlled without a tourniquet.

Four pressure points, two for each side of the body, can be used to stop bleeding. Press the artery against the bone at the pressure point. It acts just like stepping on a water hose.

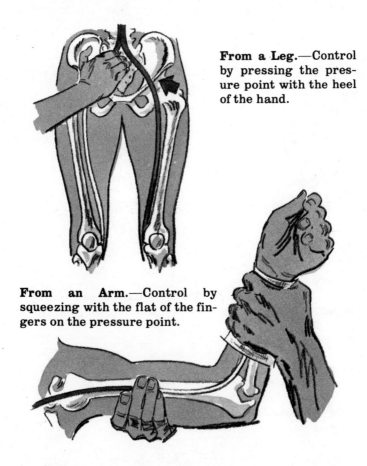

From a Leg.—Control by pressing the presure point with the heel of the hand.

From an Arm.—Control by squeezing with the flat of the fingers on the pressure point.

Poisoning by Mouth

The first thing to do is to dilute the poison. Get the victim to drink a glass of water. Get expert help right away. In large cities phone the poison control center.

What Poison?—Look for the bottle or can. The label may tell the antidote. Follow the directions.

Vomiting.—It can be very dangerous to make the victim vomit. Some poisons do real harm when they come back up.

If you are sure the poison is too much medicine (like aspirin), it will help if you make the victim vomit. Press down on the back of his tongue with your finger or a spoon. **REMEMBER**—Cause vomiting only for an overdose of medicine. And **never** if the victim is unconscious.

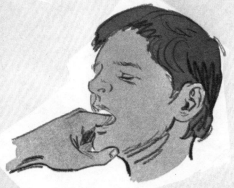

Rescue Breathing

You might save a life if you can do rescue breathing. Use it on a person who has stopped breathing. You breathe your own breath into the victim's lungs. Speed in starting is impor-

Step 1.—Clear victim's mouth of anything that might stop his breathing.

Step 4.—Let the victim breathe out. In step 3 the victim's chest should rise. It should fall in this step.

tant. Don't waste time moving the victim to a comfortable place. In a water rescue, for example, you can start rescue breathing while carrying the victim from the water to dry land. Learn the six steps shown.

Step 2.—Tilt head back as far as you can. Lift with the hand beneath neck. Push down with the hand on the forehead.

Step 3.—Use your thumb and forefinger to pinch the nostrils shut. Place your mouth over the victim's mouth. Blow 12 times a minute for an adult or 20 times for a child.

Step 5.—If air isn't getting into the lungs, check tilt of head (step 2). If still blocked, slap his back to clear the throat.

Step 6.—If unable to breathe through his mouth, breathe through his nose. On a child, breathe through both his nose and mouth.

Everyday First Aid

Learn to handle common injuries by practicing on yourself. Then you will be able to help yourself and others.

Cuts and Scratches.—Even a small cut or scratch can be dangerous. It lets germs get through your skin. Germs can cause infection. But germs don't like soap and water. So wash the cut. If you are on a hike, use water from your canteen. When the skin dries, put on an adhesive bandage.

Larger Cuts.—Wash with soap and water. Put on a sterile dressing big enough to cover the cut. Hold it by the corners. Don't touch the part that will cover the cut. If you do, the dressing won't be sterile. Hold the dressing in place with adhesive tape. If you don't have any, use a cloth bandage. Tie it in place with a square knot.

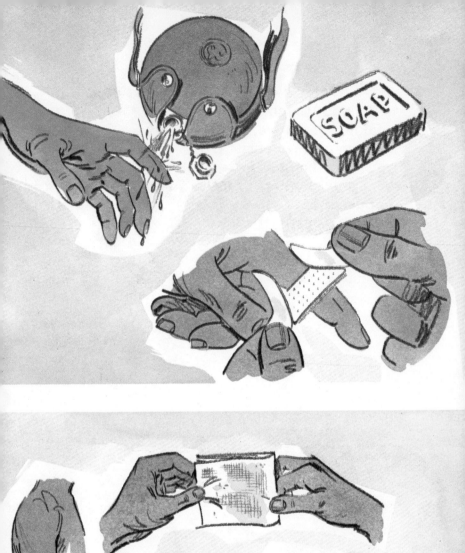

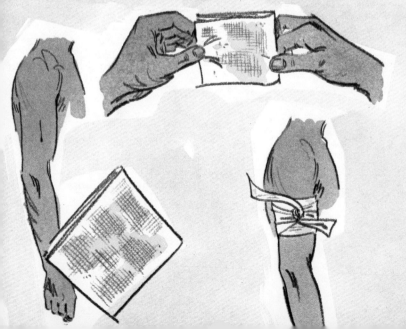

Burns and Scalds

If you touch a hot coal in a campfire, what do you get? A burn. If you spill boiling water on your hand, what happens? A scald. If you stay out in the sun too long, then what? Sunburn. All hurt. And all can be dangerous.

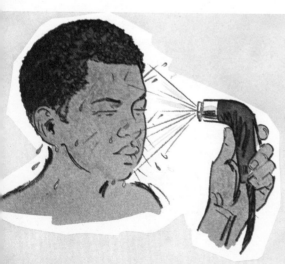

Chemical Burns.—Wash off right away. Use lots of water. Put on a sterile gauze pad. Hold it in place with a bandage. If the chemical gets in your eye, spray water into it or lie back and pour tap water into the eye. Put on a loose eye bandage. Get medical help.

Ease the Pain.—If the skin isn't broken, run cold water on the burn or scald. If you can, put a few ice cubes in water. Keep the burned part in cold water until it quits hurting.

Blisters.—Don't break the blisters. Don't put on grease or ointment. Just cover the blisters with a gauze pad. Hold it in place with layers of bandage. Cover it with aluminum foil, a plastic bag, or plastic wrap to keep air out.

Charred Flesh.—Wrap a clean cloth around the burn. Put it right over the burn and anything else that is stuck to it. Treat for shock. Get help. This burn is very serious.

Blister on Heel

Stop blisters before they form. Watch for soreness and redness. Cover the spot with an adhesive bandage before a blister forms.

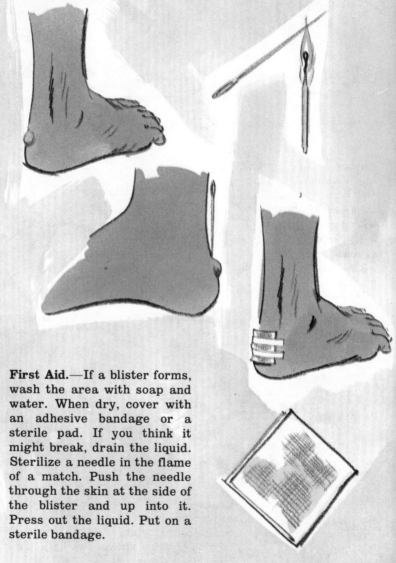

First Aid.—If a blister forms, wash the area with soap and water. When dry, cover with an adhesive bandage or a sterile pad. If you think it might break, drain the liquid. Sterilize a needle in the flame of a match. Push the needle through the skin at the side of the blister and up into it. Press out the liquid. Put on a sterile bandage.

Sprained Ankle

A stumble may cause a sprained ankle. It's painful and it swells up right away.

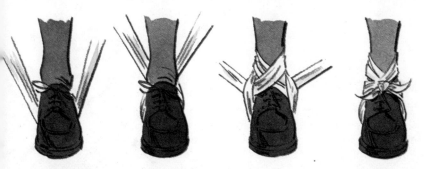

First Aid.—Don't take off your shoe. Tie an ankle bandage around your ankle and shoe. The shoe and bandage will support your ankle. If you are barefoot, lie down. Put your foot up on a rest. Cold, wet cloths will make it feel better. See a doctor; it could be a broken ankle.

Bites and Stings
MILD

Insect bites hurt long after the bite. Household ammonia or a paste of baking soda will make it feel better. Calamine lotion also helps.

The Stinger.—Sometimes part of the stinger of a bee, wasp, or hornet breaks off. Try pulling it out with tweezers or scrape it off gently with your fingernail.

DANGEROUS

Ticks.—These are dangerous because they often carry a serious disease. They can give this to you when they fasten on you. If you feel a tick crawling on you, brush it off. If a tick has fastened on you, don't pull it off. The head may break off and stay under your skin. This could cause infection. Cover the tick with grease or oil. It will let go. Wash the area with soap and water.

Tick

Scorpions, Spiders, and Allergic Reactions.—Treatment for scorpion stings, black widow and brown recluse spider bites, and allergic reactions are the same. Learn what these scorpions and spiders look like. A person with an allergic reaction to a bee, wasp, or other sting feels sick and may have trouble breathing.

1. If the bite is on an arm or leg, tie a constricting band above the bite. It should be just tight enough to stop the blood in the skin — not under it.

2. Put ice water or ice in a cloth on the bite.

3. Take the band off after 5 minutes.

4. Keep the arm or leg lower than the body.

5. Take the person to where he can get medical care. Be sure he keeps breathing. Give rescue breathing if needed.

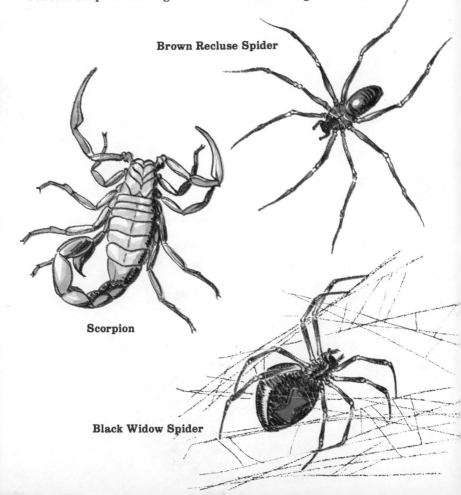

Brown Recluse Spider

Scorpion

Black Widow Spider

Snakebite

Any snake will bite if it is cornered. For non-poisonous snakes, treat like a puncture wound. Let it bleed. Wash it with soap and water. Cover with a sterile gauze pad held in place with adhesive tape or a bandage. Treat for shock.

If the bite is from a poisonous snake, take the following steps:

Rattlesnake

Copperhead

Coral Snake

Cottonmouth Moccasin

Step 1.—Get the victim to lie down and stay very quiet. Make him comfortable. Calm him down. Put the part that was bitten lower than the rest of his body.

Step 2.—Put a constriction band 2 to 4 inches above the bite. Make it just tight enough so it's not easy to push your fingers between the band and his skin.

Step 3.—Apply ice packs or cold cloths to the bite. This will also slow the spread of the poison. Get medical help. Tell them that it is snakebite and the kind of snake, if known. They may need time to locate the antivenin.

DESPERATE CASES

In desperate cases where medical help will be long delayed, treat as follows:

1. Carry out steps 1, 2, and 3 from previous treatment.

2. Sterilize a sharp knife or razor blade.

3. Wash the bite area with soap and water.

4. Make shallow cuts on the fang marks. Cuts should be about ¼ inch long running up and down the limb, not across. They should only break the skin.

5. Apply suction by mouth or suction cup for about an hour.

Animal Bites

Dog and rat bites are the most common. Carelessness around "tame" animals in the wild can make them bite. Even home pets such as hamsters will bite if poorly handled. An animal bite leaves a puncture wound. And there is always a chance of rabies. Rabies can kill the person bitten. The bite of a dog or wild animal may contain rabies germs. Preventative shots are very painful. But they are not needed if the animal doesn't have rabies. So it is important to find the animal and have it checked.

First Aid.—Wash the bite under running water. Use soap if you have it. Be sure that the animal's saliva is all washed away. Cover bite with a sterile gauze pad. Hold in place with a bandage. Get medical help.

Skin Poisoning

Learn what the poison plants look like where you live. If you touch them, you may get a rash. Your skin will get red and it will itch. Tiny blisters will form and spread.

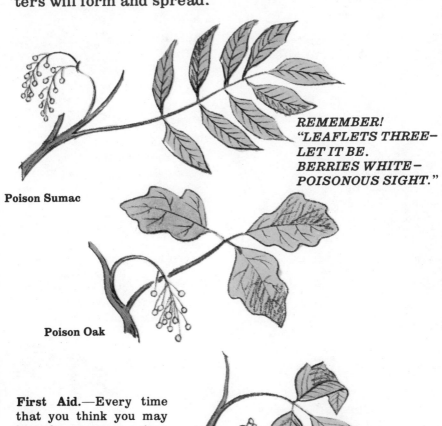

Poison Sumac

REMEMBER!
"LEAFLETS THREE—
LET IT BE.
BERRIES WHITE—
POISONOUS SIGHT."

Poison Oak

First Aid.—Every time that you think you may have been near a poison plant, wash with soap and water. Then use rubbing alcohol. If a rash develops, put on calamine lotion. If it gets worse, see your doctor.

Poison Ivy

Something in the Eye

Anything in your eye is painful and serious. It's usually easy to take a speck of dirt from the white of your eye. But don't fool with the rest of it. See a doctor. Your eyes must serve you for the rest of your life.

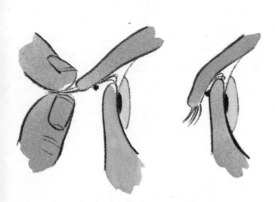

Treatment.—Don't rub. Blink your eyes. Let the tears flow and flush out the object. For an object under the upper lid, pull the lid out and down. The lower lashes may brush the speck out. If the object is under the lower lid, place your thumb just below the lid and move it down gently. Take out the speck with the corner of a clean handkerchief. If that fails, cover the eye with a sterile gauze pad. Hold it in place with a bandage. Go to a doctor.

Nosebleed

Keep your cool. A nosebleed looks bad, but it's no big deal.

Treatment.—Pinch the nostrils together. A cold cloth on the nose will help. If bleeding is severe or doesn't stop, get medical help.

Puncture Wounds

Step on a nail and you have a puncture wound. These are also caused by pins, splinters, fishhooks, knife stabs, and gunshot. All are dangerous. They are often deep and don't bleed freely. They are hard to clean. The germs of lockjaw (tetanus) may have been carried into the wound.

Splinters.—A splinter will hurt until it comes out. Take it out with a pair of tweezers or a sterile needle. Wash with soap and water. Bandage.

Fishhooks.—If snagged by a fishhook so the barb has gone through the skin, cut the line. Go to a doctor, hook and all. If it happens in the backcountry, push the hook so the barb comes out through the skin. Cut off the barb with wire cutters. Take out the remains.

First Aid.—After taking out the cause of the wound, squeeze gently around the wound. That will make it bleed and clean out dirt. Wash with soap and water. Bandage. See a doctor. You may need a tetanus antitoxin shot to prevent lockjaw.

Bandages

Sterile dressings need something to hold them in place. That's what adhesive tape or a roll of gauze is for. You can do this with your neckerchief, too. Make a cravat as shown earlier in this section. Tie it tightly over the dressing, using a square knot.

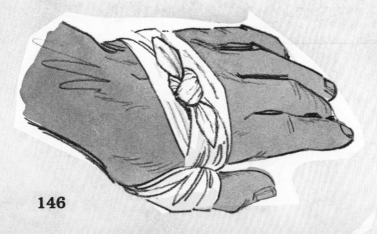

Arm Sling

The patient should lie down. Tie an overhand knot in the point of the bandage. This makes a cup for the elbow. Tie the ends together with a square knot. Slip over the victim's head as shown. Slip injured arm through the loop. When the patient stands up, adjust the knot on the side of the neck. The hand should be a little higher than the elbow.

Cravat Sling.—Make a cravat. Tie it around the neck. **Note:** This sling does not support the arm as evenly as the triangular type.

Pin Sling.—You can make a quick sling with a safety pin. Pin the sleeve to the front of the shirt or coat.

147

TYPICAL
FAMILY
EXPENSE

RENT

SAVINGS

TAXES

FOOD

CLOTHING

RECREATION

Getting along with your family is very important in your life. Young people often "turn off" their parents because they don't understand them. Learn about your family and what it takes to make it succeed. Then you'll know some of the problems your parents face.

FAMILY LIVING

REQUIREMENTS AND PAGE REFERENCES

1. Explain what is meant by the following terms:
   family   duty to family   family problems   **150-153**
2. Talk with your leader about duties and responsibilities you and other members of your family have at home. Talk with your parents or guardian about other duties you may take on in the next 3 months.
3. Show that you can look after yourself, members of your family, and home by doing the following:
   a. Inspect your home and grounds.
      List any dangers seen.   **154-155**
   b. Explain why garbage and trash must be disposed of properly.   **156**
   c. Look after some children younger than yourself for at least 3 hours. Use good health and safety practices.   **161**
   d. List some of the things your family spends money for. Tell your responsibility to your family's finances.   **160**
   e. Explain what your family does for recreation. Make a list of things your family might do at very little cost. Do one of these with a member of your family.   **162-163**
4. Explain how a person or a family where you live might get help in the following emergencies or problems: **157-159**

medical	police
legal	lack of money
housing	serious family problem
fire	utility

YOUR FAMILY

Unless you live alone like a hermit, you belong to a family. It is made up of the people living with you. Father, mother, brothers, and sisters are the family for most people. But relatives like grandparents and aunts and uncles may also be in the family. There are even some places where there aren't any relatives. Boarding schools or orphan homes are like this.

Your family is a team. It provides food, shelter, clothing, and group activities. Every member should be part of the team. You know what happens to a ball team when guys don't do their part. The same thing happens to a family, except the family doesn't just lose a ball game. Failure in your family makes changes in all your lives now and in the future.

There's nothing much more important than

being part of a warm, loving family. Don't be afraid to openly show in words and actions your love for the members of your family. Be grateful when they show their love for you. In the family, members are part of a team, yet they are individuals. Each has his own abilities and goals. The family works to support each member, and each member works for the family.

Team Jobs

What are some of the things this family team has to do? Food must be bought or grown. Meals have to be cooked. Someone has to clean the floors, windows, walls, furniture, dishes, utensils, and plumbing fixtures. Laundry must be done. Garbage and trash must be taken out.

Some families have jobs that others don't —like shoveling snow, mowing lawns, and painting and fixing up.

All of these, from food to fix-up, are big family jobs. They really belong to everybody. Sure, mom usually does some and dad others. But everyone—you too—takes a piece of the action. When everyone does his part, you really have a family team—a team that can handle the jobs that face it.

Your Jobs

There are other jobs that belong to you and only you. These include taking care of things that belong to you. Keep your living space neat and clean. Hang up your clothes. Put away your things. Make your own bed each morning. If you have litter from a craft project, clean it up. Dirty dishes from a snack you had are your responsibility. Your rule should be, "If it's mine or I did it; I'll clean it up." You see, if you don't, do it someone else will have to, and that's not fair.

You also have a duty to respect the rights and feelings of others. Keep your noise level down — radio, TV, record player, even your voice. Don't take over the TV or telephone. Don't use someone else's things without asking. Get home when you said you would so your parents won't worry. Share your things with others. Lay off the senseless fighting with your brothers and sisters.

When everyone in the family respects the rights of others, you have a team that's not torn apart with yelling and shouting.

Family Problems

A family problem is something that disturbs the happiness of the family. It could be something like sickness or money problems that you can't do anything about. But many times it's what someone did or didn't do. These can be prevented.

If you pick the wrong friends and get in trouble, your problem is a family problem. When you let your schoolwork slide and get poor grades, your problem is a family problem. If you damage someone else's property, your problem is a family problem. These are the kinds of things you can stop.

Your parents face serious problems every day. You don't know about most of them, because they try to protect you from worry. You can really help them by not making more problems in the things you do and the way you act.

Sometimes you may see things very differently from your parents. Remember, though, a good team has players with different abilities, ideas, and ways of doing things. The big thing is for a team to have unity even though the members may have different points of view.

HOME INSPECTION

Knowing the most common kinds of accidents will help in your home inspection. Especially if you know what causes them. Remember, finding the danger is only the first step. It won't do any good unless the things you find are changed.

Here are the major problem areas:

Falls. — Slippery bathtubs and showers. Cluttered stairways. Broken or weak stair railings. Loose throw rugs. Toys like skates and marbles underfoot. Improperly lighted areas.

Fires. — Matches where children can reach them. Trash near stoves and heaters. Oily rags. Overfused and overloaded electrical circuits. Wrong use of extension cords. Frayed electric wires. Ashtrays emptied wrong. Grease fires in kitchens.

Wounds.—Using or storing knives and tools wrong. Guns loaded and not locked up. Broken glass and tin cans. Falls against sharp things. Bumping into clear-glass doors. Animal bites.

Poisons. — Medicine, pesticides, and cleaning items where children can get them. Leaded paint used where children can eat it. Unvented gas or oil heaters. Cars run in closed garages.

GARBAGE AND
TRASH DISPOSAL

Many health and safety problems are caused by improper disposal of garbage and trash. Rats, flies, and other disease-carrying vermin are attracted by garbage and uncovered food. Never leave this out where it will bring rats, flies, and roaches into your home or neighborhood. Keep it sealed in plastic bags or garbage cans with tight lids.

Trash in your home is messy and dangerous. It can cause bad falls and is a fire hazard. Broken glass and tin cans can cut like knives.

HANDLING EMERGENCIES AND PROBLEMS

Your Scout motto is Be Prepared. Are you? If you had a fire in your home, could you quickly get help? Or would you waste precious time looking up a phone number? Who would you call if you smell gas in your basement? It would be nice if there were a single answer to these questions, but there isn't. Towns across America handle problems in different ways.

One goal of this skill award is for you to dig out the answers yourself. Dig them out before you have an emergency or problem. In some of these things you'll get the old run-around when you try to find out. Keep at it and you'll finally get the information you need. Then and only then will you be prepared.

Find out who is responsible for each of the things in requirement 4. Then list their names, addresses, and phone numbers. Keep this list where you can get it quickly when needed.

Medical, Police, Fire

Handle problems related to police, fire, and medical as described in the First Aid Skill Award chapter, page 123.

Legal

Legal problems may be handled by your family lawyer, your Legal Aid Society, or a neighborhood law office. A typical legal problem might involve damage done by your dog. Your family might have a legal problem about credit payment misunderstandings.

Housing
Housing responsibility is under many different departments of city government. Call the mayor's office. Describe the problem, and you will be told what department handles it. These problems include things like:

Building code violations
Landlord violation of housing standards
No heat or water
Dangerous health or sanitation conditions

Lack of Money
Not enough money for the things your family must have is a problem that a family counseling agency is set up to handle. Your church and your relatives might also be able to help.

Serious Family Problem
A family counseling agency, friends and relatives, or your church could also help with other serious family problems.

Utilities
Utility problems are those of electricity, gas, telephone, and water. In some towns these are owned and run by private companies. In others the city may be responsible. Find out which is true in your home for each utility.

Then list the names, addresses, and phone numbers so you'll have them when needed.

What kind of utility problems might make you call? Here are some typical electrical problems: power off, damaged wires in house, kite caught on wires, a cat up a power pole, and a burned-out streetlight.

Some typical water problems are no water, not enough water pressure, water leaks, broken water main, and hydrant leak or break.

Some natural gas problems are pilot light out and won't relight, gas smell, appliance won't start, and no gas.

Telephone problems are tough since you might not have a phone to use to report the problem. Use a neighbor's phone or the nearest public phone. Here are some problems: line is dead, still get dial tone after dialing, obscene calls, and party-line problems.

FAMILY FINANCES

TYPICAL FAMILY EXPENSE
RENT
SAVINGS
TAXES
FOOD
CLOTHING
RECREATION

Your family is like a business. It has money coming in and going out. If more goes out than comes in, there's trouble ahead. You know what happens when the water coming into a tub is less than that going out the drain. The tub is soon empty. And the same thing happens when finances are out of balance.

Businesses have budgets. Families should, too. A budget guesses at how much money will come in and go out. Do you know what your family expenses are? Where does the money come from? Salaries for work done are the usual source of income for most families. Others have interest on invested money. Some get money from the sale of things the family grows or makes.

Talk about family expenses with your mother and dad. You may want to help the family income from your own earnings or do jobs that your parents would have to pay to have done. And you can always help by taking care of your own things. It's money down the drain to have to replace things wrecked by your carelessness.

CHILD CARE

You can help your family by caring for younger children when your parents are away. This is a responsible job. The safety and lives of the children are in your hands.

- Know where your parents can be reached
- Have emergency phone numbers handy
- Know a neighbor who could help if needed
- Act like an adult and not one of the children
- Find out when the children are to go to bed
- Find out if the children are to eat anything
- After the children are in bed, check them every hour
- Keep the children out of danger areas
- Lock the doors. Don't open for anyone unless you know them.
- Stay awake until your parents return

If you don't have younger children at home, you can still use this information. Maybe you'll have a chance to care for the neighbor's children — or even to help at a day care center or church nursery.

FAMILY RECREATION

Recreation helps build the family team. In the freedom of fun, family members can talk more easily with each other. Parents relax. Some of the stiffness between adults and children goes away. Family recreation helps build family spirit and unity. You can help make this kind of fun by suggesting things to do.

Start by listing some of the things you can remember that the family has done. Some were lots more fun than others. Right? Check those. You'll want to do them again.

Now, figure out other things your family

could do. Don't be afraid to think big. List things like trips to interesting places, family picnics, bowling, swimming, a boat trip, or a visit to relatives. And think small, too. How about things that can be done at home? Playing some indoor games after supper, making things, or having a birthday party for a family member could be just right.

Many kinds of fun cost money, but not all of them. Your local newspaper probably runs a weekly list of community activities. Lots of things here will be free.

Whatever you do should be fun for everyone. When you suggest family activities think about things the whole family likes to do.

164

Most people in America live in communities. You probably do. And, if you don't, it is likely you will sometime. So it's pretty important to know about the things that make them work.

COMMUNITY LIVING

REQUIREMENTS AND PAGE REFERENCES

1. Explain what is meant by the following terms:

public utility	169	volunteer or private agency	170-71
public service	169	governmental agency	170
resource	171	tradition	172-173
ethnic group	172	community problem	166-67
government	166	community organization	171

2. Do three of the following:
   a. Make a list of organizations and agencies working in your community. Visit one. Tell what it does. **170-171**
   b. List the activities that take place in your community during a month. Explain the reason for each. Take part in one. **174**
   c. Make a list of some community problems. Explain how each affects you, your family, and the community. **166-167**
   d. Tell something of the history, traditions, contributions, and ways of living of the various ethnic groups in your community. **172**
3. Describe the essential public services in your community. Visit a plant or agency providing one of these services. **169**
4. Show that you know how to get around in your town or region. Show that you know how to use the following: **175**
   a. A map of your town or region
   b. A transportation schedule

Note: "Community" includes your neighborhood, town, housing development, or rural area.

YOUR COMMUNITY

There are 150 people living in Sawmill, Ariz. New York City has over 8 million. Both are communities. People in both have certain needs. The needs of the people in New York City are very different from those in Sawmill, not just because of size, but also because New York is really a combination of thousands of smaller communities.

People have gathered together since caveman days. At first it was for safety from danger. In the Dark Ages they lived near castles for protection by the lord, his knights, and the castle walls. People found they liked being with one another and so more and more gathered together. As communities grew, there were more jobs. Markets sprang up, because there were more people to buy things. New kinds of dangers came with more people, so police and firemen became part of towns. Doctors and hospitals were needed. People found services like these easier to get in communities, and so towns kept growing.

As towns got bigger, they needed leaders. So

governments were formed. Leaders were chosen to make and keep laws to bring safety and happiness to the citizens.

Community Problems

All of this isn't quite as easy as it sounds. There are community problems that disturb the way most people think things should be. Things like poor schools, destruction of property, unemployment, poor transportation, and prejudice are just a few of these. Few of these community problems have clear and easy answers. It might seem simple to just build better schools and hire good teachers. Or to set up better bus schedules, build new roads, or make bigger airports. But, people who live near the airport will fight the increased size, because it will bring more noise and traffic to their neighborhood. Where will that new road go? Probably through a park or where someone's house stands. Again, there will be those who fight against the change. Most community problems are complicated. They call for planning, citizen participation, political action, and money.

Taxes

A town's money comes from its people through taxes. Some money comes directly from them through sales taxes, property taxes, and income taxes. Other money comes from the people, too, but indirectly. When a business is taxed the people still pay, because the business charges more for what it sells.

If a town's taxes get too high, it will get less, not more, money. There won't be enough people paying. When personal taxes get too high, some people move to a place with lower taxes. If business taxes get too high, their prices will get so high people won't buy. Then its taxes can't be paid, and again the taxing town loses money.

Government must be careful that the tax rate is not so high it forces businesses and people out of town. So you can see that government can't solve problems by just raising taxes and spending money. It can go a long way, though, by deciding what problems are most important. It can then tackle those first, spending the available money to solve the most critical needs. For towns to solve their problems leaders have to be good, but they can't do it alone. They need everyone's help. A community problem is the problem of all the people. So they should all work to find the best answer.

Public Utilities and Services

People in communities have special needs. Some of these are provided by public utilities. Things like water, electricity, telephones, and natural gas are considered utilities. Many are owned by private companies, but a few are owned by the community itself. Each town has only one company selling each thing. No matter where you live, you can get your electricity from only one company. That's why utilities are controlled by government rules. With only one company selling the product, it could charge as much as it wanted. You'd have no choice — either pay or go without. So, the prices a utility can charge are set by government.

Other things we need that are usually provided by the community are called public services. These are things like fire and police protection, garbage pickup, and schools. We usually pay for these with taxes. There are still oher public services like newspapers and radio and TV that are owned by private companies.

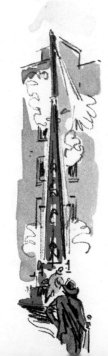

Agencies and Organizations

Needs which aren't shared by everybody are met by agencies and organizations. Some are government run, some private. The county agent's office, department of welfare, and motor vehicle department are all government-run agencies.

There are also private agencies, many of them called "volunteer." This means they depend on the help of people who work without pay. The idea of volunteer organizations has grown until most communities depend on the services they provide. Without volunteers, you wouldn't be a Scout. Your Scoutmaster is a volunteer and he is helped by many other volunteers, all helping in Scouting without any pay. All of this is guided by your Scout council, a volunteer agency.

Some services of other agencies are running blood banks, training in first aid and lifesaving, running children's day care centers, and helping in time of big trouble like floods or tornadoes.

Many volunteer agencies have a need for help you could give. When you do one of these jobs without pay, you are showing the Scout spirit of the Good Turn in a fine way.

These organizations need money to run. It comes from donations by people who believe in the things the agencies are doing. Many of the agencies belong to your United Way of America. They get money indirectly from the people and companies who give to the United Way.

Sometimes, people get together to set up a community organization. A group of parents might organize to get crossing guards at a dangerous street corner. When they get the guards, they might disband because their job is done. But other community organizations keep going, taking on other projects to help their neighborhood. For instance, a block club may help keep a block clean and in good repair.

Community Resources

People also need to relax and enjoy fine things. Many towns have community resources to meet these needs. They set up libraries, museums, zoos, beaches, and parks. These tax-supported things are for all the people to use, and they are often free. There are other community resources that are privately owned like theaters, baseball and football teams, and even some of the things provided by the community in other places. There is usually a charge for the use of private resources.

It is the job of all the people of a community

to keep these resources going. It means taking care of beaches, libraries, parks, schools, and all of the things owned and run by the community. When someone messes them up or breaks things, it costs tax money to fix them. If these costs get too high, the community will either have to charge or charge more to use them. The city might even have to close them down.

Ethnic Groups

Many communities have people of different ethnic groups. These are groups of people with the same background and language or of the same race. Usually all the people in an ethnic group are from the same country or are descendants of these people. There are, for example, blacks, Mexican-Americans, Danes, Puerto Ricans, and American Indians. These groups often have important traditions they have kept alive. A tradition is a belief or custom that has been handed down from generation to generation. It may be a kind of dance, a way of dressing, or a holiday. Whatever it is, the tradition has become a part of the life of the group. Often it gets to be part of your community — not just part of the ethnic group. New Orleans has the Mardi Gras from France. San Francisco celebrates the Chinese New Year. New York has its St. Patrick's Day Parade and Columbus Day celebration. These are big examples, but many communities have smaller ones.

Activity Participation

Now, take a close look at your neighborhood, town, or housing development. How does it compare with the things you've been reading? What are the services and agencies that make it go?

Look in the yellow pages of your phone book under "Clubs and Associations" and "Religious Organizations." Check the white pages for the name of your community, county, and state governments. Also look up "United States." Here you'll find a list of Federal agencies.

Find out, too, who owns your public utilities. Which ones are owned by your city and which by private companies? How about public services? What are they? Where are their headquarters?

Check on what is happening in your community. Most newspapers list coming events. Look at the bulletin boards in grocery stores and community centers. Walk down the street and check store windows for posters telling about things that are going to happen.

After getting all this information, do something about it. Visit a government or private agency to find out what it does. Take part in a neighborhood activity. Take a tour of a public utility. Afterward, tell your fellow Scouts what you learned.

Find out, too, about the ethnic groups in your community. You may even belong to one. Learn some of their history and traditions. Then you'll be able to understand them better. Maybe your parents or Scout leader can answer questions about them. Check your library for books about the ethnic groups in your community. Try to get to know people from different ethnic groups. They will probably be proud to tell you about the background of their group and the contribution it has made to America. The importance of this contribution is tremendous. The United States of America is not only a union of states —it is also made up of all the ethnic groups from around the world.

Getting Around

You have three ways of getting around in most communities. You can walk, go by bike or private car, or use public transportation. For the first two ways, you need to know how to use maps of your town. See the Hiking skill award for help on this.

Public transportation is another story. There are taxis, buses. subways, trains, and even boats and cable cars in some places. Find out what is used in your area. Get a copy of the schedule. It will tell where and when you can get on, and where they will take you.

Small towns don't have public transportation within the town. But most do have it to get from one town to another.

Morning or Afternoon and Evening? — Be sure the time you are looking at is right. Is it a.m. (from midnight to noon) or p.m. (from noon to midnight)? Schedules often show the difference by using bold (dark) type for p.m. Sometimes they print a.m. or p.m. at the top of the time column.

Where To? — Check on the schedule for the listing of the place you want to go. Then find the section showing where you want to start.

How Fast? — Sometimes the bus or train that leaves first gets there after one that leaves later. Check the arrival time for where you want to go. It may save time to wait for the later but faster ride.

You talk. You write. You show how. Unless others understand you, it's a waste of time. That's why it's so important to know how to communicate the right way.

COMMUNICATIONS

REQUIREMENTS AND PAGE REFERENCES

COMMUNICATION IS . . . ?

What is communication? The dictionary says it is an exchange of information. You know something and want others to know it, so you must communicate with them. Others know something you want to know—there must be communication.

So how do you communicate? First of all, you use words that others understand. You might speak English all day long in Italy, but you won't communicate until someone who understands English hears you.

If this person understands you but can't speak English, all he can do is listen. He can't ask questions, so you won't know if he understands. This is one-way communication. It's not very good—better than nothing, but still pretty poor.

Radio, TV, newspapers, and magazines are all examples of one-way communication. You can read or listen but can't talk back. This *Scout Handbook* is one-way communication.

The best communication is two way. It's the kind you have when you talk directly with someone. This can be face-to-face, over the telephone, or on ham radio.

TEACHING A SKILL

Teaching others is great! It's fun to be good at something and then help others to learn. Remember the saying "If the learner didn't learn, the teacher didn't teach." Here are some steps to help you:

Know Your Subject.—Review everything you can find about it. Practice the skill until you are really good.

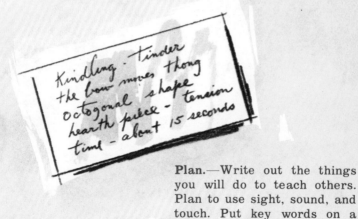

Plan.—Write out the things you will do to teach others. Plan to use sight, sound, and touch. Put key words on a card so you will stay on the track.

Follow Your Plan.—Use your notes. Speak clearly. Use simple words. Ask for questions as you go along. Demonstrate whenever you can.

KINDS OF TINDER

MOUSE NESTS
BIRCH BARK CURLS
DRY WEED TOPS
CEDAR BARK
LINT FROM CLOTH
OR CARDBOARD

Assemble Materials.—Get the things you will need to use. You may need to make drawings ahead of time. You will need program materials for you and the learner to use.

Learner Practice.—After you have shown how, let the learner try it. Make sure he does it right. Show again the things he's not doing well. If he still has problems, ask him what's wrong. He may tell you he doesn't understand something you have done.

Evaluate. — When you're through, talk over how your plan worked with your patrol leader.

INTRODUCTIONS

Introductions help strangers to get to know each other. Names are the key part of any introduction. They must be right and said clearly so they are easily understood.

Person to Person

Don't worry about a lot of formal rules, like who is introduced to whom. (Do you introduce your Scoutmaster to your parents? Or do you introduce your parents to your Scoutmaster?) Today we don't worry much about this. We are much more interested in the introduction itself. Here are some examples:

"Mr. Jones, I'd like to introduce my mother and dad."

"Mom, this is Mr. Jones, my Scoutmaster."

"Mr. Jones — my mother and father."

Speaker to an Audience

Find out things of interest about the speaker. Where has he lived? Where did he go to school? What qualifies him to speak on his subject?

Write the key points on a card. Use this so you will be correct in your introduction.

Be brief. The time you use must come out of the speaker's time if he is to finish on time. Tell the audience enough so they will feel that they know him a little better.

And finally, it is your job to thank the speaker when he is through.

MAKING AN ANNOUNCEMENT

The first step is to talk with your senior patrol leader to get time on the meeting program. You'll have to explain why your announcement is important. Tell him how much time you'll need.

When the time comes to make the announcement:

Be brief and to the point.

Tell what the event is, who it is for, when it will happen, where it will take place, and other details like cost and how to get there.

When you have made your announcement, ask for questions. Then you have two-way communication and can be sure everyone understands.

Troop announcements aren't always about events. They may also inform Scouts of decisions of the troop leaders' council, changes in rules or procedures, and reminders of things like dues.

WRITE A LETTER

A letter is a very personal kind of communication. It is usually written by one person to be read by only one other person.

Think out what you want to say before you start writing. Jot down notes of key points as a reminder. These will help keep you on the track and make sure you don't leave things out.

Set a good tone in your letter — be friendly, courteous, natural, and personal. Don't try to impress by using big words or long sentences. Write the same way you talk.

Don't be afraid to use "I" and "you." You use them when you talk. They help to make a letter warm and personal.

Be neat and write carefully. Be sure your reader will be able to read your handwriting easily. If it's hard to read, he won't struggle with it. If he doesn't read it, you haven't communicated.

Letters are written to tell others something, to try to get action, and to find out. Your letter for this requirement is to try to get action—the use of facilities. Tell a little about yourself, your Scout troop, and your adult leader. This will help impress the reader with the quality of your group. Tell when and why you want to use the facilities. Finally, make your request and ask for a reply.

TELEPHONE USE

Let the phone ring 9 or 10 times before hanging up. Give the person you are calling a chance to get to the phone.

Say right away who you are and to whom you wish to speak.

Be polite.

If what you have to say will take a long time, ask if the person you are calling has time to talk now. If not, ask when you may call back.

Be careful in your timing when you call. Don't phone too early or too late in the day or at mealtimes.

Talk the same way that you would face-to-face. Be interested in the person you are calling and in what you are saying. Your voice will show this to the other person.

When you make a call, it's up to you to cut it off when you have done what you called to do. Don't let the call run on and on in aimless chit-chat. The phone is meant for giving and getting information.

TELL A STORY

You can tell a story. But you must have something to say, and tell it so that your listeners can put themselves into your story.

Something To Say.— Don't try to make up your own stories at the start. Read adventure, mystery, or history stories in books or magazines. Then tell them in your own words.

Know Your Scenes.— The places where your stories happen should be as clear to you as your backyard. See in your mind every detail of each scene you will tell about.

Know Your Characters.—Get to know the people in your stories as well as you know your friends. Then you can describe them when you tell your story.

Tell Your Story.—When you know your story, scenes, and the people so well you can see them, just describe them. Be a reporter telling what you saw when covering a news story.

CURRENT EVENTS

Look for stories with two sides and you'll find interesting current events. These stories have disagreement in them. Some people are in favor and some against. The conflict helps make these stories newsworthy.

But where there is conflict, there can also be slanted reporting—not untrue stories—rather, not telling the whole story. Use many different news sources to be sure you get a fair report. Read more than one newspaper. Listen to several radio and TV stations.

Assemble the Facts.—Clip stories from the papers. Make notes of key points in radio and TV newscasts. Review what you have. Pick out key facts and list them. Then make up your own mind.

PROMOTING AN EVENT

Who do you want to come? Members of your group? parents? friends? the general public? Think, too, about why they should come. Your answer makes a big difference in how you will promote.

Member Promotion.—Make an announcement to the group at a regular meeting. Then form a contact committee. Get about one committee member for every 8 to 10 people that you want to talk to. Give names to each committee member. Ask that they contact each person on their list either face-to-face or by telephone. Have a "fact sheet" they can use to describe the event. Ask them to get a "yes" or "no" from each person they contact.

Parent and Friend Promotion. —Your first announcement to this group should be in writing, either mailed or hand-delivered. For follow-up, use a contact committee to get "yes" or "no" answers.

Public Promotion.—Use all the things that reach many people—posters in stores and on bulletin boards, newspapers, radio, television, and talks to public groups.

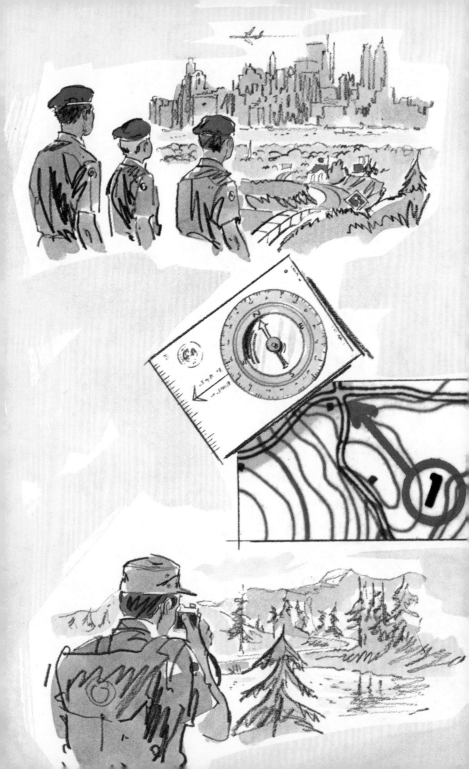

You'll be hiking and walking the rest of your life. What's the difference between the two? A hike is a walk with a purpose. Maybe it's to get to a new campsite or to explore an exciting place. You'll want to hike safely with respect for people and property. Learn to do it right. Then let's go.

HIKING

REQUIREMENTS AND PAGE REFERENCES

1. Tell what to do to take a safe hike.   **192-194**
2. Take a hike in the field.   **196-198, 200-201**
   a. Before leaving, have your plan approved by your leader (including purpose, route, and clothing).
   b. Take a 5-mile hike in the field with the troop, patrol, or two or more other Scouts. Use proper methods and courtesies.
   c. After you get back, tell what you did and learned.
3. Take a hike in your town.   **195-199**
   a. Before leaving, have your plan approved by your leader (including purpose, route, and clothing).
   b. Take a hike to a place of interest outside your neighborhood with an adult or at least two other Scouts. Use proper methods and courtesies.
   c. After you get back, tell what you did and learned.
4. Using a compass, follow a prescribed course with three different degree readings and three different distances. Finish with a 5 percent or less error.   **204-207**
5. Using a map and compass, follow a route you marked on the map far enough to prove you know how.   **208-213**

HIKE SAFETY

To begin with, there are some places that are not safe to visit. Stay away from construction sites and gang territories. Don't hike on roads with heavy traffic and don't hitch rides.

Rule of Three.—Always hike in groups of three or more. It is safer. If you are hurt, one person can go for help. The other fellow can stay with you. Walk single file on roads. Keep to the left so that you can see the traffic coming toward you.

Water.—The safest drinking water on a hike is in your canteen. If you must refill it, use water from a faucet. If in doubt, boil for 5 minutes. Or use water purification tablets, following directions on the container.

Watch Your Step.—Solid is the word for the place to step. So don't walk on loose rocks or logs. They could turn and twist your ankle. Solid is a good word to remember. If you are climbing, solid handholds and solid footholds make for a safe climb.

Landmarks.—Watch for landmarks. Different buildings, trees, vacant lots can help. Landmarks tell you where you are. Without them you could become lost. Study a map of where you are going. Take a map and compass with you.

Sunshine.—In summer the sun can spoil a hike. Protect your head and eyes. Wear light clothing. Use a cream or lotion on exposed skin.

Shadow Stick.—You can find directions without a compass. On a sunny day drive a stick into the ground so that it makes no shadow. Within 15 or 20 minutes a shadow will appear at the base of the stick. The shadow will point to the east.

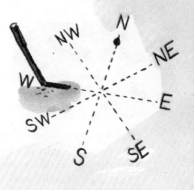

Swimming.—No swimming on hikes unless you do it right. See Swimming skill award for the Safe Swim Defense.

Lightning.—In a storm, stay away from lone trees. Lightning hits tall trees. Hilltops and rock ledges are not safe either. Low spots away from tall objects are safer places.

Keep Off. — Railroad tracks are dangerous. Don't walk along the tracks. Keep away from railroad bridges. A railroad is private property, not a road.

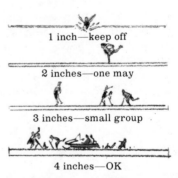

1 inch—keep off

2 inches—one may

3 inches—small group

4 inches—OK

Night Hike.—At night carry a flashlight. Tie something white around your leg. It will bob up and down as you walk. Drivers will see it before they see you.

Ice.—Be careful crossing ice. It must be thick enough to support you. River currents and lake springs make dangerous thin spots in the ice.

TOWN AND CITY HIKES

You'll want a map of where you are going. And no matter where you go: Don't be a wise guy or a loudmouth. Be courteous and you will be welcome.

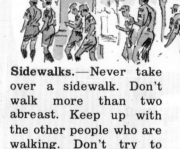

Sidewalks.—Never take over a sidewalk. Don't walk more than two abreast. Keep up with the other people who are walking. Don't try to walk faster than they do. Obey traffic signs.

Crosswalks.—Don't cross in the middle of the block. Cross only at intersections. Crosswalks and crossing areas are for your protection. You have the right-of-way at crosswalks. Be smart. Let the traffic flow.

Lost.—Ask for directions to find the way.

Toilets.—There are public rest rooms in subway and bus stations. You will find them in libraries and government buildings. Many are pay toilets. You will need "emergency change" to use one. It is as important as toilet paper on a hike in the country.

YOUR HIKE PLAN

Who needs a hike plan? You do. Anybody can just walk. What is the idea for your hike? Where are you going? What will you wear? What will you need? Other people need your hike plan too. They need to know where you will be and when you will come back.

Don't forget—
- Extra socks
- Emergency dime
- Toilet paper
- Adhesive bandages
- Handkerchief
- Map and compass
- Pencil and note pad
- A watch

HIKE PLAN OF CHRIS ANDREWS
DATE - MAY 22   8:00 A.M.
WHERE - DIAMOND POINT
ROUTE OUT - OLD BUSH HIGHWAY
ROUTE BACK - E LINE
OTHERS GOING - GARY AND BOB
PURPOSE - TEST PASSING AND FUN
PERMISSION NEEDED - PARENTS AND S.M.
DRINKING WATER - CANTEENS
EQUIPMENT - COMPASS
CLOTHING - UNIFORMS - RAINCOAT
LUNCH - SANDWICH
TIME BACK - 5:30 P.M.

CLOTHING FOR A HIKE

A Scout uniform is not required, but you cannot find a better outfit. It is comfortable. It is tough. And it stands for something. It says that you are a Scout. That's important, because people respect Scouting.

Watch Your Feet.—Shoes or boots should fit well. Don't wear new shoes. Socks should not have holes or darned places. These might cause blisters. Take extra socks in case your feet get wet.

Stay Dry.—Be prepared for rain. A poncho or raincoat and rubbers will keep you dry.

Keep Warm.—In cold weather wear several layers of clothing. Shed them if you are warm. Long underwear, sweaters, windproof jacket, mittens, and a hat with earflaps may be needed.

FOOD FOR A HIKE

Take a Lunch.—Your hike food can be fixed at home before you leave. Sandwiches, an apple, and a candy bar make a good lunch. Carry your lunch in pockets or a small, day hike bag.

Hunter's Lunch.—Be different. Forget the bread. That just makes you thirsty. Put cheese between thin apple slices for a cheese-apple sandwich. Apples, carrots, and celery will not make you thirsty. Cheese, raisins, and fig bars give you energy.

Birdseed.—Make this mixture yourself with the things you like. Put in dry, sugar-coated cereal, one small package of raisins, a half cup of unsalted peanuts or cashew nuts, and a small package of candy-coated chocolates. Enjoy a few handfuls when you are tired and hungry.

SPECIAL-INTEREST HIKE

You can hike in the city or town. Your hike plan should cover the same points as your 5-mile hike in the field. What things of special interest are there where you live?

Museum
Zoo
Park
Factory
Art gallery
Historic site
Dairy
Cattle ranch
Sewage plant

Phone ahead to be sure that you can visit without an adult.

YOUR 5-MILE HIKE

You have made your hike plan. It is approved. You may have to take a bus or a car to your starting place. Now, you are there. Walk at a steady pace. Rest every half hour. You may cover 1½ miles in that time. Get off your feet from 3 to 5 minutes and rest.

Farm Animals.—Fences keep farm animals in where they belong. Gates let people and animals through at proper times. If you open a gate, close it again. Some farm animals can be dangerous. The owner wants you to leave all animals alone.

Water.—Your body needs water—plenty of it when you hike. Drink more than you think you need when you are thirsty. Your body can handle more water than it needs, but breaks down with too little. Replace the water in your canteen each time you come to a water source. (See the "Hike Safety" section.)

Keep Out.—Scouts have no right to walk through private property. If the land is posted, stay off. If you are not sure, ask the owner.

Toilets.—If there are no toilets and you have to go, dig a hole with your heel or a stick. Cover it with dirt. Be sure it is all covered, including the paper.

Fires.—Do not light fires without permission of the property owner. Open fires are against the law in many places. Ask your fire department.

HIKE ACTIVITIES

Photo Hike.—Birds and animals will not stand still. Who can get the best picture? Hide behind something. Wait. No quick moves. Snap!

Nature Scavenger Hunt.— Make a list of some natural things you might find. Each Scout has the same list. Get as many of them as you can. The one with the most wins.

Stalking Hike.—One Scout starts before the others. He does not look back. Every now and then he stops. He counts to five. Then he looks around. If he can see someone following him, that person becomes "it." The game goes on.

Flip-a-Coin Hike.—Start down a road. Every time there is a fork or a side road, flip a coin. Heads, go right. Tails, go left. Make a sketch of your route as you go. Keep track of the time. When your time is half gone, put the coin in your pocket. Head for home following your sketch.

DIRECTIONS AND THE COMPASS

Crystal

Needle

Pivot

Housing or Case

Compass.—How does a compass work? The earth acts like a gigantic magnet. There is a plus and a minus pole. One of these is called the north magnetic pole. It attracts the north end of the compass needle. The compass needle turns on a center pivot.

Hold the compass still and level. Wait for the needle to stop swinging. It will point to the north magnetic pole. The compass needle is a small magnet. Like all magnets, it is attracted to iron and steel. Hold the compass near your belt buckle. If the needle swings toward it, wear another belt. Also look out for powerlines, railroad tracks, and other large steel objects. The power of the earth's magnetism is the only force that should act upon the compass.

Standard Compass.—The needle is the only movable part. Directions are shown on the face. Suppose you had to walk northeast. Hold the compass in both hands with your fingers at 45°. That's northeast. Hold the compass against your chest. Keep it steady and watch the compass needle as you turn. Stop when the north end of the needle points to N. Without turning your head, look up. As far as you can see straight ahead is northeast.

The Trailblazer compass is shown here. It looks like a standard compass. Don't let that fool you. You can set the black arrow in any direction. Just hold the Trailblazer in one hand and twist the clear face with the other to 45°. The black arrow is your direction of travel. The space between the marks is 5°.

Directions.—No matter where you are there are four main directions: north, east, south, and west. Between them are northeast, southeast, southwest, and northwest. Using numbers, there are 360 directions. We call them degrees. A circle above the number means degrees. North is $0°$ and $360°$. Northeast is $45°$. East is $90°$. Southeast is $135°$. South is $180°$. Southwest is $225°$. West is $270°$. Northwest is $315°$.

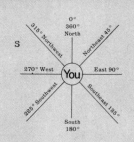

Pathfinder.—Hold this compass by the base plate. Point the direction of travel arrow away from you. Face the direction $45°$. Turn the housing until $45°$ is lined up with the direction of travel arrow. That will be halfway between $40°$ and next big line to the right. The space between the lines is $2°$. Hold the compass chest high and slowly turn. Keep your eye on the magnetic needle. When the needle points to N look up. Straight ahead of you is $45°$.

Direction of Travel Arrow

Base Plate

Compass Needle

Orienting Arrow

Compass Housing

Floating Dial.—The compass needle is under the dial. When the dial stops moving, all directions on the dial are correct magnetic readings. Face $45°$. Hold the compass in both hands chest high. Your two index fingers should point away from you. Slowly turn until you can see $45°$ between your fingers. Look up. Straight ahead of you is the direction $45°$. That direction, remember, is also called northeast.

DISTANCE

100-Foot Taped Distance

Steps and Feet.—You can measure distance. Just count your steps. Then change your steps to feet. Walk a measured 100-foot distance. Walk naturally and count your steps. Walk it again to be sure the count is accurate.

50 Steps.—If your count was close to 50, each step is 2 feet long. You can count by twos each time a foot hits the ground. If your count was 46, try to change your step length to make it come out to 50 on the 100-foot distance.

40 Steps.—If your count was close to 40, each step is 2½ feet long. You can count by fives each time your right foot hits the ground. If your count was 44, try to change your step length to make it come out to 40.

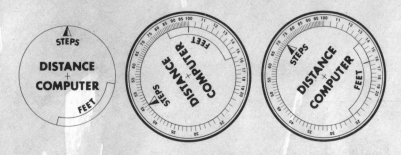

Distance Computer.—Make your own with an inside dial that turns. With this you don't need to change your step length. Turn the dial until the STEPS arrow points to the number of steps it took you to go 100 feet. Let's say 45 steps. Make a mark on the inner dial at 100. If you must measure 160 feet, turn the dial until your mark is opposite 16. Read the number of steps you must take opposite the STEPS arrow. If you took 45 steps to go 100 feet, you will take 72 steps to go 160 feet.

FOLLOW A COURSE

1-2	48°	120 FT.
2-3	185°	95 FT.
3-4	280°	160 FT.

Your Problem.—Your leader will give you a set of degree readings and distances. It is up to you to follow the instructions. The degree readings will be magnetic. Be sure that you know how to use a compass and measure distance.

Your Solution.—Let's say the problem is the one shown here. First, find the direction 48° from your starting point. Take your time. Find something in that direction to look at as you walk. Count the right number of your steps to measure 120 feet. Stop. Find 185° from there. Step off 95 feet. Stop. Find 280° and step off 160 feet. Put a marker down at that spot.

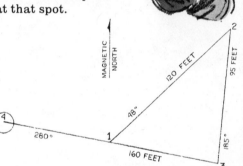

Right or Wrong.—This course measured 375 feet. Your error cannot be greater than 5 per cent of that distance. Your marker must be within 18 ¾ feet of the correct spot. You won't know where that is.

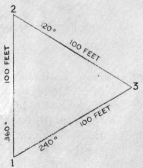

Practice.—You might be able to complete the course without practice. If you need some help, try this. Start by facing 360°. Follow that direction for 100 feet. Change direction to 120°. Step off another 100 feet. Change direction again to 240°. Step off 100 feet. You should be within 15 feet (5 percent error) of where you started.

207

MAPS

What Maps Do.—A map is a picture of the land. Usually the top of the map is north. The bottom is south. The left side is west. The right is east. If you know how to use a map, you can do a lot of things. You can find out how far it is from one place to another. You can tell what direction to go. Everything shown on the map is the way it is on the land. There is just one problem. Maps are laid out to true north. Your compass needle points to the magnetic north pole. This may make a difference. See the chart on the next page.

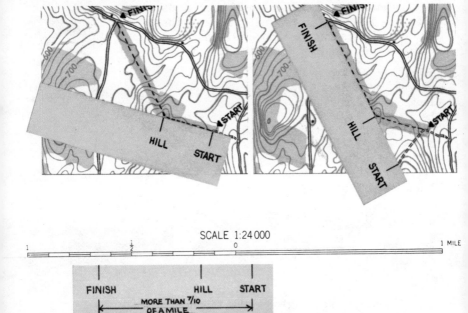

How To Use the Map Scale. — Lay a slip of paper on the map. Make a mark on the paper opposite the start. Do the same for the hill. Turn the paper to mark the finish. Now, lay the slip of paper on the map scale with the first mark at O. Read the distance at the other mark. It is more than seventenths of a mile. How far is the hill?

MAGNETIC DECLINATION OR VARIATION OF THE COMPASS

The magnetic north pole and the true North Pole are not in the same spot on earth. To find out where the compass needle points where you live, look at this list.

	Declination	North
Alabama	2° East	358°
Alaska		
Western	19° East	341°
Eastern	29° East	331°
Arizona	14° East	346°
Arkansas	6° East	354°
California		
Southern	15° East	345°
Northern	18° East	342°
Canal Zone	3° East	357°
Colorado	13° East	347°
Connecticut	13° West	13°
Delaware	9° West	9°
District of Columbia	8° West	8°
Florida	0°	360°
Georgia	0°	360°
Guam	2° East	358°
Hawaii	11° East	349°
Idaho	19° East	341°
Illinois	3° East	357°
Indiana	0°	360°
Iowa	6° East	354°
Kansas	10° East	350°
Kentucky		
Eastern	2° West	2°
Western	2° East	358°
Louisiana	6° East	354°
Maine	18° West	18°
Maryland	8° West	8°
Massachusetts	14° West	14°
Michigan	3° West	3°
Minnesota	6° East	354°
Mississippi	4° East	356°
Missouri	6° East	354°
Montana		
Eastern	14° East	346°
Western	19° East	341°
Nebraska		
Eastern	9° East	351°
Western	12° East	348°
Nevada		
Southern	15° East	345°
Northern	18° East	342°

	Declination	North
New Hampshire	15° West	15°
New Jersey	11° West	11°
New Mexico	12° East	348°
New York	11° West	11°
North Carolina		
Eastern	5° West	5°
Western	1° West	1°
North Dakota		
Eastern	9° East	351°
Western	13° East	347°
Ohio		
Eastern	5° West	5°
Western	1° West	1°
Oklahoma		
Eastern	7° East	353°
Western	11° East	349°
Oregon	19° East	341°
Pennsylvania		
Eastern	9° West	9°
Western	6° West	6°
Puerto Rico	8° West	8°
Rhode Island	14° West	14°
South Carolina	3° West	3°
South Dakota		
Eastern	9° East	351°
Western	13° East	347°
Tennessee		
Eastern	1° West	1°
Western	4° East	356°
Texas		
Eastern	7° East	353°
Western	11° East	349°
Utah	15° East	345°
Vermont	15° West	15°
Virginia		
Eastern	6° West	6°
Western	3° West	3°
Virgin Islands	11° West	11°
Washington	21° East	339°
West Virginia	4° West	4°
Wisconsin	2° East	358°
Wyoming	15° East	345°

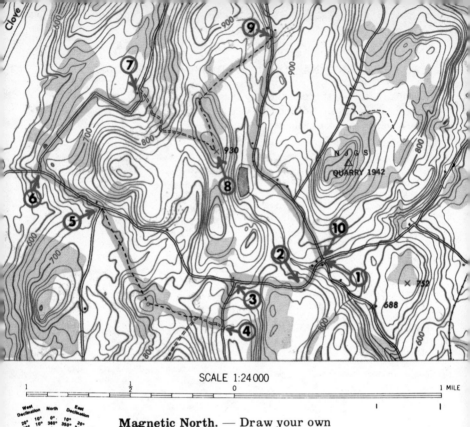

Magnetic North. — Draw your own magnetic north arrow here. See page 209.

Take This 5-Mile Hike Without Moving a Foot

1. From point 1 to point 2 will you be going uphill or downhill? (At point 1 you are at 760 feet.)
2. What direction will you go from 2 to 3?
3. How far is it from 3 to 4?
4. How high is the hill between 4 and 5?
5. What is the direction from 5 to 6?
6. How many turns are there in the road from 6 to 7?
7. How many feet will you have to climb from 7 to 8?
8. Where will you find water between 8 and 9?
9. How far is it from 9 to 10?
10. How long will it take you to hike from 1 to 10? (Walking speed is about 3 miles an hour.)

Map Symbols.—Map makers use signs and colors to show what is on the land.

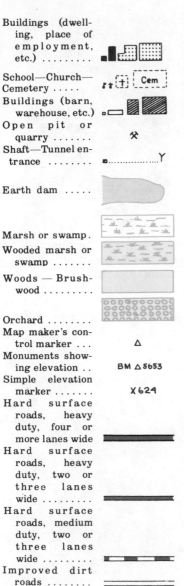

Buildings (dwelling, place of employment, etc.) ....

School—Church—Cemetery .....

Buildings (barn, warehouse, etc.)

Open pit or quarry ....

Shaft—Tunnel entrance ....

Earth dam .....

Marsh or swamp.

Wooded marsh or swamp ....

Woods — Brushwood ....

Orchard ....

Map maker's control marker ...

Monuments showing elevation ..

Simple elevation marker ....

Hard surface roads, heavy duty, four or more lanes wide

Hard surface roads, heavy duty, two or three lanes wide ....

Hard surface roads, medium duty, two or three lanes wide ....

Improved dirt roads ....

Unimproved dirt roads ....

Trail ....

Bridge, road ....
Drawbridge, road
Footbridge .....

Waterwell-spring

Large rapids ....

Small rapids ....

Topographic Maps.—The best maps for hiking are made by the Government. They show the hills and valleys.

Contour Lines.—Topographic maps give you a pilot's view of the earth. The first contour line is 20 feet. Between each line is another 20 feet. Where the lines are close together, the hill is steep. Where they are far apart, the land is almost flat.

To Orient a Map. — Set the compass to north. In this case it's 11°. Place compass on the edge of the map and turn map and compass until the red arrow points to N. Now, all directions on the map fit the directions of the land.

To Read a Direction. — With the map oriented, move the compass to where you want to go. Hold the plate steady and turn the compass housing until the red arrow points to N. In this example, the direction is 345°.

FOLLOW A ROUTE

Read a Map.—Begin with a road map. Study the scale and the symbols. Find on the map two roads or streets that are not far from where you live. Stand near the corner where these come together. Turn the map so that the map shows the roads running in the same direction they do on the ground. This is orienting a map by inspection. That means that you look at the land and the map. You do not need a compass.

Practice.—Trace your route on a map when you ride in a car or bus. Fold the map to the area where you are. Hold the map so that the map street and real street lead straight ahead. Every time the driver turns, turn your map so you are looking down the new road.

Pass Your Test.—Now you are on your own. Your leader will give you a map. Study it. Mark out a route on the map. Then show your leader that you can use the map and compass. Start out on the route that you have marked. Keep going until he says: "You know your stuff."

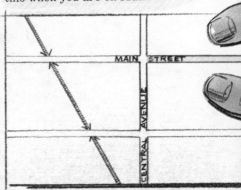

Going West.—Hold the map like this when you are on Main.

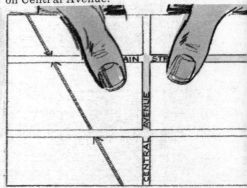

Turning South.—Now hold the map like this when you turn left on Central Avenue.

Millions of people across America today enjoy camping. They pile their gear into the car and head for lakes, streams, mountains, and forests. You have many years of camping ahead of you. It's important to know how to be comfortable, healthy, and safe outdoors. Camping is great when you know how.

CAMPING

REQUIREMENTS AND PAGE REFERENCES

1. Present yourself to your leader before going on an overnight camping trip. Show the camping gear you will use (including food and shelter). Explain how you will use the gear. Show the right way to pack and carry it.   **216-221**
2. Go on an overnight camping trip.
    a. Go on an overnight camping trip with your troop, patrol, or other Scouts using the same equipment. Carry it on your back for at least 1½ miles to your camp. After camping, carry it 1½ miles back.
    b. Pitch a tent correctly in a good place that you picked. Sleep in it overnight. Store it correctly after use.   **230-232**
    c. Make a bed on the ground. Sleep on it overnight.   **234-235**
    d. Follow good health, sanitation, and safety practices. Leave a clean camp.   **236-245**
3. Whip the ends of a rope. Tie a taut-line hitch, bowline, clove hitch, sheet bend, and square knot. Show their correct use on a camp-out.   **225-229**

YOUR CAMP PLAN

You had a hike plan when you went hiking. It's even more important to have a plan when you go camping. Your equipment list is longer, and you need more food. Your plan should cover:

- Your own equipment and pack
- Patrol or group equipment
- Menu and food lists
- Transportation
- Campsite arrangement and permission to use it
- Fire-building arrangements (permit if needed)
- Tour permit, if needed
- Time of leaving and return
- Parents' permission
- Plan of activities
- Things you need for activities

A store isn't just around the corner. The things you forget to bring you do without.

You will have your own equipment list. And you'll need to plan for your share of group gear and food. You'll probably be a member of a patrol when you go camping—or at least part of a group of two or three other guys.

How long you will stay will determine what you need.

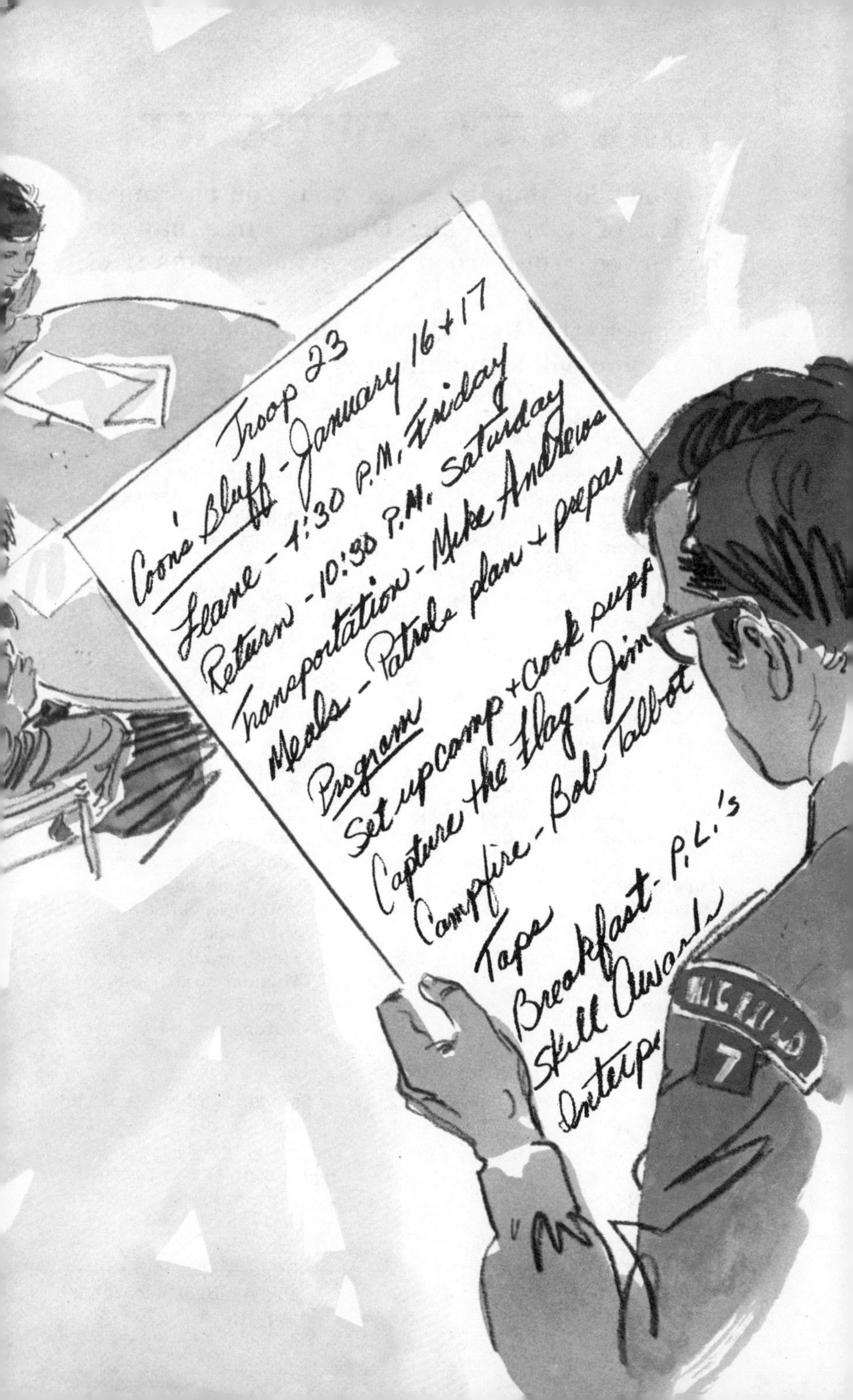
Troop 23
Coon's Bluff - January 16 + 17
Leave - 1:30 P.M. Friday
Return - 10:30 P.M. Saturday
Transportation - Mike Andrews
Meals - Patrols plan + prepar
Program
Set up camp + cook supp
Capture the Flag - Jim
Campfire - Bob Talbot
Taps
Breakfast - P.L.'s
Skill Awards
7

YOUR OWN EQUIPMENT

Don't let this list scare you. You can make a lot of it yourself. Other things can be borrowed. Your troop may even own many of these.

Check the list. Decide the needs for the camp you will be making.

Wear
—Uniform
—Comfortable hiking shoes
—*Sweater or jacket
—*Rubbers, lightweight
—*Raincoat or poncho
—*Rainhat or rainhood
*Or carry where it is easy
   to get.

Carry in Pockets
—Jackknife
—Matches in waterproof case
—Handkerchief
—Wallet and money (include
   change for pay phone)
—Toilet paper in plastic bag
—Adhesive bandages

Top of Pack or Its
Outside Pocket
—Extra socks
—Knife—fork—spoon
—Cup—bowl—plate
—Flashlight

Fastened To Pack or Frame
— Sleeping bag or 2-3 warm
   blankets

Inside Your Pack
—Waterproof ground cloth,
   plastic
—Moccasins or sneakers
   Plastic or cloth bag con-
   taining:
—extra shirt

—extra pants
—pajamas or sweat suit
—extra socks
—change of underwear
   Toilet kit with:
—washcloth
—comb
—soap
—towel
—toothbrush and tooth-
   paste
—washbasin, plastic or
   canvas

You May Also Want These:
—Watch
—Map
—Compass
—Camera, film
—Dark glasses
—Notebook, pencil
—Songbook
—First aid kit
—Musical instrument
—Canteen
—Nature books
—*Scout Handbook* or *Field-
   book*
—Mosquito dope and net-
   ting
—Swim trunks
—Length of rope
—Air mattress or straw
   tick
—Air pillow
—Bible, Testament or
   Prayer Book according
   to faith

PATROL OR GROUP EQUIPMENT

This list is suggested for a patrol. Adapt it for the size of the group you'll be camping with and the length of your stay.

Patrol Center
—Small U.S. flag and patrol flag
—Patrol dining fly, 10 by 10 feet
—Poles, tent pegs, and guy lines for dining fly
—Ax and bow saw
—Cooking gear

Health, Safety, and Sanitation
—Two plastic sheets, at least 4 by 4 feet
—First aid kit
—Toilet paper in plastic bag
—Screw-top water container, collapsible plastic or desert water bag
Cleanup materials:
—scouring pads, nonrusting
—liquid soap in plastic container

—sanitizing tablets for rinse water
—hot pot tongs
—roll of paper towels in plastic bag
—tote-litter bag with plastic liners
—plastic bags, different sizes

Tentage
—Two-man tents
—Poles, tent pegs, and guy lines as needed

You May Also Want These:
—Dutch oven
—Reflector oven
—Griddle
—3-5 canteens (where needed for dry camps)
—Lantern
—Roll of aluminum foil

CARRYING YOUR EQUIPMENT

Bedroll. — You can fasten your sleeping bag or blankets either on top of or under your pack. They should be in a waterproof cover to protect them from rain or snow.

Hip Strap.—Add a hip strap to your pack and you'll add comfort. You can make one from any wide belt. It must reach around your waist. Fasten it to the center of the pack-frame brace.

Pack Frame.—You'll probably want to carry your gear in a pack-sack on a pack frame. On long hikes, packs alone can be hot and uncomfortable. Use a pack frame.

Little Bags.—Your pack is a bag to hold many different bags. The smart camper packs things alike in small bags in his pack —all socks, for example, in a single bag. Do the same with underwear, eating gear, toilet articles, etc. Use clear plastic bags so you can see what's inside. Don't forget to carry an empty bag for dirty clothes.

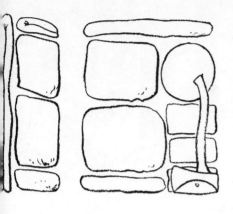

Packing.—Put the last things you'll need on the bottom of your pack. Soft packages go in the part of the pack that will be touching your back. Put things you might need right away in the pack pockets or on top.

26 pounds per load
5⏋130 your weight

Weight.—It depends on the length of your trip and the ruggedness of the trail.

Carry about one-fourth of your weight on short trips.

Plan for only one-fifth of your weight on backpacking trips where you hike most of the day.

Clothing.—Your camp clothing will be about the same as for hiking. The main difference is in amount and the need for night clothing.

You'll want pajamas, changes of underwear, and socks. You'll sleep warmer in the sweat suit type sleeping gear shown.

YOUR CAMP

Put yourself in this picture. Or just on the edge. Maybe out in a boat on the lake. Or hiking through the woods. You might be cooking supper. Wherever you are, you'll find camping know-how on the following pages.

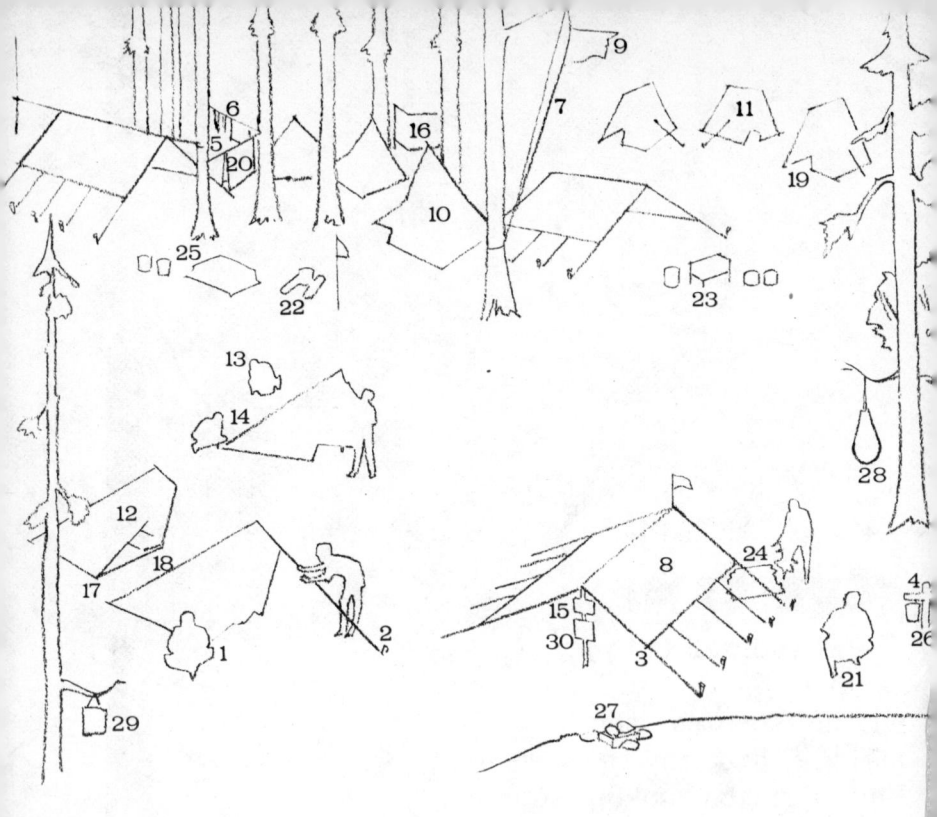

FOLLOW THE NUMBERS

This is a sketch of camp. It numbers the features of camping know-how. You can check out each one.

Look up the matching numbers on the following pages. For example, find number 6 on the sketch. It shows the knot holding two ropes together to make the clothesline. Turn to 6 later on. It will show you how to tie the knot. It's a sheet bend.

ROPES AND KNOTS

There are ropes and knots allover camp. Look at the camping scene again. Tents are shaped and held down by ropes and knots. A rope flies the flag and holds up blankets to be aired. Rope makes a lashing for the fire bucket support and holds up the latrine screening.

You'll need to know how to tie a few basic knots. Most of them will be useful for the rest of your life. These knots have been picked because they meet the test of any good knot. They are easy to tie. They hold when used right. They are easy to untie.

Always whip or backsplice the ends of a rope so they will not ravel.

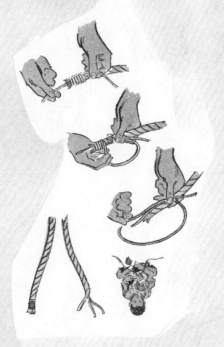

1. **Whipping.** — To whip a rope use about 2 feet of waxed linen thread. Make a loop and hold at end of rope to be whipped. Wrap the thread tightly around the rope. Work from the end of the rope back. Make turns until the whipping is as wide as the rope is thick. Then pull on the ends hard enough to tighten the whipping.

2. Bowline.—The bowline is the best knot for forming a loop that won't slip.

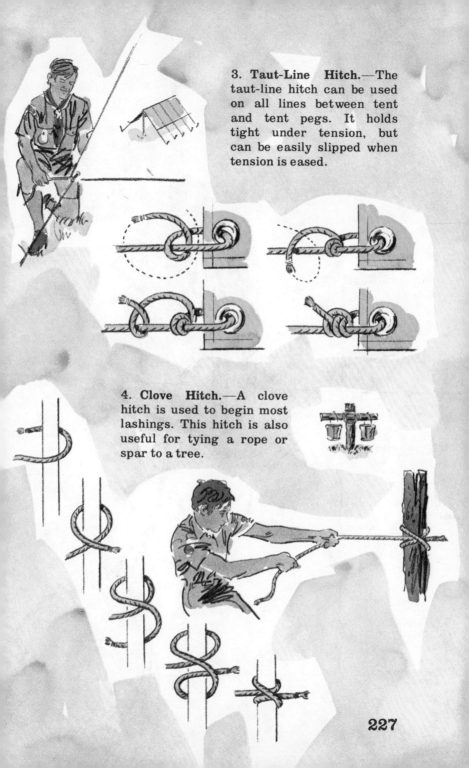

3. Taut-Line Hitch.—The taut-line hitch can be used on all lines between tent and tent pegs. It holds tight under tension, but can be easily slipped when tension is eased.

4. Clove Hitch.—A clove hitch is used to begin most lashings. This hitch is also useful for tying a rope or spar to a tree.

227

5. Two Half Hitches.—Use this for fastening a rope to a post or ring.

228

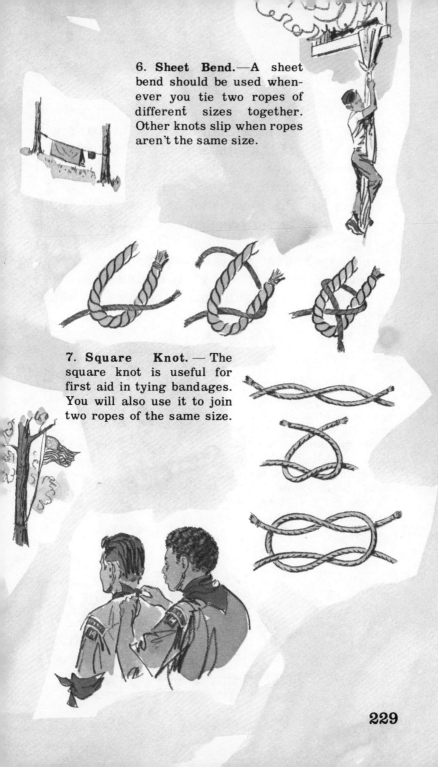

6. Sheet Bend.—A sheet bend should be used whenever you tie two ropes of different sizes together. Other knots slip when ropes aren't the same size.

7. Square Knot. — The square knot is useful for first aid in tying bandages. You will also use it to join two ropes of the same size.

SITES AND TENTS

Gently sloping, grass-covered land with a view makes an ideal campsite. Rainwater will drain away, yet the site is level enough for comfortable sleeping. If the site is steep, you will slide or roll out during the night.

Tents should have shelter from prevailing winds. Those under trees should be pitched with care. None should be under trees with dead branches which might fall during a storm.

Never pitch tents in a gully or under an overhanging cliff. The gully could become a raging river and the cliffs a landslide.

8. **Dining Fly.**—The dining fly is the first thing you set up. It will protect your gear as you make camp. Unpack under it. Get out tools and equipment you need to get ready for cooking. Then buddies set up their own two-man tents.

9. Flags.—The U.S. flag is part of every Scout camp. Bring a small flag and fly it on a line looped over a branch. Patrol flags should be flown at each patrol site.

10. Trailblazer. — The Trailblazer is light, easy to pitch, and good in a wind.

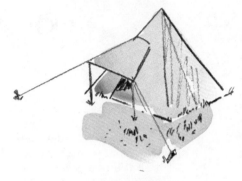

11. Voyager.—The Voyager is an improved "A" or wedge tent. Side pullouts give extra room inside. You can get it with sod cloth or floor and mosquito netting.

12. Overnighter. — The Overnighter is an inexpensive, light, two-man tent, excellent for overnight camping.

13. Tent Site.—Check the ground carefully before pitching your tent. Make sure there aren't any roots, rocks, or anthills. Get rid of sticks or pebbles. They will seem to grow to the size of logs or boulders during the night.

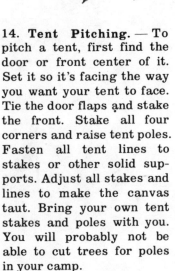

14. Tent Pitching. — To pitch a tent, first find the door or front center of it. Set it so it's facing the way you want your tent to face. Tie the door flaps and stake the front. Stake all four corners and raise tent poles. Fasten all tent lines to stakes or other solid supports. Adjust all stakes and lines to make the canvas taut. Bring your own tent stakes and poles with you. You will probably not be able to cut trees for poles in your camp.

15. First Aid.—A first aid kit is important on every camping trip. Your Scoutmaster will have a troop first aid kit for troop trips. When on your own, carry your own or a patrol first aid kit.

16. Latrine.—A latrine will have to be set up if there are no public toilets. It should be screened from your site to give privacy. The screening could be natural brush or a tied-up piece of canvas. When you dig your latrine, pile about half the dirt at the end of the trench. Save the sod to put back before you leave. Put the other half of the dirt on a plastic sheet. Carry it to your campsite. Use the dirt as a fire base if your fire area is grassy. A small shovel or wooden paddle should be stuck in the dirt by your latrine. Sprinkle a light covering of dirt after each time the latrine is used. Put toilet tissue on a stick to keep it off the ground. Cover with a plastic bag to keep it dry.

FLOORS, BEDS, AND BEDDING

A dry, comfortable bed is important for a good night's sleep. You will use a sleeping bag or blankets.

17. Tent Floor.—A sod cloth and ground cloth will protect you from drafts and crawling insects. Many tents without floors have a sod cloth around the edge. Put your ground cloth down so it is over the sod cloth.

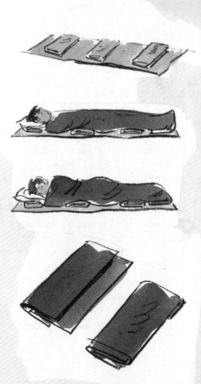

18. Ground Beds. — Use pieces of clothing or equipment for padding. Put extra thicknesses under the small of your back, your head, and your middle thighs. Put your bedroll over the padding. To sleep warm have as many covers under you as you need over you. With two wool blankets you can make a kind of sleeping bag by clever folding. Follow the steps in the illustration. The last step is to lift your feet so the end flops under your legs. When you let down your feet they'll hold the end in place. Blanket pins will help hold things together during the night.

19. Air Mattress.—Test your air mattress by lying on it after it's blown up. Let out air slowly until it feels comfortable. A polyurethane pad is a good substitute for an air mattress.

20. Clothesline.—String a line between two trees. Use it to dry out damp clothing, towels, and swim suits. Air your blankets or sleeping bag in the morning.

FIRES AND FOOD

You will need protected fire and food storage areas to make your camp a success. Plenty of water and firewood should be handy.

21. Rock Fireplace. — A rock fireplace is set up after you have cleared your fire area of things that will burn.

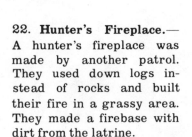

22. Hunter's Fireplace.— A hunter's fireplace was made by another patrol. They used down logs instead of rocks and built their fire in a grassy area. They made a firebase with dirt from the latrine.

23. Charcoal Stove. — A third patrol used charcoal. They started their charcoal as you started your wood fire, with tinder and kindling. Don't use liquid fire starters.

24. Woodpile.—The woodpile should be handy to your fire. Sort and pile wood by size. You might want to stake your woodpile to keep it together.

25. Protection.—Throw a plastic sheet or piece of canvas over your woodpile at night and during wet weather. Weight the edges with rocks or sticks so it won't blow away.

26. Water Buckets.—Keep
a couple of buckets of water
near your tent for instant
fire protection. Keep them
from being knocked over by
lashing a "T" support of
deadwood.

27. Food Cooler.—Make
a simple food cooler by
shaping a holding basin at
water's edge. Put food to be
cooled in watertight con-
tainers. Weight them with
rocks to hold them down. In
warm weather, don't use
foods that will spoil.

28. Food Storage.—Protect your food supply from bugs and animals. One way is to hang it in a bag on a line over a branch.

29. Drinking Water.—Hang the desert water bag where air can freely blow around and cool it. Use a plastic water container during cool weather or if cool drinking water is nearby.

30. Duty Roster.—Use a patrol duty roster. Your patrol leader fills it out and patrol members do the jobs. No one should do all the cooking, cleanup, or wood gathering. Pass the jobs around.

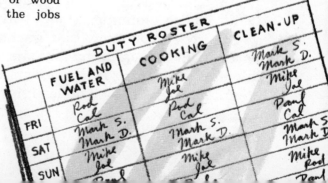

DUTY ROSTER	FUEL AND WATER	COOKING	CLEAN-UP
			Mark S. Mark D.
		Mike Jal	Mike Jal
FRI	Rod Cal	Rod Cal	Paul Cal
SAT	Mark S. Mark D.	Mark S. Mark D.	Mark S Mark D
SUN	Mike Jal	Mike Jal	Mike Rod

CAMP CLEANUP

You'll want to live in a clean camp. It's important to leave a clean camp. Don't litter while you're camping. Don't leave litter when you're gone. You know that garbage, cans, and bottles will be dug up by animals soon after you leave. Dishwashing is an important part of camp cleanliness. It's easy if done right.

Rough Clean. — Wipe out your utensils with paper towels, a rubber scraper, or leaves. Burn soiled towels and leaves.

Wash.—Hot dishwater and soap are needed. Use a dishmop to clean plates, cups, silverware, and pots.

Rinse. — Hold the plates with hot pot tongs. Dunk them in another kettle of water that is nearly boiling. This will heat them so they will dry by themselves. You won't need a dish towel.

Sanitize.—You can be sure your rinse water will sterilize dishes by adding a chemical sanitizing agent. You can get it from your Scout distributor.

Dry.—Spread out your utensils so they can air-dry. Then store them.

Garbage.—Pollution control laws are not the same in each state. Check your own laws about getting rid of trash and garbage by burning. Many campsites have garbage cans and regular pickup. Some leftover food can be put out for birds and animals.

Paper.—Where permitted, you can get rid of most trash and dry garbage by burning. Turn it with a stick so it burns easily.

Wet Garbage.—You must dry wet garbage before it can be burned. Put it close to your fire. As the side near the fire dries, push the pile closer so the dried part burns. Pour grease at the side of your fire. Watch for a flare-up if it hits the flame.

Tin Cans.—Put empty tin cans on your fire to burn out scraps of food. Take the hot cans out with a stick. When cool, flatten by stepping on them.

Tote-Litter Bag. — Wash out empty glass jars. Put them with the flattened cans in your tote-litter bag. Get rid of them at home or at the next trash can. Be sure your tote-litter bag has a plastic liner. You may be bringing back nonburnable wet garbage from your last meal. If law prevents burning, you may have to bring it all back.

Waste Water.—Getting rid of waste water is done according to the camp. In a campsite not used often, carry waste water to the edge of the camp. Scatter it out on the ground. Scatter, don't pour. In a campsite that is used a lot there will be a waste-water sump.

BREAKING CAMP

Keeping a clean camp and leaving a clean camp go hand in hand. You'll leave it the way a good camper should always leave a site—as good as or better than when he came.

Fires.—Put out your fire with water. Sprinkle it rather than pour. When the fire is out, stir the ashes with a stick. Then sprinkle more water on them. Test with your bare hand. It must all be cold enough to touch. Put the ashes, charred wood, and dirt in your latrine hole. See the Cooking skill award for more ideas on this.

Latrine.—Put all dirt back in your latrine hole and pack it down. Put the sod back and firm it in place.

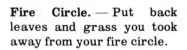

Fire Circle. — Put back leaves and grass you took away from your fire circle.

Woodpile. — Take apart any camp gadgets you made. Put the deadwood on your firewood pile which you are leaving for others.

Tents. — Brush all dirt, grass, and leaves from your tent while folding it. If it's dry, you can store it in its tent bag. If wet or even damp, you'll have to dry it at home before storing. Hang it in a dry garage, basement, or outdoors on a dry day. When dry, store it in its tent bag.

Storage.—Put everything you used in good shape. Then store or return it to the patrol equipment officer. If you put away a dull ax, it will be dull next time. You'll forget that frayed tent line unless you fix it before storing the tent.

Bacon sizzles over a campfire; stew bubbles in a kettle; and biscuits turn golden brown in a Dutch oven — man, that's livin'. A good cook is the most popular guy on any trip. Learn how to cook and you can be the one who sings out "Come and get it." For the rest of your life you'll have it made.

COOKING

REQUIREMENTS AND PAGE REFERENCES

1. Do the following in the outdoors:
   a. Sharpen a knife and ax correctly. Give the rules for the safe use of these tools.   252-257
   b. Use a knife, ax, or saw correctly to prepare kindling or fuel wood.   257
   c. Start a fire using proper precautions on a good fire site. Use proper tinder, kindling, and fuel. Use this fire to cook a simple meal of at least a meat and vegetable.   258
2. Show you know how to cook by doing the following indoors or outdoors:
   a. Cook an egg.   263-264
   b. Cook a vegetable.   264-265
   c. Cook some kind of meat.   266-267
   d. Make a cup of hot cocoa.   270
   e. Cook a dessert.   271
3. Explain what is meant by a balanced menu.
4. Show you know how to buy food by doing the following:
   a. Plan a balanced menu for three meals—breakfast, lunch, and supper.   248-251
   b. Make a food list based on your plan for a patrol of eight Scouts.   250-251
   c. Visit a grocery store and price your food list.   251
   d. Figure out what the cost for each Scout would be.   251
5. On a camping trip(s) with two or more friends or family or your patrol, cook for this group a full breakfast and full dinner or supper.   268-273
6. In each test where you cooked, wash the dishes, if used. Properly get rid of the water, trash, and garbage. Put out your fire. Clean up.   240-243,260

NOTE: When laws do not let you do some of these tests, they may be changed by your Scoutmaster to meet the laws.

GOOD NOURISHMENT

A balanced menu is one that gives you the vitamins, minerals, and other foodstuffs needed for good health. You can live quite awhile on hot dogs and hamburgers, but in time you'd get sick because of the things missing in your diet.

Water is important to good health, so drink plenty each day, in addition to the items in the basic four.

The Four Basic Food Groups

1. **Meat, Poultry, Fish, Eggs.** —At least two helpings every day. At least three eggs a week.

2. **Milk and Milk Products.** —At least 1 quart of milk each day. Also some cheese, ice cream, and other milk products.

3. **Vegetables and Fruit.** —Citrus fruits or tomatoes every day. Dark-green or deep-yellow vegetables at least every other day. Potatoes, other vegetables, and fruit twice a day.

4. **Bread and Other Flour Products.**—At least four helpings each day.

PLANNING MENUS

In planning your menu, use the basic four food groups. Be sure to use all the things considered important. There are many choices. A breakfast of fruit juice, cereal with milk, bacon and eggs, and cocoa has fruit from group 3, meat and eggs from group 1, flour products from group 4, and milk from group 2.

Food List.—Once the menu is planned, make a food list. First, list all the items you need. Then plan for the number who will eat. How many eggs for the breakfast, how much bacon, how many quarts of milk for the cereal and cocoa? Put amounts by each item on your list.

Food :

6 doz eggs
4 lbs of c
3 boxes (
2 lbs.
lb.

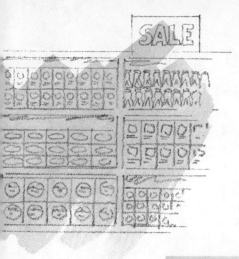

Price It Out.—Your next job is to check costs. Visit a grocery store with your list. You might let the owner or manager know what you are doing. He could be helpful. You don't have to buy anything. In picking package size, keep packing for the trip and amount needed in mind.

$$8 \,\overline{) \,\$17.90 } \;\; \$2.23+$$

Cost for Each Person. — When you have priced your menu, add up the amount and divide by the number who will be eating. This will give you the food cost per person.

...ed meat

...Flakes

...con

...loin steak.

...ed beef

WOODS TOOLS

The knife, ax, and saw were the tools of the pioneers who settled this land.

You don't have the same need for these tools today. But you should know how to use and care for them.

Scout Knife.—The official Scout knife with its strong cutting blade, bottle and can opener, screwdriver, and leather punch is a fine knife for campers. Keep it clean by wiping the blades after use. Take dust and grit out of the blade slots. Oil the blade joints and spring as needed.

Sheath Knife.—This was the knife of the trapper and hunter. It was used to skin and cut up wild game. Today it is used mainly as a camp kitchen knife for slicing, paring, and peeling. Keep it in its sheath when not in use. Carry it in your pack on the trail. If you wear it on your belt around camp, carry it over your hip pocket—never at the front of your body.

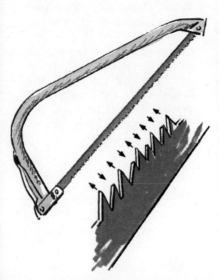

Bow Saw. — Here is the ideal tool to cut wood into lengths. Keep your hands away from the blade when sawing. It has a dangerous habit of jumping out of the cut. If the blade sticks in the cut, it needs fixing. Use pliers to slightly bend each tooth back the way it was when new. The saw will then make a wider cut. For packing or storage, cover the blade with its plastic guard or a folded piece of heavy cardboard.

How To Sharpen a Knife.—A sharp knife is safer and easier to use than a dull one. Lay the blade on a sharpening stone. Raise the back of the blade slightly and push across the stone with a cutting motion. Repeat, making sure every bit of the blade is sharpened. After working one side of the blade, do the same on the other side. Keep changing sides until the blade is sharp. Keep your fingers below the face of the stone.

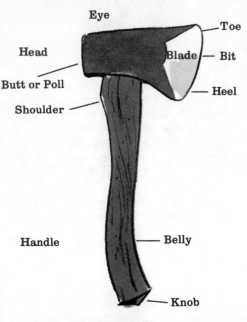

Eye

Head

Butt or Poll

Shoulder

Toe

Blade — Bit

Heel

Handle — Belly

— Knob

Scout Hand Ax.—This tool is used most often to make small firewood out of larger pieces of wood. Use the saw to cut firewood into lengths and the ax to split the lengths into kindling or fuel wood. It can be used for trimming and even felling, but a saw is better.

Ax Handle. — If your ax has a wooden handle, make sure the head is tight. Use proper wedging. If the head becomes loose because the handle dries out, soak it in linseed oil. For temporary swelling, soak in water. Keep the handle free of knicks and splinters by sanding.

How To Sharpen the Ax.—Use a file. Work from the head toward the blade. When one side is bright, turn the ax over and do the other side. Finish the job with a sharpening stone.

Cover the Blade.—Always mask (cover the sharp edge) your ax when not in use. You can mask it with its sheath or by driving it into a log, leaving the handle near the log.

Pack It.—Carry your Scout hand ax in its sheath in your pack. A larger ax in its sheath can be tied to the outside of your pack with the blade toward the rear.

Care and Safety.—Keep all woods tools off the ground. Moisture and dirt cause rust. Take pride in the condition of your woods tools. Never throw them at trees or into the ground. Why work for hours to get a good sharp blade and then mess up the job? Never put woods tools in or near your fire. The heat can make the edge soft and useless. Be sure you have lots of swinging room before starting to cut with an ax. You could have a bad accident if your ax caught on an overhead branch. Keep people away from you when chopping. Be careful when passing an ax to another person. Don't let go until you are sure he has it. Pass it so the blade doesn't point at either one of you.

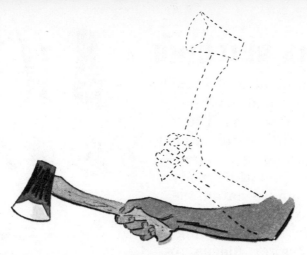

Arm Action.—The Scout hand ax is just that: an ax to be used in the hand—not two hands. If the wood you are trying to cut is so big you need two hands to swing your hand ax, then it's too big for that kind of ax. You need a saw or a bigger ax, or your ax needs sharpening. Use the hand ax by putting motion into it from the elbow through the wrist to the axhead. You don't lift your whole arm to use your hand ax.

Chop on Wood.—Use a chopping block to give a solid base under the wood you are cutting. It also protects your ax blade from hitting the ground. In splitting, put the ax bit at the end of the stick. Lift the stick and the ax together and bring them down together on the chopping block. Just as they hit, twist the ax slightly in the stick.

FIRE BUILDING

To build a fire and cook a meal you need a safe fire area. You'll need tinder to catch the match flame. There must be body kindling to catch the flame from the tinder. When that's going, use bigger pieces to give constant heat.

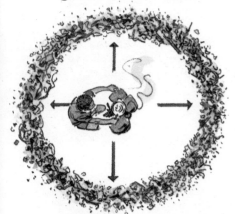

Fire Area.—Find an open space about 10 feet from the nearest brush or tree. There should be no branches above the fire area. Clear a 10-foot circle of dry leaves, grass, twigs, pine needles, etc. You'll put all this stuff back when you break camp. Use mineral dirt 3 or 4 inches thick as a fire base. Put this dirt back before you leave.

Tinder.—Tinder is stuff that flares up when you touch it with a lighted match. Paper is tinder. But you'll want to prove you can start a fire with native tinder. Use dry bark, dead weed tops, and twigs. Or make shavings from split dry wood.

Hot Coals.—Hardwoods or charcoal make the best cooking fire. Hardwoods burn down into coals that give lots of heat. They are easy to control and last a long time. Charcoal acts the same way.

Kindling.—This is the next size up. Small dead branches still on the tree make good kindling. It's called "squaw wood," because Indian women collected it for their fires. Take only wood that snaps easily when you bend it. Remember the saying "If you can't snap it, scrap it."

Lean-To Fire.—Push a stick into the ground at an angle. Aim the top of the stick into the wind. Put a lot of tinder under the lean-to stick. Lean more tinder and small kindling against the stick. Lean small fuel wood on the kindling. Hold a batch of tinder in one hand. Light it. When it flares, shove the burning tinder into your fire from the open end of the tinder pile.

Fuel.—Use deadwood near your camp. Saw it into 10- to 12-inch lengths. Then split it into pieces. Where wood fires aren't permitted, use charcoal for fuel. Never use a charcoal fire in an unventilated area.

Fire Stick.—Another way to start a fire is to put a stick across a couple of small rocks or logs. Put the tinder under this stick. Lean more tinder and kindling against the stick on the downwind side. Light as with the lean-to method.

259

PUTTING OUT THE FIRE

You built your fire in a safe place. You were with it from the moment you touched a match to it until you were ready to put it out. Putting out your fire is one of the most important parts of fire building and cooking.

Cold Out.—Your fire must be **COLD OUT** —cool enough for you to touch with your bare hand.

With Water.—Sprinkle water on your fire. Stir the wet embers with a stick. Sprinkle again and stir again until soaking wet ashes are the result. Turn half burned twigs and drench all sides. Give everything the **COLD OUT** test.

Without Water.—Work mineral soil (soil with nothing in it that will burn) into the ashes. Stir, stir, stir again until the last ember is out. Rub burned sticks against the ground until all sparks are out. Give everything the **COLD OUT** test.

PREPARING TO COOK

Make a Kitchen.—Spread a plastic sheet to work on. Keep food and utensils on it. Use it to air-dry your dishes after washing.

Pots and Pans.—Soap the outside of pots and pans before using over an open fire. This will make it much easier to clean off the black, cooked-on soot. Soak a small piece of soap in water until soft. Rub the soft soap on the outside of the pot with your hand, covering it thoroughly. Be sure none of the soap gets inside.

COOKING

Learn basic skills, and it will be easy to cook camp meals. The skills are boiling, broiling, frying, baking, roasting, and stewing. And there's one more skill—follow the recipes! You can practice on an electric or gas stove at home. Then graduate to a fire outside. The main difference is in the way you control the heat. On your stove, you just turn the heat up or down.

Over a fire you change the heat by moving things closer to or farther from the fire. See "Hand Thermometer" below. An even heat is important. With leaping flames you can't control the distance between the heat and your pan. One second the flames are touching the pan and the next they are a foot away. Coals—steady, glowing coals — are the answer.

Hand Thermometer.—Hold your bare hand over the coals. Count 1 and 2 and 3—OUCH. The seconds you can stand to hold your hand over the fire are your guide. Raise or lower your hand to find the temperature you want.

Hand Removed	Temperature About	Heat
Between 4 and 5 seconds	300°	Low
Between 3 and 4 seconds	350°	Medium
In less than 3 seconds	400°	High

Eggs

Poached.—Bring about 2 inches of water in a pan to a boil. Reduce heat until water is simmering. Break egg into a cup and then slide it out into the hot water. Remove pan from the heat and let stand for about 4 minutes. While standing, spoon hot water over that part of the egg above water. Remove cooked egg from water and put on toast.

Soft-Boiled.—Put eggs in pan. Cover with water. Bring water to a boil. Then take pan off fire. Let stand 4 minutes. Take out eggs, and they will be soft-boiled if used right away.

Hard-Boiled.—Cook as soft-boiled but let stand 20 minutes in hot water.

Fried.—Heat butter or bacon grease in frying pan until it sizzles. Reduce heat to low. Break egg in pan. Cook until white is firm. If a hard yolk is wanted, turn the egg over. Season with salt and pepper.

Scrambled.—Break 8 eggs into a bowl. Add 1/2 teaspoon salt, a pinch of pepper, and 8 tablespoons of milk. Beat until well mixed. Pour into greased frying pan. Make sure none sticks to skillet by turning mix from bottom to top. When egg is in cooked chunks, it is done. This recipe will serve eight people or four hungry Scouts.

French Toast.—Break 6 eggs into bowl and beat. Add 2 cups milk and 1 teaspoon salt. Beat. Dip bread slices in the mix until both sides are coated. Fry on greased frying pan or griddle until golden brown on both sides. Serve with butter, syrup, jam, or jelly. This will coat about 20 pieces of bread.

Vegetables

Boiled.—Most vegetables, including potatoes and rice, can be prepared by boiling. Use just enough water to cover. Keep the lid on so water won't boil away.

Fried.—Vegetables to be fried should be sliced, diced, or cut up into small pieces. Deep-fried vegetables need enough grease to cover them. For regular frying, use just enough to stop sticking. Turn vegetables often when frying.

Baked.—Break skin on vegetables such as potatoes by jabbing with fork to let steam out without exploding the vegetable. Wrap in foil and put in oven or outside fire. Bake about 45 minutes. If fork goes in vegetable easily, it's done.

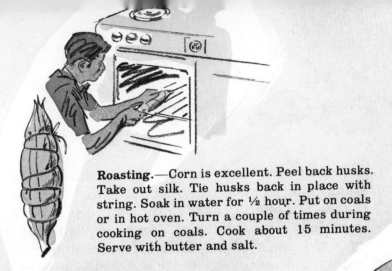

Roasting.—Corn is excellent. Peel back husks. Take out silk. Tie husks back in place with string. Soak in water for ½ hour. Put on coals or in hot oven. Turn a couple of times during cooking on coals. Cook about 15 minutes. Serve with butter and salt.

Baked in Coals.—You can bake potatoes by putting them right in the coals. Punch a hole in the skin. Make sure the potato is all covered by coals or ashes, or it will burn. When it's easy to put a fork into the potato, it's done.

Rice.—Cooking regular rice is tricky. But converted or instant rice is a cinch. Beginning chefs should use instant rice and follow package instructions.

Meats

Most meat 2 inches thick or less can be fried:
steak, chops, sliced ham, bacon, and chicken.
Use just enough grease in the pan to stop sticking. Meat good for frying can be broiled. Put it
over the coals of an outside fire or under the
broiler unit of an oven. Meat should be from 3
to 6 inches from the heat. Put it very close at
the start to sear the meat. That helps to hold
in the juices. Then move it farther away.

Kabob.—Don't forget kabob when thinking of broiled meat.
Sure, its more than just meat, but meat is the main ingredient. Cut ¼ pound of lamb or steak into 1-inch cubes. Peel an
onion, cut it lengthwise, and take apart the leaves. Make a
skewer from a straight stick about as big as a pencil. Sharp-
en one end to a point. String meat, onions, cherry tomatoes,
and sliced carrots on the stick. Put over coals at high heat.
Cook about 15 minutes. Turn once or twice during cooking.
Season to taste with salt and pepper. Sometime, try sliced
peppers, mushrooms, pineapple, and peach halves with ham.

Stew.—Brown chunks of meat in a pan over the fire. When brown, put them in a kettle with diced potatoes, carrots, onions, and beans (almost any vegetable in season). Simmer just below the boiling point for an hour or so. Salt and pepper to taste.

Roast.—Large chunks of meat are usually cooked by slow roasting. Put meat in pan with a cover. Roast in oven or just off the direct heat of a campfire. Timing will depend on size of roast and heat source. A 4-pound beef roast on low heat will take about 3 hours. You might add water during roasting to keep moist. This is then called braising instead of roasting.

Tarzan Steak.—Another method of broiling is to put meat directly on the coals. Blow the ashes off, and then put the steak right on the coals. Cook about 5 or 6 minutes on each side. Season with salt and pepper.

Control the Flames.—When broiling over coals, grease may drip and flare up and char the meat. When this happens, squirt base of flame with water to kill it. Use an old plastic, liquid-soap bottle filled with water.

Breadstuff

Biscuits.—Mix prepared biscuit dough according to instructions on the package. Keep plenty of *dry mix* on your hands to keep dough from sticking to them. Don't mix or work the dough any more than needed. Bake in a reflector or Dutch oven. You can use your *Scout cook kit* by putting the bowl over the frying pan and covering it with coals. You can also bake in foil by wrapping dough loosely to allow room to expand in the foil.

Twist. — Mix biscuit dough so it's a little on the thick side. Form dough into a long sausage shape and twist around a stick about as big around as an ax handle. Push stick in ground at a slant close to fire. Turn stick from time to time to cook all the way around.

Toast.—You can make toast directly on your coals if there's no flame. Blow surface ash off and put bread on coals. As soon as you see a flicker of smoke, lift bread with fork and turn it over. Keep doing this until toasted to suit your taste.

Biscuit Cup.—Round the end of a stick about the size of a ball bat. Mix biscuit dough and cup it over the rounded end of the stick. Put stick in ground and cook the same as twist. Put some stew in the biscuit cup for a real treat.

Pancakes.—Mix batter according to instructions on the ready-mixed package. Heat skillet or griddle and melt enough grease on it to wet it allover. Pour batter on griddle until it spreads to about 4 inches. When bubbles appear at center and break, sneak a peek under one of the edges. If it's brown, turn and cook the other side. Serve with butter or margarine and syrup or jam.

Cereal, Soup, Cocoa, and Salad

Oatmeal.—Bring 3/4 cup of water to a boil. Pour it over 1/2 cup instant oatmeal in a bowl. Stir until well mixed. Sprinkle with salt and stir in. Serves one.

Farina.—Pour 1/4 cup farina into 1 cup boiling water. Add pinch of salt. Boil gently 5 minutes, stirring often. Serves one.

Powdered Soup.—Dried or powdered soups come in many different package sizes. Follow package directions as to amount of water, cooking time, and quantity.

Condensed Soup.—A half can of condensed soup will serve one person. Pour soup into a pan and add an equal amount of water (or milk). Cook according to instructions on the can.

Stew Juice.—When you are making stew add plenty of water to the kettle. Before serving the stew, pour off the liquid into a separate pan and serve as soup.

Cocoa.—There are three kinds of prepared cocoa products:

   Type 1—Add hot milk to the mix.

   Type 2—Add hot milk to a mixture of cocoa mix and sugar.

   Type 3—Add hot water to the mix. This kind is the handiest for camping trips.

Salads.—Most salads aren't cooked. They are made of fresh vegetables and fruit. You need them for a balanced diet. Lettuce, tomatoes, onions, radishes, celery, and carrots are all good in a vegetable salad. Add prepared salad dressing and season to taste.

Fruit

Stewed Fruit.—Cover dry fruit such as prunes, apricots, peaches, or apples with water. Bring to a boil. Then reduce heat to keep just below boiling. Cook about 20 minutes. Add sugar just before it is done.

Baked Apple.—Core an apple. Put brown sugar with a little cinnamon added in the hole left by the core removal. Or fill with tiny "red hot" candy. Wrap in aluminum foil. Put directly on the coals or in your oven. Bake about 30 minutes.

Baked Banana.—Slice a peeled banana in half lengthwise. Put jam or jelly on one flat side. Put the two halves back together. Put the peel back around the banana. Wrap in aluminum foil. Bake on the coals about 10 minutes.

Fresh Fruit.—Look for wild blueberries, raspberries, and similar fruit. They go good on your breakfast cereal. If they're out of season, bring some bananas, oranges, or apples with you.

OLD FAVORITES

Spaghetti.—Cook 1½ pounds spaghetti in boiling, salted water about 6 minutes. Bite a piece to see if it's done. Drain all water. Good spaghetti sauce calls for many ingredients. When cooking outdoors, you will probably want to use a commercially prepared sauce. Put spaghetti on plates. Pour hot sauce over it. Serves eight.

Macaroni and Cheese.—Cook 1½ pounds macaroni in boiling, salted water about 15 minutes. Bite test as in cooking spaghetti. To make a sauce melt 3 tablespoons butter or margarine. Add 3 tablespoons flour, stirring until smooth with a fork. Add 1½ cups milk slowly to heated mixture. Cook until it boils. Stir during cooking. Add 2 cups melted American cheese and 1 teaspoon Worcestershire sauce to the mix. Pour sauce over macaroni. Serves eight.

Chili.—Fry 3 pounds hamburger and 2 cups diced onions in melted butter or margarine. Add two No. 2 cans kidney or pinto beans and 2 cans tomatoes. Add 3 tablespoons chili powder. Cook while stirring until ingredients are all mixed and heated. Salt and pepper to taste. Serves eight.

Corned Beef Hash.—Chop 4 cups corned beef and 6 cups boiled potatoes. Mix together in kettle large enough to hold all the ingredients. Melt ½ cup of butter or margarine and add with enough milk (fresh or canned) to come up an inch or two in the kettle. Heat to just below boiling point. Put on kettle cover. Cook at least a half hour. Stir from time to time. Just before serving, break in 8 eggs. Cover again. Cook another 3 or 4 minutes. Serves eight.

Fish Chowder.—Cook 4 strips bacon until crisp. Remove from pan, crumble, and save for later. Put bacon grease in soup kettle. Add 1 cup chopped onions and brown. Add 3 cups water and 3 large diced potatoes. Cook until potatoes are tender. Cut 2 pounds fish filets into small squares. Add to mixture along with 3/4 cup diced celery. Cut 2 tomatoes into wedges. Add along with 1 can canned milk and the bacon. Heat below boiling point until very hot. Season the chowder with salt and pepper to taste. Serves eight.

A Foil Meal.—Slice a large potato, medium onion, and a couple of carrots. Put about half the slices in the center of a sheet of aluminum foil. Salt and pepper. Put a thick hamburger patty on top of the sliced vegetables. Put the rest of the sliced vegetables on top of the hamburger. Salt and pepper again. Close foil around the food. Put the package on a bed of coals. Cook about 10 minutes. Take off coals and open the package. Add more salt and pepper to taste. You can eat from the package.

Natural laws rule all life on earth. Breaking these laws can bring disaster to mankind. You need to understand these laws of nature and to appreciate your interdependence with your environment and life everywhere.

ENVIRONMENT

REQUIREMENTS AND PAGE REFERENCES

1. Explain how animals (mammals, birds, fish, reptiles, insects) depend upon plants. In the outdoors, find and name 10 different kinds of wild animals or signs of them. Describe the environment where each was found.   **276-297**
2. Explain the relationship of plant life with the environment in which it grows. Tell the importance of plants to man. In the outdoors, find and name 10 different kinds of plants. Describe where each was found.   **276-297**
3. Do two of the following:
   a. Make a closed terrarium that includes animals. Describe how you made it. Tell what you saw happen for a month.   **301**
   b. Make an aquarium that has plants and animals. Describe how you made it. Tell what you saw happen in it for a month.   **300**
   c. Keep a daily weather record for your neighborhood for a month. Include rainfall, sunshine, days with smog, temperature, wind speed and direction, and humidity. Tell how the weather affects you and your environment.   **298-299**
   d. See and name 10 kinds of wild birds. Tell what each was doing when you saw it.   **304**
   e. Grow a plant cutting in a plastic bag. Describe what you saw and learned.   **302-303**
4. Do one of the following:
   a. Make a display of at least 20 newspaper and magazine clippings on national or local environmental problems.
   b. Help an adult group with one of its ecology projects.
   c. Name the major kinds of pollution in your town. Report one cause.   **310-312**
   d. Report on the study of a 10-square-foot plot that has plants you can see. List the plants and animals you found.   **305**

LAND FOOD CHAIN

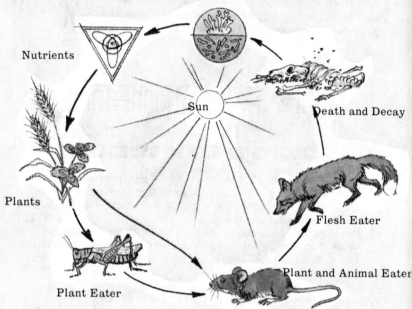

Nutrients

Sun

Death and Decay

Plants

Flesh Eater

Plant Eater

Plant and Animal Eater

Animals need food to live. Some such as deer, squirrels, and seed-eating birds live on plant life. Others like foxes, shrews, hawks, and owls eat the flesh of other animals. They all depend on plant life, even the flesh-eating animal. The food he eats lives on plant-life.

Energy from the sun is needed by all living things. Animals get their energy from food. The mouse eats a root and gets energy from it. The mouse is eaten by a fox. The fox gets energy from the mouse. Body wastes from both the mouse and the fox return to the soil as food for plants, called nutrients. When animals die their remains also return to the soil. The nutrients from the animals will be used by plants.

AQUATIC FOOD CHAIN

This is almost the same as the land food chain. But it happens in water with water animals. Water plant life grows with aid from the sun's energy. Plant life is eaten directly or indirectly by animals. It supplies the energy needed for their life.

The nutrients come from animal body wastes and decomposed plant and animal life. Nutrients are in the water and soil at the bottom.

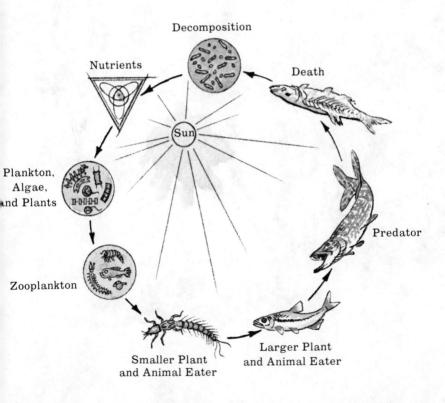

Decomposition

Nutrients

Death

Sun

Plankton, Algae, and Plants

Predator

Zooplankton

Smaller Plant and Animal Eater

Larger Plant and Animal Eater

IMPORTANCE OF PLANTS TO MAN

COMMUNITIES OF NATURE

Plants and animals live together in natural communities. They depend upon one another. Natural communities are not all alike. Rain, kind of soil, temperature, sunlight, interaction of plants and animals, and even man influences the make-up of these communities.

Some are typically forest. Others are desert, prairie, or marsh. There are even differences in these typical communities. A northeastern forest community is very different than a forest on the west coast.

Look carefully at these communities on the following pages. Learn to identify the plants and animals common to each. Then ask yourself some questions about each community. What made it the way it is? Why are some plants and animals in one community but not another? What would happen to the animals in a forest community if the trees were removed? What changes take place when a swamp is drained? Or a dam built on a river? What happens when there are more animals than food in an area?

When you understand these kinds of things you'll know why the laws of nature are so important to man.

SIGNS OF WILDLIFE

Do you really see? See with your mind as well as your eyes? If you came on the scene above, what would it say to you? Could you see in your mind the wildlife that has been there? How many signs of wildlife can you see?

Try to identify the wildlife before looking at the bottom picture. Then look at the picture below. How did you do? Do you know why certain animals were in certain areas? Places where you find an animal are known as its habitat. Know the habitat and it will help you name the animals usually found in it.

CITY

SEASHORE AND OCEAN

1. Herring Gull
2. Porpoise
3. Bald Eagle
4. Common Tern
5. Semipalmated Sandpiper
6. Dead Horseshoe Crab
7. Rockweed
8. Left-handed Welk
9. Deer Mouse
10. Razor Clam
11. Common Starfish
12. Sand Shrimp
13. Ghost Crab
14. Scallop Shell
15. Moon Shell
16. Sand Dollar
17. Skate Egg Case
18. Fiddler Crab
19. Hermit Crab
    (in Moon Shell)
20. Common Mackerel
21. Portugese Man-of-warır
22. Bluefish
23. Soft Shell Clam
24. Porgy
25. Sand Shark
26. Flounder
27. Mole Crab
28. Sea-anemone
29. Kelp
30. Sea Lettuce
31. Limpets
32. Common Mussels
33. Sea-urchin
34. Oyster Drill
35. Oyster
36. Rock Barnacle
37. Blue Crab
38. Periwinkle
39. Blue-green Algae

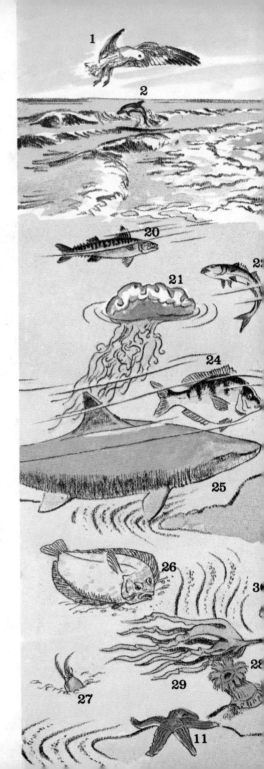

STREAMS AND LAKES

MARSHES AND SWAMPS

1. Red Maple
2. Poison Sumac
3. Pussy Willow
4. Mallard Duck
5. Marsh Hawk
6. Black Willow
7. Cattails
8. Great Blue Heron
9. Red-winged Blackbird
10. Arrowhead
11. Reeds
12. Black-crowned Night Heron
13. American Coot
14. Spatterdock
15. Bank Swallow
16. Muskrat
17. Sora Rail
18. Sedges
19. American Bittern
20. Water Snake
21. Damselfly
22. Rushes
23. Dragonfly
24. Pied-billed Grebe
25. Pintail Duck
26. Green Heron
27. King Rail
28. Cottonmouth
29. Mink
30. Wild Rice
31. Snapping Turtle
32. Painted Turtle
33. Leopard Frog
34. Bullfrog
35. Wild Celery
36. Sundew
37. Pitcher Plant
38. Spring Peeper

WESTERN DESERT

1. Saguaro Cactus
2. Gila Woodpecker
3. Red-tailed Hawk
4. Turkey Vulture
5. White-winged Dove
6. Paloverde
7. Cholla Cactus
8. Yucca
9. Barrel Cactus
10. Peccary
11. Spotted Skunk
12. Ocotillo
13. Diamondback Rat
14. Creosote Bush
15. Kit Fox
16. Mesquite
17. Staghorn Cholla
18. Yuma Antelope S
19. Desert Tortoise
20. Elf Owl
21. Road-runner
22. Prickly Pear Cact
23. Collared Lizard
24. Gila Monster
25. Beaver Tail Cactu
26. Gambel's Quail
27. Sidewinder
28. Black-tailed Jack
29. Cactus Wren
30. Zebra-tailed Liza
31. Kangaroo Rat
32. Garter Snake
33. Centipede
34. Tarantula
35. Scorpion
36. Horned Lizard (t

EASTERN WOODLANDS

1. Red-eyed Vireo
2. Blue Jay
3. Screech Owl
4. Gray Squirrel
5. Cooper's Hawk
6. Scarlet Tanager
7. Sassafras
8. Gray Birch
9. Black-capped Chickadee
10. White Ash
11. Dogwood
12. White Pine
13. White Oak
14. Spicebush
15. White-tailed Deer
16. Hairy Woodpecker
17. American Beech
18. Viburnum
19. Shagbark Hickory
20. Sugar Maple
21. Wood Thrush
22. Rhododendron
23. Raccoon
24. King Snake
25. Long-tailed Weasel
26. Ruffed Grouse
27. Ferns
28. Box Turtle
29. Ringneck Snake
30. Eastern Chipmunk
31. Wood Frog
32. Ovenbird
33. White-footed Mouse
34. Shrew
35. Red Eft

WESTERN EVERGREEN FOREST

1. Lodgepole Pine
2. Ponderosa Pine
3. Goshawk
4. Douglas-fir
5. Golden Eagle
6. Quaking Aspen
7. Engelmann Spruce
8. Great Horned Owl
9. Abert Squirrel
10. White Fir
11. Steller's Jay
12. Western Tanager
13. Elk
14. Mule Deer
15. Clark's Nutcracker
16. Bobcat
17. Red Squirrel
18. Fisher
19. Oregon Junco
20. Porcupine
21. Black Bear (brown)

FIELDS

1. Cottonwood
2. Red-tailed Hawk
3. Barn Swallow
4. Walnut
5. Pheasant
6. Pin Cherry
7. Bobwhite
8. Crow
9. Red Fox
10. Cottontail
11. Wheat
12. Sumac
13. Apples
14. Multiflora Rose
15. Blackberry
16. Bluebird
17. Corn
18. Meadowlark
19. Striped Skunk
20. Leopard Frog
21. Lichen
22. Meadow Vole
23. Garter Snake
24. Lark Sparrow
25. Pasture (grasses)

PRAIRIES

1. Lark Bunting
2. Coyote
3. Sagebrush
4. Grama-grass
5. Pronghorn Antelope
6. Prairie Falcon
7. Bison Skull
8. Thirteen-lined Ground
   Squirrel
9. Burrowing Owl
10. Jackrabbit
11. Prairie Rattlesnake
12. Horned Lark
13. Badger
14. Prairie Dog

296

WEATHER STATION

Know your climate and you'll better understand your own environment. Weather records will help you to learn. Use information from lo-

WEATHER RECORD

WEATHER RECORD

Date _____

	a.m.	p.m.	
Temperature			
Relative humidity			
Wind direction			
Wind velocity			
Rainfall			
Sunshine			
Smog			

Weather Record Chart. — Record daily. At the end of the month use information to interpret your weather.

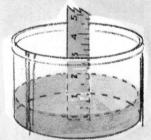

Rain Gauge. — This can be as simple as a No. 10 can or a coffee can. Whatever you use must have top, sides, and bottom the same diameter. Measure rainfall daily with a ruler. Empty can after each measurement.

You can estimate wind velocity by using the Beaufort Scale.

Beaufort Scale*

When you see this:	The wind's miles per hour is:
Calm; smoke goes straight up.	Under 1
Direction of wind shown by smoke drift, but not by wind vane.	1 to 3
Wind felt on face; leaves rustle; wind vane moves.	4 to 7
Leaves and small twigs move steadily; small flag held straight out.	8 to 12
Dust and loose paper raised; small branches are moved.	13 to 18
Small trees sway; waves form on lakes.	19 to 24
Large branches move; wires whistle; umbrellas hard to use.	25 to 31
Whole trees in motion; hard to walk against the wind.	32 to 38
Twigs break from trees; very hard to walk against the wind.	39 to 46
Small damage to buildings.	47 to 54
Much damage to buildings; trees uprooted.	55 to 63
Widespread damage from wind.	64 to 72
Violence and destruction from wind.	73 and up

*Original scale modified to simplify.

cal newspapers, radio, or TV, if available. If not, set up a simple weather station. Take readings twice a day for temperature, relative humidity, and wind. The others on the chart can be done once each day.

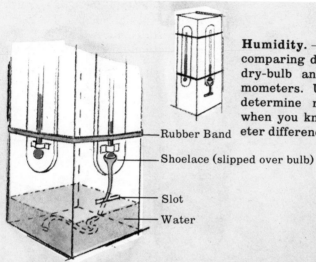

Humidity. — Measure by comparing difference between dry-bulb and wet-bulb thermometers. Use the chart to determine relative humidity when you know the thermometer differences.

Rubber Band

Shoelace (slipped over bulb)

Slot

Water

TABLE OF RELATIVE HUMIDITY—MEASURING MOISTURE

Difference between wet-bulb and dry-bulb readings	Temperature of air, dry-bulb thermometer, Fahrenheit							
	30°	40°	50°	60°	70°	80°	90°	100°
1	90	92	93	94	95	96	96	97
2	79	84	87	89	90	92	92	93
3	68	76	80	84	86	87	88	90
4	58	68	74	78	81	83	85	86
6	38	52	61	68	72	75	78	80
8	18	37	49	58	64	68	71	74
10		22	37	48	55	61	65	68
12		8	26	39	48	54	59	62
14			16	30	40	47	53	57
16			5	21	33	41	47	51
18				13	26	35	41	47
20				5	19	29	36	42
22					12	23	32	37
24					6	18	26	33

AQUARIUM

Materials needed:
 Fishbowl
 Clean sand and gravel
 Rocks and stones
 Local aquatic plants
 Snails
 Minnows

Set up as shown. Don't try to put in more than 1 inch of fish for each 10 square inches of water surface. Use tap water from which chlorine is removed by letting water stand for a day or by adding special chemicals. Add water to replace that lost by evaporation.

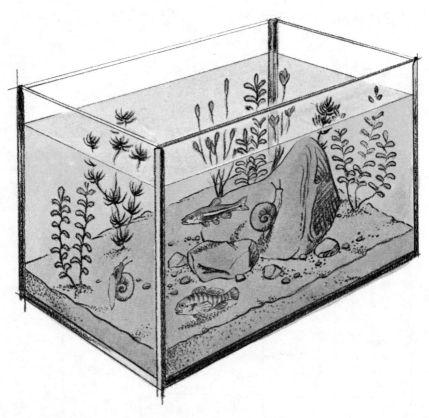

TERRARIUM

Materials needed:
- Gallon jar or other container
- 1 cup of coarse gravel
- 1 cup of fine wood charcoal
- 3 cups topsoil
- 2 ounces tap water
- Some small rooted plants
- Grass or small flower seed
- Salamander, land snail, cricket, etc.

After setting up as shown, screw the lid on tight. Put the terrarium in a window but out of direct sunlight. Open as needed to feed your "animal."

PLASTIC BAG GREENHOUSE

Materials needed:
 2-quart plastic freezer bag
 Peat moss
 Sand
 Plant cuttings

Mix. — Mix 2 parts peat moss and 1 part sand to fill about 4 inches of the plastic bag.

Water. — Add water to mix. Work in thoroughly. When mix is squeezed tightly, you can squeeze out only a few drops of water.

Yew and juniper—January
Geraniums, lantana, roses—late May through August
Forsythia, mock orange, viburnum, holly,
    azaleas, camellias—mid-June to mid-August
Ivy, philodendron, Chinese evergreen—any time

Cuttings. — A cutting should be this year's growth. It should snap into a clean break. Take off leaves from lower one-third to one-half.

Stem Preparation. — Cut sliver 1 inch long from side of bottom end. Dip end from which you took the sliver in hormone mix. (You can buy it at a garden store.)

Planting. — Put cuttings 2 to 3 inches deep in soil in bag. Water leaves lightly. Seal bag with rubber band. Put on window sill, shaded from direct sunlight. It should be ready to transplant in 1 to 3 months, depending on the plant.

BIRD FEEDERS

It's fun to watch birds that are near you. You can do this at your own bird feeder. The kinds depend on where you are, food used, and time of year.

Use any good bird identification book. You can get one at your library or buy your own. They come in paperback.

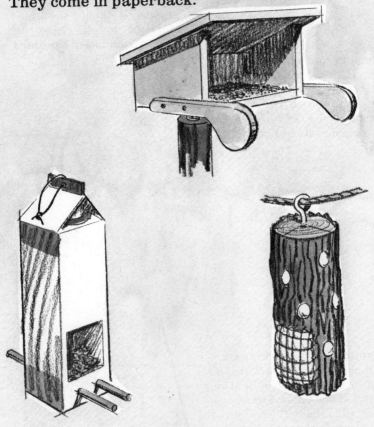

PLOT STUDY

A whole town may be under your feet. Not a town of living people, but a town of living creatures. It's exciting to study this town. To look at it in detail. To see the different kinds of insects and other small animals and watch what they are doing.

Mark off with string a 10-square-foot plot of land. Ten square feet is 5 feet long and 2 feet wide. Pick land on which there are living plants.

Now start checking on what's in the area you have marked. Start with the plants. List the kinds of plants in the area. Then look for living creatures. List all you can see. Use a magnifying glass to look for the smaller ones.

Use a shovel and carefully remove the sod from an area about 1 foot square. Dig up the dirt in that space and check it out for more living things. Put the dirt and sod back when you are through.

You are an astronaut on a huge spaceship called earth. It has support systems to give you water, oxygen, soil, and other things needed for life. The resources of your support system cannot be replaced from another spaceship, world, or galaxy. They are all you and the people of the future will ever have.

CONSERVATION

REQUIREMENTS AND PAGE REFERENCES

1. Make a drawing that shows how water moves in a cycle. Tell what water pollution is. Tell how it affects you.   **308-309**
2. Make a drawing that shows how oxygen moves in a cycle. Tell what air pollution is. Tell how it affects this cycle.   **314-315**
3. Explain how air, water, soil, minerals, plants, and animals work together to make a glass of milk.   **314-317**
4. Take a walk around your neighborhood for 2 hours. Make a list of things you see that please you. Make another list of those you feel could be improved. Plan and carry out a project, approved by your patrol leader before you start. This project will help improve your neighborhood.   **318-319**
5. In addition to requirement 4 do one of the following:
   a. Ragweed control   **320**
   b. Litter prevention   **320**
   c. Erosion control   **321**
   d. Solid waste recycling   **321**

THE CYCLES

There are a few cycles you need to know to see the real need for conservation. A cycle is a process which continues in a circle with no start or end. It is like a bike wheel. One of these circles is the hydrologic cycle. No matter where you start in the cycle, if you follow what happens to water, you come back to your starting point.

Precipitation is rain, hail, sleet, or snow. These droplets fall to the earth from clouds moved by differences in air pressure which makes wind.

Surface runoff takes place when the droplets fall faster than the soil can soak them up. The excess runs downhill to streams, rivers, and finally, to lakes and oceans.

HYDROLOGIC

Precipitation

Surface Runoff

Soak-in

Stream to Oceans

Percolation is what happens to the droplets that don't run off the land. This water is used by plants. It also moves deeper into the ground to become part of the groundwater supply. When all space in the ground is filled with water, it flows along cracks to come up as springs, or in rivers, lakes, or the ocean.

Evaporation is the process by which water in lakes, oceans, or any other body of water or surface is changed into vapor. This vapor rises into the air. It finally forms clouds. Wind and high temperature speed up evaporation.

Transpiration is the loss of water from plants to the air. It is another way vapor enters the air. The water entered the plants from the groundwater supply.

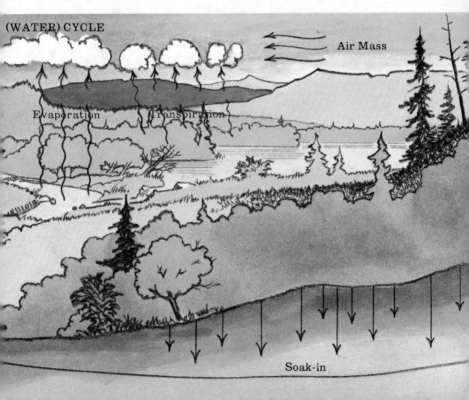

(WATER) CYCLE

Air Mass

Evaporation   Transpiration

Soak-in

WATER POLLUTION

Pesticides

Fertilizer

Erosion

Detergents

Litter

Industrial Wastes

Feed Lot Wastes

Raw Sewage

Household Wastes

Man pollutes at the surface runoff and percolation stages. It is here that man dumps raw sewage, industrial wastes, detergents, pesticides, fertilizers, and litter such as cans, paper, and bottles.

Man has polluted his water supply for centuries. There used to be a tiny bit of pollution in a huge water supply. Today we have great amounts of pollution in the same water. Now there are so many people making so much pollution that the water can't clean itself.

310

Water may carry chemicals that are eaten by the tiniest water animals. Larger animals eat thousands of the smaller ones and so the chemical builds up and is magnified in each larger animal. When you finally eat a large fish, the accumulation of the chemical enters your body.

Water pollution puts an end to water sports. There is no swimming and there are no fish to be caught. Silt fills in lakes, and you can't even enjoy camping by a polluted stream. It stinks.

AIR POLLUTION

Man pollutes not only the water. He also pollutes the air when he burns fossil fuels like gasoline, oil, and coal. If they don't burn completely, they give off chemicals that pass into the air.

Air pollution around big cities is so bad it makes smog. Smog is unhealthful to man, injures plants needed for food, and attacks building materials and cloth. Smog even cuts down the amount of sunlight reaching the earth.

WEB OF NATURE

All life forms are tied together. Plants, mammals, birds, insects, and even microorganisms depend on each other for life. They are so closely tied, they are called the "web of nature."

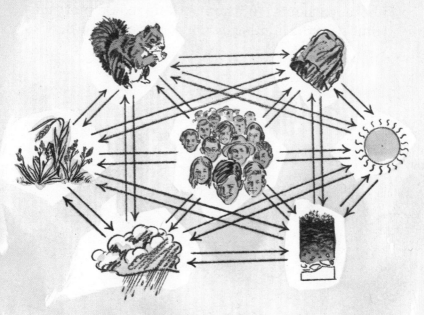

You are in this "web of nature." Your very life depends on the other things in the web. You must be concerned about anything that might destroy or damage any of these resources — soil, air, water, plants, animals, and rocks. You need to understand the close relationship of each of these to the others and to you.

HOW PLANTS MAKE FOOD

Sunlight is the source of all energy. It joins with chlorophyll in plants to make sugars from water and carbon dioxide. The process is called photosynthesis. Without it life could not continue. Sunlight also warms the air and soil so

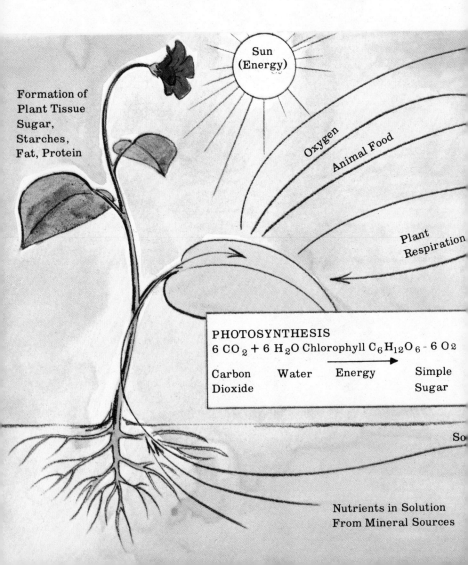

Formation of
Plant Tissue
Sugar,
Starches,
Fat, Protein

Sun
(Energy)

Oxygen

Animal Food

Plant
Respiration

PHOTOSYNTHESIS
$6 CO_2 + 6 H_2O$ Chlorophyll $C_6H_{12}O_6 - 6 O_2$

Carbon   Water   Energy   Simple
Dioxide   Sugar

So

Nutrients in Solution
From Mineral Sources

plants can grow, and gives the energy to evaporate water in the water cycle.

Air contains carbon dioxide, oxygen, and other ingredients. Plants use the carbon dioxide and give off oxygen. Man and other animals use the oxygen and give off carbon dioxide. Air is also part of the soil. It is needed for plant-

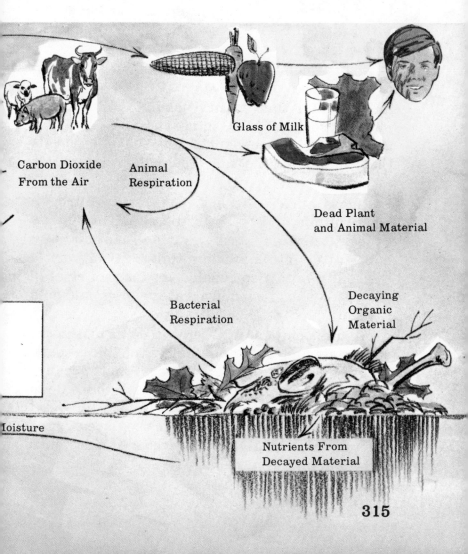

Glass of Milk

Carbon Dioxide From the Air

Animal Respiration

Dead Plant and Animal Material

Bacterial Respiration

Decaying Organic Material

Moisture

Nutrients From Decayed Material

root growth and for the millions of microorganisms living in soil. Moving air is part of weather, as the clouds with their rain or snow are carried by the wind.

Water is needed for both plant and animal growth. Plant roots soak up water which carries food from the soil to the plant leaves. Water is needed to start plant seeds growing. It is basic to animal life. Man can live for weeks without food. He will last only a short time without water.

Soil is the base for most plant growth. It contains minerals like nitrogen, potassium, potash, and calcium that plants need. When you eat plants, you get the minerals you need for growth. Animal products also have minerals that come from the soil. The calcium in milk is an example.

Plants enrich the soil. Some take nitrogen from the air and fix it in the soil. Tiny plants called bacteria break down dead plant and animal matter into materials that become part of the soil. Plants also cushion the force of rainfall on the ground, slow down water runoff, and hold the soil.

Animals help plants to grow. Some loosen the soil so air and water can get to the plant roots. Insects pollinate plant flowers that produce seeds. Manure from animals and their dead bodies return to the soil to give food for plant growth. When animals breathe they use oxygen from the air and give back carbon dioxide which is used in photosynthesis.

The Food You Eat

All the food you eat comes from the plant-food cycle. A glass of milk, your breakfast eggs, a hamburger — all are made by animals which have changed simple plant sugars into animal food products. The bread, cereal, and vegetables you eat are plant products your body uses directly for growth.

You can put any food product into the cycle and trace its relationship to the parts of the cycle. Let's try it with a glass of milk. The cow ate grass and drank water. The sugars produced in the grass by photosynthesis were used by the cow to make milk. You drank the milk. Your breathing passed off carbon dioxide into the air where it was used by plants. Manure from the cow was used to fertilize the soil. And the soil along with water and sunlight grew grass. And so the cycle is completed.

NEIGHBORHOOD PROJECTS

Now then, what can you do about it all? It depends a lot on where you live and how old you are. But everyone can do something. You might think you are too small and alone to make a change in your town. Maybe you would be if you were alone. But, you aren't. The things you do as a Scout can influence others — other Scouts, and other citizens of your town — to do something about the unfavorable things they see around them.

You are asked to take 2 hours to walk around your neighborhood as an observer. Make two lists — one of things that please you and the other of things you think could be better.

Some pleasing things might be clean and litter-free streets, sidewalks, and even vacant lots. Trees, flowers, grass, and clean brooks or

streams or rivers are also pleasing. Look up at the sky on a cloudless day or night. If it's nice and blue during the day or the stars are bright at night, you have clean air.

You probably won't like any of the opposites of the pleasing things. Litter, few growing things, dirty air and water, too much noise—all are things that could be improved. There are many others, but it is up to you to find them in your 2-hour walk.

After you have your lists, look at the things that could be improved. Is there anything on the list you could do something about? Pick something and plan in detail the steps you could take to improve it. Write out your plan. Have it approved by your patrol leader. After he has given it an OK, start to work, using others to help you if needed. Then you will be doing something for conservation and for your community.

To earn the Conservation skill award you must also do one of the following named projects. If you picked one of these for your community improvement project, you will do one of the other three. You must do this plus the one you did for requirement 4.

Ragweed Control.—Ragweed pollen makes it very hard for many people to breathe. You can help by getting rid of ragweed. Study the picture so you can identify ragweed. Find where it grows and cut it off. Don't pull it up by the roots. This loosens the soil, making it easy for new seeds to start. Do the first cutting in midsummer when it can be first identified. Cut it again in late summer if it regrows.

Litter Prevention. — There are many steps you can take in a litter control project. Make and give litter bags to neighbors. Make anti-litter posters and put them in store windows. Give talks to neighborhood groups about the Outdoor Code shown in the "To Be a Scout" chapter.

Erosion Control.—You can help prevent stream and lake siltation by controlling erosion. Build diversions to slow water runoff. Plant grass and shrubs in eroded areas. Put protection (riprap) along streambanks that are being eroded.

Recycling.—Carry out a solid waste recycling project. Collect aluminum and tin cans, bottles and other glass, and paper. Turn it in at your nearest collection center. Set up a campaign to get your friends to do the same thing. Offer to pick up solid waste weekly.

Your body is a wonderful machine. It is much more complex than any manmade machine. It is yours for the rest of your life. You won't have another one, so take care of it. Machines simpler than your body need to be in top running condition. Decide now to get in shape. Decide now to stay in shape.

PHYSICAL FITNESS

REQUIREMENTS AND PAGE REFERENCES

1. Within the past year, have had a health examination by a doctor licensed to practice medicine. If he told you some things to do, tell what you are doing about them.   **324**
2. a. Record your best in the following tests: **325-327**
   Push-ups   Pull-ups   Sit-ups
   Jump-reach   Run-walk
   b. Set goals to reach during the next 30 days.   **328**
   c. Decide on daily exercises. Keep a record of how you are doing for the 30 days or until your goals are met.   **328-329**
3. Explain the foods needed in the daily diet of a boy your age. Tell how this diet helps your body.   **248-249**
4. Satisfy your adult leader that you have good daily health habits.   **331-334**
5. Explain how the use of tobacco, alcohol, and drugs can be harmful to you.   **335-343**

YOU CAN IMPROVE

Machines run smoother and last longer when they have regular checkups and care. Your body needs this same kind of care. Your doctor is the man to do this. He will find out if your body is in good running condition. If it is not, he will tell you or your parents. And he'll tell you what to do to get it running right again.

If a mechanic told your dad his car needed new plugs, he'd put them in. If your doctor tells you to do things to improve your health, do them. Surely, your body is more important to you than your dad's car is to him.

Can you really improve your fitness? Can you build yourself up so you don't get tired so quickly when running or hiking? You bet you can! Lots of guys have done it.

You need a goal and a way to get there. Your plan to earn the Physical Fitness skill award will take 30 days or more.

Test yourself at the start. Then, set fair goals for regular practice and exercise. Finally retest yourself. Find out how much you have improved.

Push-Ups.—Keep your body straight and tense. Bend your elbows and touch your chest (not waist, thighs, legs, or chin) to the floor. Count each time you come upright. Record your test score on the chart.

Sit-Ups.—Lie on your back. Have someone hold your ankles, or put your feet under something heavy. Clasp your hands behind your neck. Sit up. Touch your right elbow to your left knee. Lie down. Sit up. Touch your left elbow to your right knee. Count one for each time you lie back flat. Don't do more than 100. If you can do 100, record that as your test score. If you do less than 100, mark that number on the chart.

Pull-Ups.—Use a solid bar high enough that your feet don't touch the floor. Grasp it with your thumbs toward one another. Count one pull-up each time your chin is over the bar. Record your test score.

Run-Walk.—Start by running 50 steps and walking 50 steps, repeating until you have gone about half a mile. This was a Scouting test many years ago. It was called Scout's pace and was used to go a mile without getting tired. Run more and walk less each day. By the end of 30 days you should be running all the way. You may even work up to running a mile.

Jump-Reach.——Fasten some string with tape or a thumbtack so it hangs from the ceiling. Stand under it. Jump and hit it with one hand. After each successful jump, cut the cord shorter. The string should be just out of reach when you jump as hard as you can. Each day jump about 10 times. Cut a little more off each time you hit it.

YOUR 30-DAY FITNESS TEST

Record your first test score on the chart. Set your goals. For pull-ups, push-ups, and sit-ups your total month's goal should be about 30 times the number you did on the first test. Suppose you did five pull-ups. Multiply by 30. Your 30-day goal should be about 150. If you do five pull-ups a day for 30 days you will do 150 in all. You could miss a day. Then you would have to do 10 the next day. Keep track each day by marking totals on the chart.

Your run-walk goal should total about 15 miles. If you go a half mile each day, you will cover 15 miles in 30 days. Mark each tenth of a mile you run on your scoresheet.

Your jump-reach goal will be the number of jumps during the 30 days. It isn't the number of times you hit the string. A good goal would be about 300. This would be 10 jumps a day. Put one mark for each five jumps. Do this and you will really shorten the string in a month.

YOUR 30-DAY FITNESS SCORESHEET

Keep track by marking in groups of 5 like this ⊢⊢⊢

	Pull-Ups (mark 1 for each)	Push-Ups (mark 1 for each)	Sit-Ups (mark 1 for each 50)	Run-Walk (mark 1 for each ½ mile)	Jump-Reach (mark 1 for each 10 jumps)
First Test				✕	✕
30-Day Goal					
30-Day Total					
Second Test				✕	✕

HEART RECOVERY STEP TEST

Your heart speeds up when you exercise. If you are fit, your heartbeat should go back to normal soon after you stop exercising. You can test your fitness by checking your heartbeat recovery.

Try the test at the start of your 30-day plan. Test again at the end. Your score should be lower the second time.

Test.—Step up and down for 4 minutes on a solid bench, box, or chair. Do this fast enough to do 30 step-ups each minute. Rest for exactly 1 minute. Then count the number of heartbeats in the next 30 seconds. Multiply by two. A score of 120 is pretty good.

Pulse Count.—You will need to count your heartbeats by taking your pulse count. Just below your jawbone is an artery you can easily feel. Use it to count your heartbeats.

GOOD DAILY HABITS

Good daily health practices are important to fitness. Being clean is one of these. Soap and water get rid of dirt and germs, and germs cause infection and disease.

Bathe regularly—every day if you can. If not daily, bathe after you get hot and dirty or sweaty from heavy exercise.

Wash your hands before meals, after using the toilet, before going to bed, and whenever they get dirty. Keep your fingernails neatly trimmed and clean. Your hands can carry germs through your mouth into your body.

Shoes cover your feet most of the time. When your feet sweat the wetness can't get out, and the wastes carried by your perspiration build up. Wash your feet every night that you don't take a bath or shower. Change to clean socks every day. Then the dirt and sweat from the previous day won't be put back in your shoes. Cut your toenails straight across to prevent ingrown toenails. Be sure your shoes and socks fit right.

Wash your hair about once a week—more often if it gets dirty. Brushing it every day will help to keep it clean. This will stimulate oil glands to aid good grooming.

Brush your teeth every night before going to bed. Rinse out your mouth after each meal to help get rid of pieces of food that can cause decay. Have a dental checkup twice a year. Your dentist can find cavities while they are still small and save you trouble later on.

It's also important to your health to get enough sleep. The amount needed isn't the same for all people. The purpose of sleep is to rest your body so you are ready to go full steam the next day. If it's hard to get up in the morning or if you feel tired during the day, you need more sleep. Most Scout-age boys need from 9 to 10 hours every night.

Sight is one of your most important possessions. If your eyes bother you in any way, see a doctor. Don't take a chance with home remedies.

Your ears are delicate instruments. Don't put anything into them. If you have ear trouble like running ears, earache, too much wax, or poor hearing, see a doctor.

Some Scouts have trouble with their ears when they swim. Wear earplugs if regular swimming bothers your ears. Hold your nose whenever you jump into the water feetfirst. This will keep water from being driven up your nose under high pressure.

Your posture is important, too. Stand tall with your head up, shoulders back, and stomach muscles tight. This gives room for your lungs to fill properly. It will help prevent backache. This habit will help you as you get older. You'll avoid that ugly "pot belly."

Good health practices become good health habits when you do them over and over—day after day. When they are so automatic you do them without thinking, they become habits to serve you all your life.

SEXUAL MATURITY

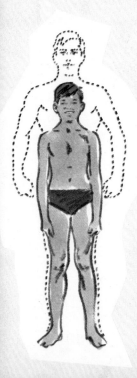

Sometime in your early teens you stop being a child and start growing up. This happens because certain glands in your body act to speed up your growth in height and muscle. Your voice deepens, shoulders broaden, your beard starts growing, and changes occur in your sex organs.

This is all a natural thing, and happens to all boys sooner or later. The exact time that it happens is different from one boy to another. If it happens to you earlier or later than it does to your friends, don't worry about it. It is perfectly natural.

You may have questions about sexual matters such as nocturnal emissions (also called "wet dreams"), masturbation, and even those strange feelings you may have. Talk them over with your parents and/or spiritual advisor or doctor. Don't rely on the advice of friends who think they know all the answers, but may not really know as much as you do. In these matters, it is always smart to get facts and not fiction.

HARMFUL HABITS

Be proud of keeping your body fit and strong. You know that good food and health habits will help.

There are things that you can do to keep fit. There are other things that make you weak. Tobacco, alcohol, drugs, and drug-type things are known to be harmful. None of them are good for your body.

Smoking

Smoking will shorten your life. There's not one single good reason to start smoking. Even if your "friends" smoke, don't. They may try to get you to start. They think they'll look a little smarter if they can get a lot of others to start.

You say, "But lots of grown-ups smoke. Why do they do it?" Most of them started before they really knew the dangers. They have become dependent on the habit and keep on smoking even though they know it's bad for them.

It's important that you don't start. Smoking is a tough habit to kick. If you don't start, you won't have to fight to quit later. Most cigarette smokers would stop today if they could break the habit easily.

Alcohol

Alcohol makes it harder for a person to think straight and act quickly in an emergency. Many auto accidents are caused by drivers who couldn't use good judgment or react to an emergency because they had been drinking.

A person who has been drinking can't judge what will happen and so is a danger to himself and to others. Drinking can become a serious habit. A person who drinks excessively does great damage to himself.

Teen-agers sometimes think that if they take a drink they'll look grown-up. Somehow, it just doesn't work that way.

Drinking is another habit you won't have to fight if you don't start.

Drugs

Drugs have great value in the care and treatment of illness. Doctors prescribe drugs to ease pain, to relax the muscles, to quiet nerves, and to cause physical changes in the body.

But some drugs are also abused. They are used without being prescribed by a doctor. They are used for "kicks." It is this abuse of drugs that is a serious problem today.

Drugs are tricky. Nobody can predict how they will hit you. The effect varies from person-to-person and from time-to-time in the same person. This makes abusing drugs extremely risky.

Even for those who may just be experimenting, there is the possibility of becoming dependent upon or addicted to drugs. There is no way to tell how far you may go if you experiment with drugs.

Let's look at drugs and drug substances so you can understand what they do to the mind and body.

Marijuana

This comes from the Indian hemp plant. It is often smoked as a cigarette or in a pipe. It can be put in food or drink. Users often find they feel uneasy or uncomfortable without it. Marijuana affects the user's self-control. Heavy use by some has produced boredom, disinterest in things and friends, and dropping from normal activities.

Hallucinogens

These change how you taste, smell, see, hear, feel, and think. The sensations they create are often called "trips." They are like dreams you can't wake up from. These dreams may be like nightmares. You can't tell how a person will react to a dose of hallucinogen, DMT, STP, and MDA. There are many others. Some doctors class THC, a strong ingredient in marijuana, as a hallucinogen.

LSD is one of these drugs. While using it, a person may lose control of himself. He doesn't know what is real. He may get real scared or think he can do strange things like flying. "Flashback" is always possible. This means a person may have a reaction days or months after the last dose.

Stimulants

Any drug that excites or overworks the brain is a stimulant. It can cause convulsions when taken in overdose. Some dangerous stimulants are known as "pep pills."

Abuse of stimulants may cause liver and brain damage. They make your blood pressure much higher. They cause loss of appetite. Users of stimulants often suffer from loss

of weight and have malnutrition. They lose their sense of values and personal identity. They may get emotionally disturbed and act strangely.

Sedatives and Tranquilizers

Sedatives are drugs that when properly prescribed may help bring about sleep. One group of sedatives is called barbiturates, and also known as "goof balls" or "sleepers." An overdose of sedatives can kill. There are many accidental deaths from their abuse.

Tranquilizers calm and relax people. But they have to be properly prescribed by doctors for certain problems. Some of these pills may produce dependency on drugs. They never should be used without the advice and prescription of a doctor.

Narcotics

These drugs have the ability to relieve pain and bring sleep. They include opium and its active ingredient, morphine. They also include heroin, which is a form of morphine. The dangers of narcotic use are extreme. An overdose can kill. The addict can never be sure how strong the narcotic he buys is. Many dis-

eases are caused by using dirty needles for shots. A person on narcotics can't fight diseases such as tuberculosis and pneumonia.

A dependence on narcotics builds and builds in the user. He must have more and more to satisfy his problems. An addict who can no longer get narcotics really suffers. He shakes, sweats, and throws up. His eyes and nose run. His muscles ache and jerk. He has a bad belly-ache and diarrhea. He may have hallucinations and delusions.

Other Abusable Substances

Many other chemicals and drugs affect one's mind and body. They are not meant to be used by the human body. They have very bad effects when used that way. Blind-ness, damage to lungs and kidneys, and even death have been reported from misuse.

Drug Abuse

Why do kids try drugs? Usually just for "kicks," to try to get a little excitement, or maybe out of curiosity. Some try them to go along with the crowd they are in.

Usually those who try drugs are searching for those things they can't find in their regular lives. Those who really know and will level with you say it's better to get those feelings from something real than to try the dangerous way from drugs.

Some kids foolishly use drugs to try to "get out of the dumps." Every person suffers pain. You have. Everybody feels lonely and discouraged sometimes. You have. We all have.

Most of us stand up to these things. Most overcome them. Some foolishly run away or cop out. A few turn to drugs and usually get into deeper and more serious problems than they originally had.

People who face their problems squarely have something going for them. They often have good friends they can count on. They may have religious beliefs to give them strength. They might have a moral code such as the Scout Oath and Law to guide them. They usually have families to help. Give your parents a chance. They love you even though you may feel they don't show it. Try talking with your parents. Then, when you feel really low, it will be easier to talk things over with them.

Taking drugs doesn't change your problems one bit. When the drug wears off you are face to face with them again, sometimes much worse.

On the other hand, the satisfactions and relief you get from friends and family, from accomplishment, and from standing up to your problems and solving them are real and lasting.

Reaching an Understanding

Learn about drugs and how they act on your body and mind from real sources, not from rumors or false ideas of uninformed "friends."

Try to find real solutions to problems instead of a poor substitute like drugs.

Find real friends and stand by them.

Develop warm and open relations with your parents and other members of your family.

Speak out against drug abuse, and practice what you preach.

No one has ever said that using drugs is good for your body. Everything points the other way—drugs destroy fitness. You want a fit mind and a fit body. You will not find these in the abuse of drugs.

Fitness is a lot more than having a strong body. Fitness calls for an alert mind—a mind that will make the right decisions. And most important to fitness is a set of moral standards. These will let you live in peace with yourself.

The things you do for this award will help you to have fun in the water. You'll learn how to swim safely with your patrol, troop, and family. You will use simple rescue methods with which you can help other people who might be in trouble in the water.

SWIMMING

REQUIREMENTS AND PAGE REFERENCES

1. Tell what precautions must be taken for a safe swim with your patrol, troop, or family.   **346-347**
2. Jump feetfirst into water over your head. Swim 100 yards with at least one reversal of direction. For the first 75 yards, use any stroke. For the last 25 yards, use a resting backstroke. Float for a minute with as little motion as possible.   **348-353**
3. Show water rescues in the following ways: **354-355**
   a. Reaching.
   b. Throwing.
   c. Going with support.
4. Show rescue breathing.   **130-131**

SAFE SWIM DEFENSE

Swimming is safe! Swimming is dangerous! It's strange, but both of these are true statements. Swimming is quite safe when proper care is taken, but very dangerous when it is not.

The Safe Swim Defense has brought safe swimming to millions of Scouts. The same plan, with small changes to adapt it to family use, can bring safe swimming to your family.

Seven steps are shown. The eighth step is good discipline at the swimming area. This means there are rules to protect swimmers, and the rules are followed. Good discipline doesn't spoil the fun. It makes sure the fun won't be dangerous.

Step 1.—An adult supervisor must be in charge of all Scout swims. He must have passed water-safety training or use assistants who have.

Step 5.—The lookout has an important job. He stands where he can see and hear all areas. He directs any help needed during the swim.

Step 3.—The bottom is checked and cleared of any dangers. Areas are set and marked: no more than 3½ feet deep for nonswimmers — just over the head for beginners — deep water for swimmers.

Step 2.—Each swimmer shall have had a physical examination in the last year to be sure he is fit.

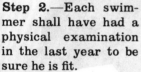

Step 4.—The good swimmers act as lifeguards. Two stand on shore with a lifeline. In an emergency, one carries out the line. The other feeds it out and then pulls in his partner and the swimmer being helped.

Step 6.—Swimmers are divided into ability groups before the swim. They swim in areas according to ability. A nonswimmer is just learning. A beginner can swim 50 feet. A swimmer can swim 100 yards, including 25 yards on his back. He must also be able to float.

Step 7.—In the buddy plan, each Scout is paired with another boy with the same swimming ability. Buddies check in the swimming area together. They stay near one another for the whole swim. They check out together. At the buddy signal, buddies grasp hands and raise them overhead so the lifeguard can check the number in each area against the names on the check-in board.

LEARNING TO SWIM

The first step in learning to swim is to gain confidence. You need to know that water will hold you up. To know you can breathe without choking. To know you can move through the water easily. When you know these things you will have that confidence you need.

Jellyfish Float.—In waist-deep water, take a deep breath. Bend down and grab your ankles with your hands. Put your chin down on your chest. You won't sink. You'll bob up and float with your back out of the water.

Breathing.—Breathing while swimming is different. You breathe in through your mouth and out through your nose and mouth. Try it in waist-deep water. Take a breath through your mouth. Put your face in the water. Breathe out through your nose. Then turn your head so your face is above water and breathe in through your mouth. Repeat by blowing air out underwater.

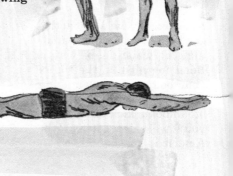

Gliding.—Now, try gliding on top of the water. Take a deep breath. Push off with your feet and stretch yourself with your arms way out in front. Don't kick—just see how far you can go by this coasting glide.

Leg Kick.—Practice the leg kick by resting your hands on the bottom with your legs straight out. Move your legs up and down. Keep them straight but not stiff. Move your legs from your hips, not your knees.

American Crawl.—Practice the arm stroke while standing in waist-deep water. Bend forward so the top of your body is in a swimming position. When you add the steamboat kick and glide, you will be doing the American crawl.

Steamboat.—Now try gliding with the leg kick added. You'll find you can travel quite far with just one breath.

Backstroke.—The elementary backstroke is great for swimming a long way without getting tired. Power comes from the arm stroke plus a strong leg kick as you bring your legs together. A glide between stokes makes it a resting stroke.

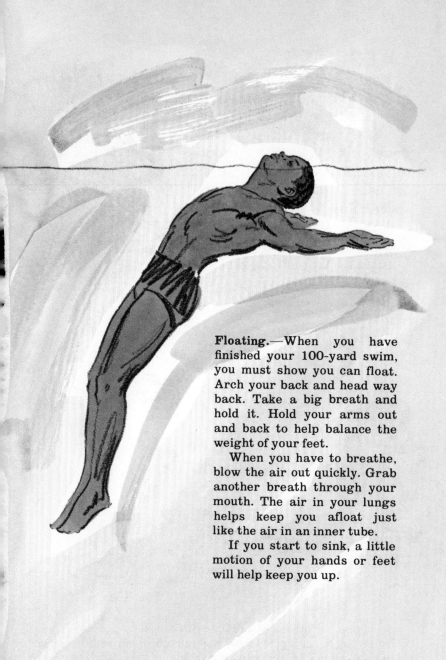

Floating.—When you have finished your 100-yard swim, you must show you can float. Arch your back and head way back. Take a big breath and hold it. Hold your arms out and back to help balance the weight of your feet.

When you have to breathe, blow the air out quickly. Grab another breath through your mouth. The air in your lungs helps keep you afloat just like the air in an inner tube.

If you start to sink, a little motion of your hands or feet will help keep you up.

RESCUES

Never try a swimming rescue if you can do it a better way. And a better way is always without risk to your own life. These better ways are reaching, throwing, or going with support. Don't try a swimming rescue unless you have been trained in lifesaving.

Reaching.—You stay in touch with shore or a dock or pier. You reach with a pole, an oar, a shirt, or even yourself to the person in trouble. But you always hold on to your base.

Throwing.—When the person is too far to reach and you have a ring buoy or a rope, throw it. Keep hold of one end so you can pull the person in. If you don't have a buoy, a rope coil can be thrown quite far.

Going With Support.—For longer distances, use a boat, surfboard, or something else that floats. Keep your eye on the person you are going to help.

SPECIAL SCOUTING OPPORTUNITIES

NATIONAL HIGH-ADVENTURE PROGRAM BASES

Attendance at these is restricted to Explorers and Scouts who will be at least 14 years old by September 1 of the year they take part. Many councils organize trips to these bases. Troops also may use the bases with their eligible boys taking part with their own Scoutmaster or other qualified adult.

358

Philmont. — This base has 137,000 acres of the old West. It is near Cimarron, N. Mex. An expedition on foot or horseback takes you into the wilderness of the Sangre de Cristo range of the Rocky Mountains. You can fish, rock climb, get firsthand information about geology and archaeology, pan for gold, do burro packing and hundreds of other exciting things.

Charles L. Sommers Wilderness Canoe Base. — This is the jumping-off place for exciting canoe trips in the water wonderland of northern Minnesota and the Quetico forest area of Canada. These are rugged trips for experienced canoeists.

Northern Wisconsin National Canoe Base. — Here you outfit for canoe adventure on the lakes and streams of beautiful northern Wisconsin. A great training program is given as needed. There are trips of varying degrees of difficulty.

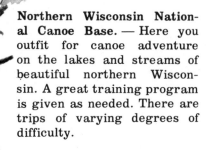

Maine National High Adventure Area. — This newest base is located on beautiful Grand Lake Matagamon in the Maine wilderness. The program features wilderness backpacking, camping, and canoeing. The program, length of stay, and group-size requirement are all flexible.

RELIGIOUS EMBLEMS PROGRAMS

These emblems are awarded by the related religious groups. They are not a Scouting recognition. Each faith has its own requirements for earning its emblem. Most call for religious knowledge and service. Listed below are the emblems, the faith represented by each, and where to write for information. Many council offices also have these materials as a service.

Ad Altare Dei. — Roman Catholic — Priest or Scoutmaster.

Alpha Omega. — Eastern Orthodox Catholic — Relationships Division, Boy Scouts of America, North Brunswick, N.J. 08902.

Ararat.—Armenian—Armenian Church, Diocese of America, 630 Second Ave., New York, N.Y. 10016.

"Duty to God." — Church of Jesus Christ of Latter-day Saints, 525 Foothill Drive, Salt Lake City, Utah 84113.

God and Country.—Episcopal—National Council Episcopal Church Center, 815 Second Ave., New York, N.Y. 10017.

God and Country.—Protestant—Minister or Scoutmaster.

"In the Name of God." — Islamic—Islamic Committee on Scouting, 7016 Heather Heath, Birmingham, Mich. 48010.

Ner Tamid.—Jewish—Rabbi or Scoutmaster.

Pope Pius XII.—Roman Catholic—Restricted to high-school-age Explorers and Scouts—Priest or Scoutmaster.

Pro Deo et Patria.—Lutheran—Lutheran Council of the U.S.A., 315, South Park Ave., New York, N.Y. 10010.

Religion in Life.—Unitarian Universalists or members of other liberal groups—Unitarian Universalist Assn., 25 Beacon St., Boston, Mass. 02108.

Sangha.—Buddhist—Buddhist Churches of America, 1710 Octavia St., San Francisco, Calif. 94109.

Ad Altare Dei

Alpha Omega

Religion in Life

God and Country

Ararat

Pro Deo et Patria

God and Country

Pope Pius XII

Ner Tamid

"Duty to God"

Sangha

"In the Name of God"

ORGANIZED GROUP ACTIVITIES

These happen outside or away from your troop.

Exploring. — When you have completed the eighth grade or are 15 years of age or older, you may join an Explorer post. As an Explorer you are still a member of the Boy Scouts of America, and may also be in a Scout troop. Explorer posts often specialize in some form of vocational exploration. Their activities and membership may include girls who meet the same school or age requirement.

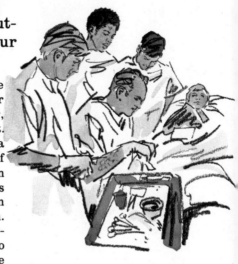

Order of the Arrow.—This is a national brotherhood of Scout campers. To become a member, you must meet certain qualifications in camping and Scout advancement and be elected by the Scouts in your own troop. Talk to an Arrowman for firsthand information.

Alpha Phi Omega.—This is a national college service fraternity active on many campuses. It is based on the ideals of the Scout Oath and Law.

The Eagle Scout Association.
—Eagle Scouts may join the
National Eagle Scout Association. Many local councils
have active chapters on both a
formal and informal basis.

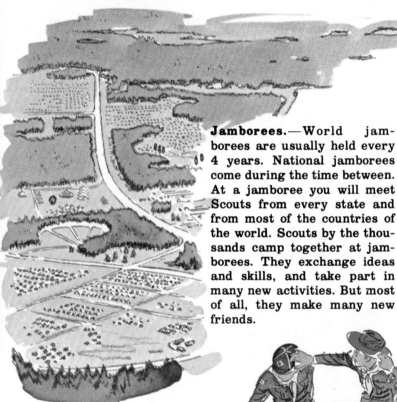

Jamborees.—World jam-
borees are usually held every
4 years. National jamborees
come during the time between.
At a jamboree you will meet
Scouts from every state and
from most of the countries of
the world. Scouts by the thousands camp together at jamborees. They exchange ideas
and skills, and take part in
many new activities. But most
of all, they make many new
friends.

Den Chiefs.—These are
Scouts who help den leaders
run the Cub Scout program
for boys 8 through 10 years
old. They gain leadership
experience and are doing a
real Good Turn to Cub Scouts.

ACTIVITIES
AND SKILLS

Interpreter.—You may wear this strip if you show your knowledge of a foreign language by:

1. Carrying on a 5-minute conversation in the language.
2. Translating a 2-minute speech or address.
3. Writing a letter in the language.
4. Translating 200 words from the written word.

BENGALI

Mile Swim BSA.—Swim a continuous mile under safe conditions and in the presence of a special counselor approved by your council. He will get the emblem for you.

Hornaday Award. — This award is presented to a Scout who has done exceptional and distinguished service in conservation. It is made by the Boy Scouts of America on recommendation of the local council.

Lifeguard BSA — For Scouts who hold Swimming, Lifesaving, and Rowing merit badges and meet requirements outlined on the application.

Council Trail Medals.—Many councils have developed local historic trails and sell medals to Scouts who hike these trails. Note that hiking these local trails *does not* qualify you for the Historic Trails Award.

Paul Bunyan Axman.— Awarded to Scouts who teach others the skills of axmanship and who demonstrate special ability with a three-quarter ax.

50-Miler Award.—This is presented to Scouts in a troop which makes a wilderness hike, canoe, or boat trip of not less than 50 consecutive miles in at least 5 days. Additional requirements include group service projects on the trail.

Historic Trails Award.—To earn this award, troop members must locate, improve, mark, and camp on a historic trail or site.

College Scholarships.—There are scholarships for Scouts available in many colleges and states. If you are old enough to apply for college, write to the Scouting Division, Boy Scouts of America, North Brunswick, N.J. 08902.

HEROISM AWARDS

These awards given in the name of the National Court of Honor are for unusual Scout-like action and for saving life.

The Honor Medal is awarded to Scouts who saved life or attempted to save life at the risk of their own. They must have shown heroism, resourcefulness, and skill. In exceptional cases the Medal is awarded with crossed palms.

The Certificate for Heroism may be awarded in place of the Honor Medal where less risk was involved to the person making the rescue.

The Medal of Merit is awarded to Scouts who performed an outstanding act of service not necessarily at the risk of life. They must have used the skills and ideals of Scouting.

The Certificate of Merit is a local council award for meritorious action.

THE EARLY YEARS

Scouting started in the imagination of an English general, Sir Robert Baden-Powell. Early in his army days he wrote a book for soldiers about how to track, stalk, and live in the outdoors. He called his book *Aids to Scouting*. Baden-Powell didn't realize when he wrote his book that ideas in it would be put to practical use a few years later.

During the Boer War between the English and the descendants of Dutch settlers in South Africa, Baden-Powell was in charge of the defense of a key town, Mafeking. His troops, badly out-numbered and completely surrounded by the enemy, were under constant attack day after day. Using every trick in his book, Baden-Powell and his men held out for over 7 months until another army group broke through army lines to relieve them. The people of England has been anxiously following the news of the long battle and went wild with joy when they learned that the siege of Mafeking had been lifted.

Baden-Powell returned to England as a great hero, cheered by crowds wherever he went. His fame had led boys to read and use the book he had written for soldiers and this bothered him. He believed that boys should read books for boys, not for soldiers, so he decided to rewrite his *Aids to Scouting*.

First, he read things others had written for youth, and he met with youth leaders to share ideas. Among them were author-artists, Ernest Thompson Seton and Daniel Carter Beard, men who had started

programs that attracted boys. They used nature lore, pioneering, hiking, and camping to do this.

B-P, as Baden-Powell was known, decided to try out his ideas. In 1907 he brought together a group of boys at Brownsea Island for the first Scout camp. Here he learned that boys were eager to do the things he called Scouting.

His book, *Scouting for Boys*, was the result of his experience, imagination, testing, and work with others. It was an instant hit in England and Scout troops sprang up allover the land. Copies of his book were soon being read by boys around the world.

In 1909 an American business-man, William D. Boyce, was pass-

ing through London on his way to Africa to go on a safari. One day he came out of his London hotel room into a heavy fog. He was hesitant about crossing a busy street, and a boy with a light came up to him and asked whether he could be of help. Boyce accepted the offer. Later he tried to pay the boy for his help, but the boy refused it saying he was a Scout, and that Scouts didn't take pay for being helpful. Boyce asked him more about Scouting, and the boy told him about Baden-Powell. Boyce asked to be taken to Baden-Powell's office. When they got there, the boy disappeared into the fog. He has been known ever since as the unknown Scout. There is a statue in England honoring him.

Boyce liked what he heard about Scouting from the British Scout people. He studied the books that had been given him, and decided to do what he could to get Scouting started right in the United States. On February 8, 1910, the Boy

Scouts of America was legally incorporated in Washington, D.C. by W. D. Boyce. This date is celebrated as our Scouting birthday.

Ernest Thompson Seton and Dan Beard took a big part in the new organization. They combined their own youth groups with Scouting, and became active themselves in the new organization. Seton wrote the first Scout handbook for the Boy Scouts of America using material from Baden-Powell's book and his own *Birchbark Rolls*. Seton was the first Chief Scout of the Boy Scouts of America. Beard was named National Scout Commissioner.

Not long after Scouting started in the United States, James E. West was appointed the executive officer (Chief Scout Executive). West had grown up in an orphan home and was handicapped by a badly crippled leg. In spite of this he graduated from law school and was a successful attorney before joining Scouting. West led the Boy Scouts of America from 1911 until he retired in 1943. His wisdom and strong leadership helped to build Scouting into the largest boys' organization in the country.

MERIT BADGES

Any Number. — Any number of merit badges, from one on up may be worn on a merit badge sash. The sash is worn only on ceremonial occasions and not in regular troop activities.

374

Up to Six. — You may wear up to six merit badges on the right uniform shirt sleeve.

The requirements shown on the following pages have been simplified for ease of reading. They may not match word for word those in the merit badge pamphlet. Where the intent is the same, you may use either set. Where it is different, the requirements in the book with the latest printing date should be used.

Merit badges can be earned by any Scout regardless of the progress award he holds.

To earn any merit badge, you must present satisfactory evidence (acceptable to your counselor) that you have met the requirements. You will do many of these in the presence of your counselor.

Merit badge subjects with a 4-H FFA designation under the title may be earned by a 4H'er by completing a club project in that subject, or by an FFA member by meeting these requirements through the FFA program.

A

Agriculture

4-H FFA

1. Explain the nature of soil, its texture, its need of water, of air, and of plant and animal life. Tell what the soil does for the plant. Tell how soil may be improved.

2. Make a seed tester. Test the germination of three varieties of seeds. Test 100 seeds of each.

3. Identify and describe 10 weeds of your town. Tell the best way to get rid of them.

4. Identify six insect pests. Tell what plants they often infest. Tell the best way to control them.

5. Tell the purpose of plowing, cultivating, harrowing, disking, draining, and harvesting. Describe the farm machines used in each case.

6. Describe the different ways plants are propagated. Explain where plants get their food. Tell how they grow.

7. Read a weather map. Know weather signs. Make your own observations.

8. Identify 10 birds where you live. Tell their value to the farmer.

American Business

1. Do the following:

(a) Explain four features of the free enterprise system in America. Tell its benefits and responsibilities. Describe the difference between freedom and license. Tell how the Scout Oath and Law apply to business and free enterprise.

(b) Describe the industrial revolution. Tell about the major developments that marked the start of the modern industrial era in the United States. Tell about five people who had a great influence on business or industry in the United States. Tell what each did.

2. Do the following:

(a) Visit a bank. Talk with one of the officers or staff. Chart the organization of the bank. Show its relationship with other banks, business, and industry.

(b) Explain how changes in interest rates, taxes, and government spending change the flow of money into or out of business and industry.
(c) Explain how a proprietorship or partnership gets its capital. Discuss and explain four ways a corporation gets its capital.
(d) Explain the place of profit in business.
(e) Name five kinds of insurance useful to business. Describe their purpose.

3. Do the following:
(a) Pick two or more stocks from the financial pages of a newspaper. Pretend you have bought $1,000 worth of these stocks. Explain how you "bought" the stocks. Tell why you decided to "buy" them. Keep a weekly record for 3 months of your stocks' market value. Show any dividends declared.
(b) Write to one company whose stock you "bought." Ask for a copy of its annual report. Explain it.

4. Do the following:
(a) Draw an organizational chart of a typical central labor council.
(b) Describe automation, union shop, open shop, collective-bargaining agreements, shop steward, business agent, union counselor.
(c) Explain the part played by four different Federal or state agencies in labor relations.

5. Run a small business involving a product or service for at least 3 months. First find out the need for it. For example: a newspaper route, lawn mowing, sales of things you have made or grown. Keep records showing the costs, income, and profit.

Report:
(a) How service, friendliness, hard work, and salesmanship helped build your business.
(b) The benefits you and others received because you were in business.

Comparable 4-H, FFA, or Junior Achievement projects may be used for No. 5.

Animal Industry

4-H FFA

1. Name three breeds of draft horse and two breeds of light horse. Tell the country each came from.
2. Name four leading breeds of dairy cattle. Tell the merits of each.
3. Describe the color markings and characteristics of five different breeds of beef animals.
4. Tell what's needed for successful and money-making raising of beef on a farm.
5. Describe how hogs are made profitable.
6. Name four leading breeds of sheep. Describe them.
7. Show one first aid requirement related to farm animals.

5. Explain the following:
(a) The difference between field archery and target archery
(b) Field round
(c) Hunter's round
(d) Animal round
(e) Scout field archery round
(f) American and junior American rounds
(g) National indoor round
(h) Modified Chicago round

Archery

1. Name and explain the archery safety rules.
2. Do the following:
(a) Name the parts of an arrow.
(b) Name the parts of a bow.
(c) Describe the following: arm guard, shooting glove or finger tab, quiver.
3. Do the following:
(a) Explain proper care and how to store the bow, bowstring, arrows.
(b) Make a bowstring.
(c) Fletch six arrows.
(d) Explain the following: cast, weight of bow, fistmele, aiming, and spine.
(e) Describe the different kinds of arrows.
4. Shoot with bow and arrows ONE of the following:
(a) A field round for 14 targets. Make a score of 60 points.
(b) A Scout field archery round for 14 targets (56 shots). Make a score of 75 points.
(c) A junior American round on a 48-inch target. Make a score of 250 points.
(d) A national indoor round for 10 targets. Make a score of 30 points.
(e) A modified Chicago round on a 16-inch target. Make a score of 250 points.

Architecture

1. Write about a period of history that influenced architecture. Compare the buildings of that time with those in the United States today.
2. Write about a building you admire. Describe its arrangement, exterior, interior, and surroundings. Give the function for which the building was designed.
3. Make a sketch of a building you admire (other than the one in No. 2).
4. Measure a building. Make a drawing of it at a scale of ¼ inch equal to 1 foot. Make one plan and one detail such as a doorway or window. It may be in pencil on tracing or drawing paper. Use simple architectural letters.

Astronomy

1. Do the following:
(a) Sketch the face of the moon, indicating on it the locations of at least five seas and five craters.
(b) Within a single week sketch the position of the moon in the sky at the same hour on three different evenings. Explain the changes observed.
(c) Tell what factors keep the moon in orbit around the earth.
2. Do ONE of the following:
(a) Photograph or locate on a map of the sky a planet at approximately weekly intervals at the same time of night for at least 4 weeks. Explain any changes noticed on the photographs or map.
(b) Find out when each of the five visible planets will be observable in the evening sky during the next 12 months and compile this information in the form of a chart or table.
3. Do ONE of the following:
(a) In a sketch show the position of Venus, Mars, or Jupiter in the sky at approximately weekly intervals at the same time for at least 4 weeks.
(b) Using a compass, record the direction to the sun at sunset at approximately weekly intervals for at least 4 weeks in spring or fall (for 6 to 8 weeks in summer or winter) and relate this information to the seasons of the earth.
(c) With the aid of diagrams explain the relative positions of sun, earth, and moon at the times of lunar and solar eclipses

Art

1. Tell a story with a picture or pictures.
2. Promote a product or an idea with a picture or pictures.
3. Record in an art medium something that you have done or seen.
4. Decorate something with an original design. Put the design on Scout equipment, furniture, ceramics, or fabric.
5. Design something useful.
6. Render a subject of your choice in FOUR of these ways:
(a) Pen and ink
(b) Watercolor
(c) Pencil
(d) Pastel
(e) Oil
(f) Tempera
7. Discuss job opportunities in art.
8. Explain the ways of reproducing art.

379

and at the times of New, First Quarter, Full, and Last Quarter phases of the moon.

4. Using the shadow of a vertical pole in sunshine, lay out a true north-south line (a meridian). Then, using the line and the pole on another day, measure the altitude of the noontime sun and determine your latitude.

5. Identify in the sky at least 10 constellations, four of which are in the Zodiac. Identify at least eight conspicuous stars, five of which are of first magnitude. Then do the following:

(a) Show in a sketch the position of the Big Dipper and its relation to the North Star and the horizon early some evening and again 6 hours later the same night. Record the date and time of making each sketch.

(b) Explain what we see when we look at the Milky Way.

6. With the aid of diagrams (or real telescopes if available) explain the difference between reflecting and refracting telescopes. Describe the basic purpose of a telescope, and list at least three other instruments used with telescopes.

7. Do the following:

(a) Describe the composition of the sun, its relationship to other stars, and some effects of its radiation on the earth's weather. Define sunspots and describe some of the effects they may have on this radiation.

(b) Identify at least one star that is red, one that is blue, and one that is yellow, and explain the meaning of these colors.

8. Do ONE of the following:

(a) Visit a planetarium or observatory and submit a report to your counselor both on the activities occurring there and on the exhibits of instruments and other astronomical objects you observed.

(b) Spend at least 3 hours observing celestial objects through a telescope or field glass, and write a report for your counselor on what you observed.

9. Name different career opportunities in astronomy. Explain how to prepare for one of them. List the high school courses most useful in beginning such preparation.

Athletics

1. Write 500 words on how to train for sports.

2. Give the rules for two track and two field events. Tell what an amateur is.

3. Prepare plans for holding a sports meet. Outline duties of each official needed.

4. Serve as an official in an athletic meet or major sport.

5. Qualify in one event, for your weight, in each of the following groups:

GROUP 1	Under 75 Lbs.	Under 95 Lbs.	Under 110 Lbs.	Under 125 Lbs.	Under 140 Lbs.	Under 160 Lbs.	Under 175 Lbs.	Under 200 Lbs.	Over 200 Lbs.
Running long jump ...	10' 2"	11' 6"	12'	13'	14'	15'	16'	14'	10'
Running high jump ...	3' 2"	3' 6"	3' 9"	4'	4' 3"	4' 2"	4'	3' 6"	3'
Standing long jump ...	5' 10"	6' 3"	6' 9"	7' 2"	7' 4"	7' 6"	7' 4"	6'	5'
Standing high jump ...	2' 6"	3'	3' 2"	3' 4"	3' 6"	3' 8"	3' 5"	3'	2' 4"

GROUP 2	sec.	sec.	sec.	sec.	sec.	sec.	sec.	sec.	sec.
50-yard dash	8	7-4/5	7-3/5	7-1/5	7	6-3/5	7	7-3/5	8-2/5
100-yard dash				13	12-3/5	12-2/5	12-4/5	14	15-3/5
6-potato race	36	28	27	26	25	24	28	32	36

GROUP 3	sec.	sec.	sec.	sec.	sec.	sec.	sec.	sec.	sec.
20-yard swim........	19-3/5	18-2/5	17-4/5	17-1/5	16-3/5	16	15	15-4/5	18-3/5
40-yard swim........	47	40	39	38	37	36	35	39	40

GROUP 4									
Pull-up	3 times	5 times	6 times	8 times	10 times	12 times	10 times	6 times	4 times
8-lb. shot put........	15'	20'	24'	28'	32'	34'	36'	37'	38'
Push-up from floor ...	7 times	9 times	10 times	12 times	14 times	16 times	17 times	12 times	8 times
Rope climb 18 ft.	29 sec.	17 sec.	15 sec.	13 sec.	11 sec.	14 sec.	17 sec.	20 sec.	25 sec.

GROUP 5									
1. Baseball throw for accuracy ...... (3 strikes, 6 throws)	42'	48'	51'	54'	57'	65'	70'	60'	50'
2. Baseball throw for distance	120'	150'	175'	195'	210'	220'	230'	200'	175'
3. Basketball goal shooting (30 sec.)..	5 in 8	5 in 8	6 in 9	7 in 10	8 in 11	9 in 12	10 in 13	8 in 12	6 in 15

Atomic Energy

1. Tell the meaning of the following: alpha particle, atom, background, radiation, beta particle, curie, fallout, half-life, ionization, isotope, neutron activation, nuclear reactor, particle accelerator, radiation, radioactivity, roentgen, and X ray.

2. Make three-dimensional models of the atoms of the three isotopes of hydrogen. Show neutrons, protons, and electrons. Use these models to explain the difference between atomic weight and number.

3. Make a drawing showing how nuclear fission happens. Label all details. Draw a second picture showing how a chain reaction could be started. Also show how it could be stopped. Show what is meant by a "critical mass."

4. Tell who five of the following people were. Explain what each of the five discovered in the field of atomic energy: Henri Becquerel, Niels Bohr, Marie Curie, Albert Einstein, Enrico Fermi, Otto Hahn, Ernest Lawrence, Lise Meitner, William Rontgen, and Sir Ernest Rutherford. Explain how any one person's discovery was related to one other person's work.

5. Draw and color the radiation hazard symbol. Explain where it should be used and not used. Tell why and how people must use radiation or radioactive materials carefully.

6. Do any THREE of the following:

(a) Build an electroscope. Show how it works. Put a radiation source inside it. Explain any difference seen.

(b) Make a simple Geiger counter. Tell the parts. Tell which types of radiation the counter can spot. Tell how many counts per minute of what radiation you have found in your home.

(c) Build a model of a reactor. Show the fuel, the control rods, the shielding, the moderator, and any cooling material. Explain how a reactor could be used to change nuclear into electrical energy or make things radioactive.

(d) Use a Geiger counter and a radiation source. Show how the counts per minute change as the source gets closer. Put three different kinds of material between the source and the detector. Explain any differences in the counts per minute. Tell which is the best to shield people from radiation and why.

(e) Use fast-speed film and a radiation source. Show the principles of autoradiography and radiography. Explain what happened to the films. Tell how someone could use this in medicine, research, or industry.

(f) Using a Geiger counter (that you have built or borrowed), find a radiation source that has been hidden under a covering. Find it in at least three other places under the cover. Explain how someone could use this in medicine, research, agriculture, or industry.

(g) Visit a place where X ray is used. Draw a floor plan of the room in which it is used. Show where the unit, the person who runs it, and the patient would be when it is used. Describe the radiation dangers from X ray.

(h) Make a cloud chamber. Show how it can be used to see the tracks caused by radiation. Explain what is happening.

(i) Visit a place where radioisotopes are being used. Explain by a drawing how and why it is used.

(j) Get samples of irradiated seeds. Plant them. Plant a group of nonirradiated seeds of the same kind. Grow both groups. List any differences. Discuss what irradiation does to seeds.

Automotive Safety

1. On a car, preferably the family car, point out the following:
(a) Ten supplemental safety items which are or should be there for accident prevention.
(b) Three safety items which are or should be present to lower the chance of death or injury in an accident.

Explain the value, use, and maintenance of each.
2. Do the following:
(a) Check how all outside lights are working.
(b) Check how all inside lights are working.
(c) Find and change a fuse for the lights or horn.
(d) Check a windshield-wiper blade by smear-and-clear test. Put in a new blade. Test again.
(e) Set rearview mirrors for best vision when seated at the wheel. Eliminate the "blind" place to left rear 20 feet from the back of the car.
(f) With car stopped, check brake pedal with full pressure. Find out whether the pedal moves less than halfway. Then hold pressure 30 seconds or more to make sure it does not move farther.
3. Check used tires at a service station for inside or outside defects. Check the tires on a car (preferably the family car), including the spare, for safe con-

dition. Check pressure once a week, for a month. Keep a record. Explain what was found. Give the meaning. Tell how to correct when needed.

4. Mark how far a car would go during the time needed to decide and act, and the braking distance needed to stop a car going 60 miles an hour on dry pavement. Discuss how much more it would take in bad weather and with poor road conditions.

5. Explain or answer questions about the seriousness and the size of the traffic accident problem. Visit your police department, sheriff's office, or state highway patrol. Get facts on at least two serious accident cases. Tell what driving and safety rules were violated. Tell how these accidents might have been prevented.

6. Do the following:

(a) Show six ways in which a passenger can help in the safe operation of a car in which he is riding. Explain what you would do if you were in a car being driven in a reckless way.

(b) Using a bicycle, show four safe practices for both bicycle and automobile driving.

(c) Get the driver's manual of your state. Point out the things you must do to get a driver's license.

(d) Draw the different shapes of six traffic signs. Explain the meaning of each.

7. Do ONE of the following:

(a) Report on one important community activity for traffic safety.

(b) Report on a traffic safety project in which you took part with others.

(c) Report on a project you carried out alone in promoting traffic safety.

Aviation

1. Do the following:

(a) Describe how aviation has affected our world.

(b) Define "aircraft." Describe some kinds of aircraft in use today.

(c) List at least 10 uses of aircraft.

2. Do the following:

(a) Point out on a model plane the forces which act on an airplane in flight.

(b) Show one other principle basic to flight.

(c) Build a model airfoil wing section. Show with it the principle of lift; or build demonstration airfoils to compare the drag of streamlined and nonstreamlined surfaces.

3. Show how the control surfaces of an airplane are used for takeoff, straight climb, level turn, climbing turn, descending turn, straight descent and landing.

4. Identify the following aircraft instruments. Explain the purposes of each: altimeter, airspeed indicator, compass, turn and bank indicator, tachometer, and oil-pressure and temperature gauges.

5. Show you know the International Phonetic Alphabet.

6. Explain the differences in the operation of piston, turbo-prop, pure jet, and rocket types of engines.

7. Tell six rules of safety to follow around airplanes and airports. Describe safety rules for building and flying model airplanes. Tell safety rules for use of glue, paint, dope, and plastics.

8. Build and fly a rise-off-ground model airplane (you may use a kit but must carve the propeller yourself); or build two solid scale model planes (kits may be used).

9. Do any TWO of the following:

(a) Take a flight in an aircraft. Record the date, place, type of aircraft, duration of flight, and your impressions of the flight.

(b) On a map mark a route for an imaginary air trip of at least 3,000 miles. Start from the commercial airport nearest your home. Travel over three or more different airlines. From timetables decide when you will get to and leave all connecting points. List places of interest and geographical features to see on the trip.

(c) Visit a modern airport. After the visit tell how the facilities were used.

(d) Make a checklist for a routine preflight inspection of a light plane.

(e) Learn how to read an aeronautical chart. Measure a true course on the chart. Correct it for magnetic variation, compass deviation, and wind drift. Arrive at a compass heading.

(f) Build a gasoline-powered rise-off-ground model plane that will take off and land; or fly a radio-controlled model plane (a kit may be used).

(g) Take part in a model air meet recognized by the Academy of Model Aeronautics.

(h) Find out what job opportunities there are in aviation. Describe the qualifications and working conditions of one job in which you are interested. Tell what it offers for reaching your goal in life.

Basketry

1. Plan and weave a large basket or tray. Use reed, raffia, or splints.
2. Weave a seat for a stool or chair. Use cane or rush.

Beef Production

4-H FFA

1. Name three beef breeds. Show or explain markings and other characteristics for which each breed is noted.
2. Pick a breed of beef cattle that would be your choice for where you live. Give reasons for your choice. Give the history of the breed you choose.
3. Visit a farm or ranch. Interview a farmer who raises beef cattle under any of these systems:
(a) Feeding market cattle for slaughter.
(b) Raising feeder cattle for sale to commercial cattle feeders.
(c) Raising purebred cattle for sale as seed stock to other breeders.
Tell how the cattle were handled. Tell what rations were fed. Give weight gains, time on feed, and other items emphasized by the farmer.

4. Explain what is meant by "baby beef production."
5. Prepare an actual (or typical) cost accounting record for a specific cattle feeding program. Include:
(a) Date, price, weight, and grade of cattle when bought.
(b) Total feed used. Value of feed.
(c) Miscellaneous costs such as veterinarian's bills.
(d) Date, weight, price received. Grade of cattle when sold.
(e) Profit.
6. Draw a plan of a feedlot, hay and grain storage facilities, and loading chute for 30 or more fattening steers; OR a corral plan with cutting and loading chutes for handling 50 or more beef cows and their calves at one time.

Beekeeping

4-H FFA

1. Study a hive of bees. Remove the combs. Find the queen. Figure the amount of the brood, number of queen cells. Figure the amount of honey in the hive.
2. Show the difference between the drones, workers, eggs, larvae, and pupae at different stages. Tell the difference between honey, wax, pollen, and

propolis. Tell how bees make honey. Tell where wax comes from. Explain the part played in the life of the hive by the queen, the drones, and the workers.

3. Hive a swarm or divide at least one colony. Explain how a hive is made.

4. Put foundations in sections or frames. Fill supers with frames or sections. Take out filled supers from the hive. Fix the honey for market.

5. Write in not more than 200 words how and why the honeybee is used in pollinating farm crops. Name five crops in your area pollinated by honeybees.

Bird Study

1. Spend 3 hours in each of two different kinds of natural habitats or at different elevations. List the different bird species you identified. List the numbers of each seen. Tell why all birds do not live in the same kind of habitat.

2. Spend 3 hours on each of 5 days on a 25-acre area. List bird species which you identified by sound or sight.

3. Recognize by sound 10 birds where you live.

4. List the bird families usually found where you live during a year. Identify in the field one bird from eight of the following families: Pigeons and Doves; Woodpeckers; Tyrant Flycatchers; Swallows; Crows, Magpies, and Jays; Titmice, Bushtits; Wrens; Thrashers and Mockingbirds; Thrushes, Solitaires, Bluebirds; Wood Warblers; Weaver Finches; Blackbirds, Orioles, Meadowlarks; Finches, Sparrows, Grosbeaks, and Crossbills. Identify one bird from any other family.

5. Write a life history of 500 words on one bird other than a game bird that nests where you live.

6. Do ONE of the following:

(a) Keep records of birds seen on eight field trips during one season (3 months).

(b) Watch a bird nest for an hour a day for 10 days. Describe what you saw.

(c) Go on a Christmas census of 8 hours with a bird club. List birds seen.

(d) Go on a May big day of 8 hours with an expert. List birds seen.

(e) Visit a bird refuge. Describe its purpose. Give the management techniques.

(f) Write a 500-word life history of a game bird that nests where you live.

7. Do ONE of the following:

(a) Build a backyard sanctuary of a tenth of an acre or more by planting trees and shrubs for food and cover. Describe what birds you hope to attract and why.

(b) Build three bird feeders of different kinds. Set them out. Keep them stocked with food for 3 months in winter. Describe what birds used them. Tell what kinds of food were liked best.

387

(c) Build three nest boxes for different birds. Set them out in good places. Describe the birds that used them. Tell how many young were raised in these boxes.

(d) Take 12 clear, sharp, recognizable pictures of 12 species of birds.

(e) Build a watering device for birds. Keep it filled for 3 months. Tell what kinds of birds used it. Describe any interesting things you saw.

8. Do ONE of the following:

(a) Pick one species of bird that eats other animals. Tell its place in nature. Tell on what birds your state pays a bounty, if any. Tell if this makes sense to you.

(b) Make a migration map (flyway map) of the United States. Name some of the birds that use each flyway. Tell where they nest. Tell where they winter. Describe birdbanding.

(c) Make a list of the extinct or declining birds of the United States. Describe the chief causes of this.

Bookbinding

1. Describe the two main sewing methods of binding books by hand. Tell when each should be used.

2. Rebind a book or bind four or more issues of a magazine. Use binder's board and book cloth.

3. Make a scrapbook. Use binder's board and book cloth or a good substitute.

4. Do ONE of the following:

(a) Visit a bindery. Report what you saw on how to bind a book, pamphlet, or magazine.

(b) Write an article of at least 200 words on bookbinding as a career.

Botany

1. Make five 2-hour field trips to observe wild plant life. Keep a record, based on field notes, of kinds of flowers found. Show date, and kind of place. Record other information such as seeds, seedpods, leaf arrangements, and insect attraction. Pictures or drawings may be part of the record.

2. Name from living specimens at least 50 plants.

3. Name in three specimens all parts of a perfect and complete flower.

(a) Explain how plants are pollenized.

(b) Explain how ferns are different from flowering plants.

4. Identify specimens of 10 families of flowering plants (other than trees). Label specimens of 10 such families. (May be counted as part of No. 8b.)

5. Tell what plants are rare where you live. Tell what is being done or should be done to protect them.

6. Explain how plants use light, heat, water, oxygen, and carbon dioxide. Describe how they make their own food.

388

7. Submit or identify in the field one specimen each of fungi, algae, lichens, and mosses. Where this cannot be done, you may substitute five different kinds of ferns or desert plants.

8. Do ONE of the following:

(a) Make a seed collection of at least 20 different kinds of seeds you gathered. Label each kind. Germinate five kinds. Tell the different kinds of seeds. Describe how they are scattered.

(b) Submit specimens of 30 species of flowering plants. Include leaf, stem, flower, and root (if not of rare plant). Mount neatly. Label with both common and scientific name. Give date, place found and kind of locality.

(c) Make a study of plant life in an area of 15 square feet for 2 months. Keep record of species found, kind of place, insect attraction and seeds.

(d) Raise a wild flower or fern garden that has five different species or plants. Give: (1) Common and scientific names of each. (2) Proper way to transplant and care for.

Bugling

Sound properly on the bugle the following calls: First Call, Reveille, Mess, To the Colors, Officers, Drill, Assembly, Recall, Fatigue, Church, Fire, Swimming, Retreat, Call to Quarters, Taps.

Camping

1. Make a layout of a typical patrol campsite. Show cooking spots, dining fly, latrine, and at least three two-man tents. Explain how and why weather, season, and water supply are considered when choosing a site. Explain what care to take with regard to safe water, sanitary facilities, and emergencies.

2. Make a written plan for getting to and from a camping spot on foot or by vehicle.

3. Make a chart showing how a typical patrol is organized for an overnight camp. List assignments for each member.

4. Prepare a list of clothing you would need for an overnight camp in:

(a) Summer.

(b) Winter.

Discuss the kinds of footwear for different kinds of weather. Explain care of the feet.

5. Describe four kinds of packs. Give their good and bad points.

6. Prepare for an overnight camp with your patrol by doing the following:*

(a) Make a checklist of personal and patrol gear that will be needed.

(b) Prepare a lightweight camp menu that is right for the time of the year. Give recipes. Make a food list for your patrol. List foods you can get from your grocery store. Plan two breakfasts, three lunches, and two suppers. (Some canned foods may be used.)

(c) Pack your own gear and your share of the patrol gear and food for proper carrying. Protect it against bad weather. Show that your pack is right for getting what's needed first, comfort, weight, balance, size, and neatness. Explain how the rest of the patrol gear and food is divided among members.

(d) Show the right way to pack your full gear on a pack frame. Use a diamond hitch or other good hitch.

7. Complete the following while on an overnight camp:

(a) Present yourself with your pack for inspection. Be correctly clothed and equipped for an overnight camping trip.

(b) Working with another Scout, pitch a two-man tent. Consider weather and terrain. On this campsite, where allowed, make a latrine for your patrol. (Where not allowed as in state parks, etc., describe how to build it.)

(c) Make a comfortable ground bed. Use it for 2 nights. Use ground cloth and padding of clothing, pack, grass, leaves, or straw.

(d) Where it's allowed, build up a fireplace area of nonburnable soil. Show proper use of woods tools in getting and preparing

*May be part of a troop trip.

fuel for a cooking fire. Show how, on a rainy day, you would get, prepare, and protect your wood. Show how you would properly prepare a meal when it's raining.

(e) Build three kinds of top-of-the-ground fires. Use charcoal for one. Show how to put out a fire properly. (Where open fires cannot be used, show how to build the fires, but don't light them.)

(f) Show the right way to protect your camp, including food and gear, against animals, insects, and wet or bad weather. Discuss how you would protect yourself against kinds of weather if caught out on the trail with only a pocketknife.

(g) Strike camp. Fold or roll your tent for packing. Pack all gear. Leave a clean camp. Show the right way to get rid of garbage and rubbish.

8. Show experience in camping by the following:

(a) Camp out a total of at least 20 days and 20 nights. Sleep each night under the sky or under a tent you have pitched. (You may use a week of summer camp as a part of the 20 days and 20 nights.)

(b) On one of these camping trips, hike 1½ miles or more each way to and from your campsite. Pack your own gear plus your share of patrol gear and food. (This camp is in addition to the one for Camping skill award.)

(c) Serve as one of the cooks for your patrol for at least five meals prepared in camp.

9. Discuss how the things you did to earn this badge have taught you personal health and safety, survival, public health, conservation, and good citizenship.

391

Canoeing

1. Before doing other requirements, swim 100 yards as follows: 75 yards with any strokes. Then 25 yards on your back using an easy resting stroke. Then rest by floating as still as you can for 1 minute.

2. Point out and name each part of the canoe and paddles you are using.

3. With a partner about your size, and using a properly equipped canoe:

(a) Launch and get in the bow of the canoe properly from dock or shore (both, if possible). Give directions to your partner.

(b) Paddle on one side only 100 yards using a single-blade paddle while kneeling on one or both knees. Turn and paddle back. Show proper form in the following strokes: bow, diagonal draw, pushover, backwater, reverse sweep, quarter sweep, stop.

(c) Change paddle to other side and repeat No. 3b.

(d) Change places with your partner while your canoe is afloat. On one or both knees, in the stern, paddle 100 yards and return. Keep the canoe on a straight course.

(e) Make a proper landing at dock or shore.

4. While alone in a canoe:

(a) Show eight single-blade strokes: (1) J, (2) draw, (3) stop, (4) pushover, (5) sweep, (6) reverse, (7) scull, (8) outside pivot.

(b) Go five times around a short, irregular marked course. Paddle on one side only. Use the right strokes at the right time.

(c) Use a single-blade or double-blade paddle. Paddle over a 100-yard straight course. Return using the right strokes.

5. While fully dressed and alone in a canoe, do the following:*

(a) Jump into the water feet-first, keeping hold of the canoe with one hand. Climb back in without shipping water.

(b) Tip the canoe over in deep water about 50 feet from the landing place.

(c) Turn it right side up. Stow paddle and kneeling pad. Get in the filled canoe. Paddle with hands or paddle for 25 yards.

(d) Go overboard. Hold on with one hand. Swim and tow or push the canoe to shore.

(e) Empty the canoe. Store it properly with help if needed.

6. Get in the bow with a partner in the stern. Help two persons who have tipped their canoe over and are hanging on to it. Empty the filled canoe over your own canoe. Steady it while they climb in.

7. Discuss:

(a) Canoe trip preparations and safety.

(b) How to repair a hole or break in a canvas-covered canoe, an aluminum canoe, and a fiber-glass canoe.

(c) Other uses of the canoe such as racing and sailing.

(d) Explain lining and poling. Tell the differences between lake and river canoeing.

---

*Wear clothing used when canoeing where you live at that time of year.

Chemistry

1. Show that a candle flame uses up oxygen from the air, makes carbon dioxide, and makes water. Demonstrate that heating sawdust or wood chips makes a gas that burns.

2. Write the formulas for six compounds in water that make it hard. Write an equation that describes how a home water softener works. Show the difference in how soap and a detergent act in hard water.

3. Write the simple equation for photosynthesis. Explain what parts sunlight and chlorophyll play in it. Give the three main parts of a 10-6-4 fertilizer. Explain what each one does for plants. Draw from memory a sketch of the carbon dioxide-oxygen cycle.

4. Explain what oxygen does in the animal body. Describe how oxygen, carbon dioxide, and carbon monoxide are carried in the body. Describe the chemical changes taking place when vegetables cook, meat cooks, bread dough rises, bread bakes, and bread is chewed.

5. Carry out an experiment to show three different ways of protecting iron or steel from rusting. Tell why aluminum doesn't rust the way iron does. Do an experiment in which one metal makes another metal deposit from solution. Explain what takes place in terms of the activity series of metals.

6. Do THREE of the following:
(a) Prepare an indicator from a plant leaf or bloom. Show that it works when vinegar neutralizes baking soda solution.
(b) Compare the strengths of 5 percent solutions of baking soda and borax by titrating each with vinegar.
(c) Test two different bits of food for starch and for protein.
(d) Compare the amounts of vitamin C in two kinds of fruit juice.
(e) Show that an ink or food color has two or more colors by using paper chromatography.

7. Name two chemicals that cause air, water, or solid waste pollution near your home. Tell where these pollutants may have come from. Find one way to control one of them. Do one test to show that air or water is polluted.

8. Do ONE of the following:
(a) Visit a plant that makes chemical products or uses chemical processes. Describe the processes used.
(b) Visit a laboratory or place of business that uses chemicals. Find out how and why the chemicals are used.
(c) Visit a county agent to learn how chemistry is meeting farm problems of soil fertility and crop pests.

9. Describe two different kinds of work done by chemists, chemical engineers, and chemical technicians. Explain the differences in college courses for training each of these three kinds of people.

Citizenship in the Community

1. Tell how you would describe your town to a Scout from another state. Give a short history of your town. Tell about its ethnic and other groups, the economy, and the culture. Describe the future of your town.

2. Mark or point out on a map of your town the following:

(a) Chief government buildings.

(b) Fire station, police station, and hospital nearest your home.

(c) Schools, churches, and synagogues near your home.

(d) Main highways to neighboring cities and towns.

(e) Nearest railroads and bus stations and airport, if any.

(f) Chief industries or other major places of employment.

(g) Historical and other interesting points.

3. Make a list of community problems. Pick one in your community. From newspapers, news broadcasts, or other kinds of public information and talk, gather ideas on both sides of your chosen problem. Give your own ideas on it.

4. Chart the organization of your state government. Show all three branches. Tell what each does.

5. Do ONE of the following:
(a) Chart the organization of your village, town, city, or county government. Show top officers, courts, and departments. Show which officers are elected and which are appointed.
(b) Tell how to do SEVEN of following in your community: (1) Report a fire. (2) Report an automobile accident. (3) Call an ambulance. (4) Report damage to electric power, gas, or water system. (5) Report damage to or need of repair on streets, roads, bridges, or sewage system. (6) Get a bicycle license. (7) Get a dog license. (8) Report a contagious disease. (9) Report a mad dog scare. (10) Get a building permit. (11) Call a veterinarian. (12) Get help from your county agricultural agent.
(c) Visit one department of your local government. Report on what services it does for the community. OR, attend a court session or a public meeting of a government body. Report on what took place.

6. Tell how much it costs to run your local government for one year. Tell where the money comes from. Outline for what it is chiefly spent. What kind of taxes do your family and others in your community pay to meet this cost?

7. Show that you have taken an active part in elections of your officers and matters of business in groups to which you belong.

8. List and describe the work of five volunteer organizations through which people of your community work together for the general good. Do something for or take part in the activities of one of these organizations other than Scouting.

9. Do ONE of the following:
(a) Name the main political parties in your community or state. Explain their different points of view on one public issue.
(b) Describe one job in your community in some form of public service. Tell what qualifications are needed for the job.

10. Do ONE of the following:
(a) Draw the course of your home water supply from watershed to water tap and on to receiving stream. Show waste treatment, if any.
(b) Find out if the water supply is likely to be a problem in your town in the future. Explain why.

11. Define water pollution. Give the main causes and results of water pollution nationally and in your town. Find out what steps, if any, are taken to control pollution in your area. Tell what other steps might be taken.

12. Tell how good land-use planning is important to five of the following: community planners, highway builders, camp planners, small landowners, farmers, ranchers, recreation planners, industrial and housing developers, fishermen, and hunters.

13. Do the following:
(a) List and explain at least five privileges and forms of protection you enjoy as a citizen in your community. Describe your obligations to the community.
(b) Plan your own program of community service. Get approval of your plan from your Scoutmaster and counselor. Give 5 hours of your time in carrying it out; or give 5 hours of community service carried out by your Scouting group.

Citizenship in the Nation

1. Read the Declaration of Independence. Tell the meaning of the "self-evident truths."

2. Read the Constitution of the United States of America with its amendments.

(a) Explain its purpose as set forth in the Preamble.

(b) Chart the organization of our government into three branches as outlined in Articles 1, 2, and 3.

(c) Explain the checks and balances. Give the reason for them.

(d) Tell how the Constitution may be amended.

3. Show newspaper or magazine stories which show how three of the rights in our Bill of Rights have been protected in our country.

4. Talk over the main differences between a republic and a democracy. Tell how these differences have been adapted to our form of government.

5. Take part in a group discussion of an important national problem of the day. Report on both sides that were presented. Tell what you learned from it.

6. Do ONE of the following:

(a) Visit the National Capitol or a Federal project which serves your town or region; or a place associated with a person or event which figured in the history of our country. Get information for your visit. Report on your trip, explaining why the things you saw are important.

(b) Correspond with someone about your age who lives in another part of the United States. Exchange things such as ideas, pictures, and descriptive material. From this exchange, compare the two places. Show how they are alike and different.

7. Tell the names of the Senators from your state and your Representative in Congress. Tell how you should address a letter to them at their Washington offices. Write to one of your Congressmen, giving your views on a local or national issue of your choice. Show a copy of your letter to your counselor.

8. Tell what branch or department of the government is responsible for 10 of the following:
national parks
national forests
fish and wildlife
weather forecasting
flood control
investigation of violations of Federal laws
judgment on such violations
atomic energy
education
minting of money
appropriations for government expenses
foreign policy
supreme command of our Armed Forces
soil conservation
child welfare
public housing
water and air pollution

9. Do the following:
(a) Outline five ways in which the Federal Government serves you, your family, and your town directly. Also, talk with your parents (or guardians) and counselor about the ways in which Federal income, Social Security, excise and other taxes, as well as import duties, affect the cost of living.
(b) Explain what is meant by "resource management."
(c) List five Federal conservation agencies. List the main ones in your state. List five private conservation groups. Tell what they do. Describe three successful conservation projects in your area.

10. Tell what a citizen from another country must do to become a United States citizen.

Citizenship in the World

1. Tell how today's communication and travel have changed the interaction between countries.
2. Report on a world problem facing the United States. Report things we have done to try to solve it. How do these things affect the interrelationship of countries? Explain the place of the State Department in it.
3. Show a map of three countries with ideologies different from each other and from that in the U.S.A. Tell how each operates. Compare the rights and responsibilities of the people in each with those of citizens in the U.S.A.
4. Explain the preamble of the United Nations Charter. Outline the UN organization. Tell the things it does.
5. Tell what we mean when we speak of:
(a) International trade agreements
(b) Foreign exchange
(c) Balance of payments
(d) The European Common Market
(e) International law

(f) International treaty

(g) Diplomatic exchange

(h) Tariff policy

(i) Cultural and educational exchange

Explain how two of these affect the international program of the U.S.A.

6. Tell the purpose of two international organizations of which the United States or a United States citizen is a member. Tell what each does.

7. Tell how the resources of a country affect its economy. Tell how they affect its relations to other countries.

8. Pretend you have made a trip to another country. Make a short but full report. Tell about the following:

(a) Means of travel, passports, visas, and immunizations needed.

(b) Interesting places and things.

(c) Government plan, family life, weather, language, and schools.

(d) How the country relates to the U.S.A.

(e) How you could bring good will to this country for the U.S.A.

(f) Review the story of a hero of this country.

9. Do ONE of the following:

(a) Take part in an international event in your own area.

(b) Play host to a visitor from another country.

(c) Attend an international event in another country.

(d) Talk with another person in a modern foreign language for at least 5 minutes. Translate 200 written words in that language.

(e) Help set up and run a World Friendship Fund in your unit.

(f) Help an organization which pushes the idea of world brotherhood.

Coin Collecting

1. Do the following:

(a) Collect a type set of U.S. coins for the year of your birth. Commemorative and rare coins are not needed. Use coins from any mint.

(b) Point out the mint mark (if any) on each coin. Name the mint.

(c) Point out the initials (if any) of the designer on each coin. Name him.

2. Collect a type set of U.S. coins minted during the 20th century. Commemorative and rare coins are not needed.

3. Do ONE of the following:

(a) Make rough drawings of both sides of five different kinds of U.S. coins minted from 1792 through 1852. Draw both sides of five different colonial or state coins made before 1792. Show all designs, dates, and lettering clearly.

(b) Collect, classify, and mount 50 different coins of 10 different countries.

Communications

1. Develop a plan to teach a skill. Have it approved by your counselor. Then, create and make teaching aids. Carry out your plan. With the counselor, check to see if the learner has learned.

2. Pick an item or product. It may be real or imagined. Build a sales plan based on its good points. Try to "sell" the counselor on buying it from you. Talk with him about how well you did in telling him about the item and the wisdom of buying it.

3. Show how you would make a telephone call inviting someone who is an expert fisherman to give a demonstration on fishing to your unit.

4. Do the following:
(a) Write a 5-minute speech. Give it at a meeting of a group.
(b) Show how to introduce a guest speaker.

5. Attend a town meeting where two or three points of view are being given. Record what you hear. Make a report from your notes. Tell your troop or patrol what you think you heard.

6. Plan a troop court of honor or campfire program. Give it to the troop leaders' council for approval. Write the script. Prepare the program for reproduction. Act as master of ceremonies.

7. Prepare an autobiographical résumé that you would use in applying for a job.

8. Check careers in the field of communications. Prepare a statement on the one you like. Talk it over with your counselor.

399

Computers

1. Do the following:

(a) Give a short history of computers. Describe the major parts of a computer system. Give four different uses of computers.

(b) Describe the differences between analog and digital computers. Tell the use of each.

(c) Explain some differences between special- and general-purpose machines.

2. Do the following:

(a) Tell what a program is and how it is developed.

(b) Explain the difference between an assembler and a compiler. Tell where each might be used. Describe a source and an object program.

(c) Use a flowchart diagram to show the steps needed to set up a camp.

3. Do ONE of the following:

(a) Prepare flowcharts to find out the average attendance and dues paid at the last five troop meetings.

(b) Prepare flowcharts to work out a simple arithmetic problem. Explain to your counselor how this program could be stored in a computer. Tell how it could be used again.

4. Do the following:

(a) Name four input/output devices for computers. Explain the use of two of them in a system.

(b) Explain the Hollerith code. Show how your name and address would be punched on a card.

5. Tell the meaning of six of the following:

a. memory
b. bits
c. on-line
d. bytes
e. microsecond
f. address
g. channel
h. interrupt
i. register
j. console
k. central processing unit

6. Tell the meaning and use of 12 of the following:

a. business data processing
b. information retrieval
c. simulation
d. scientific processing
e. floating point
f. truncation
g. fixed point
h. accuracy
i. input
j. record
k. output
l. file
m. software
n. instruction
o. hardware
p. indexing
q. loop
r. subroutine
s. real time
t. time sharing
u. cybernetics

7. Visit a computer installation. Study how it works.

8. Explain what each of the following does:

(a) design engineer
customer engineer
programmer
analyst
operator
salesman

400

(b) Read two pieces of information about computers. Describe what you read.

(c) Describe jobs in the computer field.

Cooking

1. Plan menus for 3 straight days (nine meals) of camping. Include the following:

(a) A camp dinner with soup; meat, fish, or chicken; two fresh vegetables; drink; and dessert. All are to be cooked.

(b) A one-pot dinner. Use foods other than canned.

(c) A breakfast, lunch, and dinner good for a trail or backpacking trip where light weight is important. Use as much dehydrated or dry frozen foods as you can. Get them from local food stores (not specialty stores). You should be able to store all foods used for several days without refrigeration. The lunch planned should not need cooking at the time of serving. The dinner must include hot soup or a salad; meat, fish, or chicken; vegetable and starch food or a second vegetable; baked biscuits; and drink. (The menus for the other two breakfasts and two lunches shall be the kind you can prepare in camp or on the trail.)

2. Do the following:

(a) Make a food list, showing cost and amount needed to feed three or more boys using the menus planned in No. 1.

(b) List the utensils needed to cook and serve these meals.

(c) Figure the weight of the foods in No. 1c.

3. Using the menus planned in No. 1:

(a) Prepare and serve for yourself and two others, the three dinners, the lunch, and the breakfast planned in No. 1. Time your cooking so that each course will be ready to serve at the proper time.*

(b) For the meals prepared in No. 3a, for which a fire is needed, pick a good spot for your fire. Build a fireplace. Include a support for your cooking utensils from rocks, logs, or like material. (Where local laws do not allow you to do this, the counselor may change the requirement to meet the law.) The same fireplace may be used for more than one meal. Use charcoal as fuel in cooking at least one meal.

(c) For each meal prepared in No. 3a, use safe food-handling practices. Use the correct way to get rid of garbage, cans, foil, paper, and other rubbish by burning and using a tote-litter bag. After each meal, clean up the site thoroughly.

---

*The meals in No. 3a may be prepared for different trips. They need not be prepared consecutively. Scouts earning this badge in summer camp should plan around food they can get at the camp commissary.

Cotton Farming

4-H FFA

1. On a map of the United States, color the places where cotton is grown.
2. Grow a patch of cotton successfully.
3. Show how to test cottonseed for vitality.
4. Give the uses of cotton and cottonseed. Name some of the more important by-products.
5. Name the more important insect pests that damage cotton. Tell how they can be controlled.
6. Name the important cotton plant diseases. Explain controls for each.
7. Take part in four operations in connection with a cotton crop. Explain how you did the work.
8. Make a written report from watching a cotton gin in action. Tell the conditions and operations of the nearest cotton market.
9. Show how you would detect cotton goods made from long staple cotton.
10. Draw a plan for a moderate-sized cotton plantation. Show field layouts. Show a plan for 3 or 4 years' rotation of crops with the cotton.

Corn Farming

4-H FFA

1. Grow a patch of corn not less than 300 square feet, if planted to a standard variety. A smaller plot may be used if experimental. (Speak to your counselor before planting.)
2. Keep a record of costs, hours of work, type of seed, and yield.
3. Have your corn patch inspected at least once by your counselor.
4. Show your records and samples of crop. Describe modern ways to farm.

Cycling

1. Clean and adjust a bicycle. Prepare it for inspection using a bicycle safety checklist. Be sure the bicycle meets local laws.

2. Show your bicycle to your counselor for inspection. Point out the adjustments or repairs you have made. Do the following:

(a) Show all points that need oiling regularly.

(b) Show points that should be checked regularly to make sure the bicycle is safe to ride.

(c) Show how to adjust chain tension, brakes, seat level and height, steering post.

3. Describe how to brake safely with foot brakes and with hand brakes.

4. Show how to repair a flat. Use an old bicycle tire.

5. Show the following:

(a) Proper mounting, pedaling, and braking. (Include emergency stops.)

(b) Ride a straight line. Ride at least 100 feet between straight,

parallel lines 6 inches apart, 4 out of 5 times.

(c) Show proper curbside and road edge riding. Show how to watch for rear, side, and oncoming traffic.

(d) Ride an obstacle course, changing from very slow to higher speed. Do a complete turn in a 15-foot road or driveway.

(e) Show correct hand signals.

6. Describe your traffic laws for bicycles. Compare them with motor-vehicle laws. Know the bicycle-safety code.

7. Avoiding main highways, take six rides of 25 miles each. Take two each month for 3 months. You must make a report of the rides taken. List dates, routes traveled, and interesting things seen.*

8. After the 3-month period in No. 7, lay out on a road map a 50-mile trip. Stay away from main highways. Using your map, make this ride in 8 hours.

---

*Bicycle must have all needed safety features. It must be registered as required by your traffic laws.

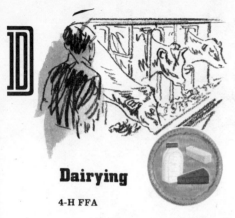

Dairying

4-H FFA

1. Tell about the management of dairy cattle.
2. Milk a cow.
3. Tell about pasteurization of milk. Tell need for care of dairy utensils and appliances.
4. Test the milk of five cows (individually) for 10 days each with a test approved by your local health authorities. Make reports.

Dog Care

1. Tell some of the characteristics of 10 breeds of dogs; OR give a short history of one.
2. Point out on a dog (or on a sketch) at least 10 parts. Give the correct name of each.
3. Present a report signed by a parent or guardian describing the care you have given your dog for 2 months. Include these items: feeding schedule, food used, housing, exercising, grooming, and bathing. Tell what has been done to keep the dog alert and healthy.
4. Present a written report showing about how much it costs to keep your dog for 2 months.
5. Explain the right way to obedience train. Show with your dog any three of these commands: "Come," "Sit," "Down," "Heel," "Stay," "Take it," "Drop it," "Get it."
6. Do at least TWO of the following:
(a) Describe what should be done to remove fleas, ticks, and lice from your dog.
(b) Describe the symptoms of the following: distemper, rabies, mange, ringworm. Explain what you would do if your dog showed these.
(c) Describe the proper treatment for sore ear, sore eye, fits, removing something swallowed by a dog, removing something stuck in its throat.
(d) Explain first aid for a dog-bite. List the things needed in every dog owner's first aid kit.
7. Explain precautions to take in handling a hurt dog. Show how to put on an emergency safety muzzle. Explain how to treat wounds. Show how to put on a simple dressing and bandage to the foot, body, or head. Explain what to do when a dog is hit by a car.
8. Tell the dangers of home treatment of a serious ailment. Report on a visit to a veterinary hospital; or report on a visit to an animal shelter.
9. Know the laws and ordinances involving dogs in force in your town.

Drafting

1. Prepare the following pencil drawings on material for reproduction:

(a) Make a rough sketch of a room. From it make a finished, scale floor plan. The drawing is to be properly titled. Show by conventional symbols all openings, equipment, and safety devices. List drawing instruments used.

(b) Make a scale drawing of some piece of craftwork. It must be so clear it can be used by someone else to make the article. The drawing is to have a bill of material. There is to be an estimate of cost.

(c) Reduce or enlarge the drawing you made for No. 1b. Show the scale used.

(d) Show drawings you made of orthographic projections. Show an isometric drawing of something other than those in Nos. 1a and 1b.

(e) Make ONE of the following: (1) A simple bar chart or graph showing your progress in scholarship, physical fitness, or financial activity. (2) A simple schematic drawing of a radio or electronic circuit. (3) A perspective drawing of your own house. Use proper proportion. Show shrubs and trees.

2. Using single-stroke vertical or slant Gothic lettering, describe in ink for reproduction the subject of your drawing in No. 1b in not less than 25 words. Lettering devices may be used.

3. Describe five ways that drawings can be reproduced. Make copies of one of your pencil drawings and ink lettering, using one of these ways.

Electricity

1. Show electrical attraction and repulsion. Make and use a simple electromagnet.

2. Explain the difference between a direct and an alternating current. Tell the common uses of each. Show one way of finding which is in an electric line.

3. Show in a simple drawing you have made how a battery cell and an electric bell work.

4. Explain why a fuse blows out. Tell how to find a blown fuse in your home. Show how to change it safely.

5. Explain what overloading an electric circuit means. Tell what you have done to make sure your home circuits aren't overloaded.

6. Join two pieces of insulated wire the right way; or fix a bad wire on an appliance or to a plug.

7. Show how to save a person touching a live wire in the home. Show first aid if he is unconscious from electrical shock.

8. Show on a floor plan of a room in your home the lights, switches, and outlets. Show which fuse protects each.

9. Read an electric meter. Figure an electric bill from meter readings.

10. Explain 10 electrical terms such as volt, amperes, watt, ohm, resistance, etc.

11. Do any TWO of the following:

(a) Connect a buzzer, bell, or light with a battery. Have a key or switch in the line.

(b) Make and run a simple electric motor (not from a kit).

(c) Build a simple rheostat. Show that it works.

(d) Build a single-pole double-throw switch. Show that it works.

(e) Hook a model electric train layout to a house circuit. Tell how it works.

Electronics

1. Do the following:

(a) Show how to read a schematic diagram.

(b) Draw a simple circuit. It should have parts such as resistors, capacitors, transistors, or tubes. Use correct symbols. Label all parts.

(c) Explain the purpose of each of the parts.

2. Do the following:

(a) Explain the right way to solder and unsolder.

(b) Wire the circuit that you drew for No. 1b.

(c) Explain how to avoid heat damage to the parts.

3. Explain ONE of the following:

(a) Remote-control:

Explain how you can use an electronic circuit for remote control. Build a device to show this. A kit may be used. Suggested—an electric eye. A model train control. A model plane control. A toy electronic organ.

(b) Electronic brain:

Explain the binary system of numbers. Make up five problems in addition and subtraction. Work them out. Change binary numbers to decimal numbers. Build a simple flip-flop circuit using either transistors or tubes.

4. Discuss jobs in the field of electronics.

Emergency Preparedness

1. Earn First Aid merit badge.
2. Do the following:
(a) Tell what you would do to prevent injury and possible loss of life to yourself and others in each of the following emergencies:

Fire or explosion at home and in a public building
Car stalled in blizzard or desert
Motor vehicle accident
Mountain accident
Food poisoning
Boating accident
Search for lost person
Lost or marooned group
Gas leak
Earthquake
Flood
Tornado or hurricane
Atomic emergency
Avalanche (snow or rock)

(b) Show that you know what to do in at least TWO of the above.
3. Show how you could safely save a person from the following:
(a) Touching a live electric wire
(b) From a room with carbon monoxide or other fumes or smoke
(c) With clothes on fire
(d) From drowning using non-swimming rescues (including ice accidents).
4. Tell the things a group of Scouts should be prepared to do, the training needed, and the safety precautions to be taken for the following emergency service:
(a) Crowd and traffic control
(b) Messenger service and communication
(c) Collection and distribution services
(d) Group feeding, shelter, and sanitation.
5. Take part in an emergency service project, either real or a practice drill.
6. Show three ways of attracting and communicating with rescue planes.
7. With another person, show a good way to move an injured person out of a remote and rugged area, conserving the energy of the rescuers.
8. Do the following:
(a) Prepare a written plan for mobilizing your troop when needed to do emergency services. If there is a plan, explain it. Tell your part in making it work.
(b) Take part in at least one troop mobilization. Describe your part.
(c) Show the personal "emergency pack" which you have prepared to be ready for a mobilization call. Show a family kit (suitcase or box) for use by your family in case an emergency evacuation is needed. Explain the need.
9. Show proper use of ropes and lines for rescue work by doing the following:
(a) Tie knots for joining lines. Tie knots for shortening or adjusting lines. Tie knots for lashings.
(b) Lower a person from a height sufficient to show how.
(c) Coil and accurately throw light and heavy 50-foot heaving lines.

Engineering

1. Tell what high school preparation is needed to get in an accredited engineering college. Read *Faith of the Engineer*. Point out in what ways this is like the Scout Oath.

2. Describe the kind of work done by an engineer. Tell how each branch of engineering helps our society.

3. Make an inspection trip to a manufacturing or processing plant or an engineering job in your town. Talk about what is happening with an engineer. Prepare a report telling about the trip. Emphasize things that use engineering.

4. Make a slide rule. Show its use in solving problems. Explain the mathematical basis for the rule.

5. Do THREE of the following:

(a) Design a cam, linkage, gear train, or other mechanical device for transforming motion. Prepare a working drawing. Build a working model from wood, plastic, or metal.

(b) Build a simple electrical or electronic device (kits may be used).

(c) Show by a drawing how the forces are distributed in a king post truss bridge carrying a 200-pound person at the center, if the two members are inclined 30 degrees above the horizontal.

(d) Explain with the aid of a drawing, and figure how much it would cost to pump 100,000 gallons of water from sea level into a reservoir whose surface is at 550 feet above sea level. Assume electric power costs 6 cents per kwhr, and the combined pump and motor efficiency is 80 percent and 5 percent of the water is lost in leaks.

(e) Write a report explaining how energy in a fuel is changed into useful work in a machine. Use drawings to show what happens.

(f) Pick a busy street or highway in your town. Study the traffic flow when heavy and light. Get from the city the predicted increase in automobiles and population over the next 5 years. Report on what you found. Include your plan of how the traffic situation in 5 years might be helped at the place studied.

(g) Set up a distilling apparatus with and without a fractionating column. Draw a graph of product purity versus percent distilled. Explain why you get better results with a fractionating column.

(h) Show how to use one device for getting engineering measurements.

(i) Set up a device for measuring heat transfer. Draw a graph showing heat transfer versus rate of flow. Explain why you get better heat transfer with a high rate of flow.

(j) In place of one activity under this requirement, the counselor may choose a similar project that will make use of engineering activities in your town.

Environmental Science

1. Explain the meaning of the following: ecology, biosphere, ecosystem, plant succession, limiting factor. Give an example of the last two.

2. With the help of your counselor, pick an area of 10 acres* for study.

3. Visit the area four times for 2 hours each time. On each visit do the following:
(a) Record the temperature, rain, and wind.
(b) List the animals you saw. Tell what they were doing.
(c) List the plants you saw. Name the kinds of rocks and soil.

4. Write about your study in 500 words or more showing:

(a) How the climate, topography, and geology have influenced the number and kinds of plants and animals.
(b) How the living and nonliving elements are interrelated.
(c) Why it is important that people understand this.

5. With your counselor, plan and carry out a project in ONE of the following:
(a) The effect of water-holding capacity of soil on plant life. The relation of plant cover to runoff. How both are related to the water and oxygen cycles.
(b) The influence of land plant life on temperature, light intensity, wind velocity, and humidity. The influence of water plant life on the water environment. How both land and water plants affect animal life.

6. Make a report, in the form of a short talk to a Scout group, on what you did in No. 5.

7. Show you understand the following:
(a) The causes of water pollution. Tell what it does to rivers and lakes.
(b) The causes of land pollution. Tell what it does to the environment.
(c) The causes of air pollution. Tell what it does to the environment.
(d) How some chemicals get into the tissues of animals miles from where they were used.

8. Describe what you and others can do to help solve a local problem of air pollution, water pollution, or litter.

9. Describe the duties of three positions in environmental science.

---

*City Scouts may pick an area in a large park, if a better place is not available.

Farm Arrangement

4-H FFA

1. Do EITHER (a) or (b).
(a) Rearrangement Plan
(1) Make a scale drawing of a farmstead as it is now. Show location of buildings. Name them and mark as permanent, temporary, obsolete, or movable. Show windbreaks, desirable trees, roads and farm lanes, electric lines, direction of prevailing winds in winter and summer, good and poor drainage spots, wells, ponds, streams. (2) On tracing paper overlay, show where you would relocate the main farmstead centers to best suit the needs of your kind of farm operation. Explain why you would relocate the centers.
(b) New Plan
(1) Make a scale drawing of a farmstead site that has no buildings. This drawing should show present location of the

following: trees (mark whether desirable or not), windbreaks, slope of land, roads, streams, ponds, direction of prevailing winds in winter and summer, high and low spots, electric lines. (2) On this plan show where you would put the farmstead centers to best suit the needs of your kind of farm operation. Explain why you would put the centers where you have.
2. Do ONE of the following:
(a) Get plans for one building that would best fit into your farmstead. Tell how you would change the plans to fit your needs.
(b) Make and explain a detailed plan for water and sanitation facilities for a farm.
(c) On a tracing paper overlay, show the best way for getting from one center of the farmstead to another. Show how to get from the farmstead to the fields, pastures, and road. Explain your drawing.

a daily service check for field use. (Do things needed for best field performance.)

(c) Prepare any farm machine for winter.

6. Visit an implement dealer. Prepare a list of the safety features found on a tractor and one other farm machine shown there. Explain the reasons for these.

Farm Mechanics

4-H FFA

1. List tools usually found in a well-equipped farm shop. Explain the uses of four.

2. Pick any farm machine and explain how power is transferred to do a job.

3. Do ONE of the following:

(a) Put a new handle in any tool found on the farm.

(b) Sharpen any cutting tool found on the farm.

(c) Build a tool rack and place to store nails, bolts, and washers.

4. Do ONE of the following:

(a) Adjust farm equipment or machinery.

(b) Pick a piece of farm machinery or equipment. Check all nuts, bolts, and screws. Tighten any that are loose. Replace those that are missing, worn, or damaged. List things you did.

(c) Repair broken or worn farm machinery or equipment.

5. Do ONE of the following:

(a) Do the following on a tractor: grease, change oil and oil filter, clean air cleaner, flush cooling system, clean radiator fins.

(b) With any farm machine, do

Farm Records

4-H FFA

1. Explain what kind of records and books should be kept for a general purpose and stock farm.

2. Keep chicken and egg production record for 1 month.

3. Make out a bill of sale for the following to Jones Produce Company, Chicago, Ill.

160 lbs. of spring fryers	$ .30 per lb.
32 doz. eggs	.42 per doz.
1 cockerel	5.75
24 pullets	2.50 ea.

4. Keep a 7-day milk record for a herd of cows (your own or a neighbor's).

5. Make out a sample of 1 year's birth record for 3 colts, 27 calves, and 15 pigs.

6. Explain what records are needed in making out an income tax report.

Fingerprinting

1. Take a clear set of prints. Use both rolled and plain impressions. Make these on an 8- by 8-inch fingerprint card.
2. Do the following:
(a) Name the surfaces of the body where friction or papillary ridges are found.
(b) Explain why plain impressions must be taken on a card.
3. Show you can identify the eight types. Collect six of these.
4. Give a short history of fingerprinting. Tell the difference between civil and criminal identification. Point out the purposes of each.
5. Get the prints of one person. Have the prints and descriptions accepted for the civil identification file.

Firemanship

1. Discuss how heat, fuel, and air are the things needed to cause fire. Explain how taking away any of these will put out fire.

2. Explain five main causes of fire in the home. Tell how to guard against each.
3. Explain the safe way to:
(a) Make a light in a dark closet.
(b) Act when you smell gas.
(c) Light and use charcoal.
(d) Burn leaves and rubbish where it's allowed.
(e) Use home gas and electric appliances.
(f) Put fuel in gasoline-powered equipment.
(g) Melt wax.
4. Make a firesafety inspection of your home. Have your parents help. Then prepare the following in writing:
(a) List things that could start a fire. Use a home firesafety checklist. Have one of your parents sign this.
(b) List how much and where there is any gasoline, cleaning fluid, paint thinner, or other flammables.
(c) Tell which were stored unsafely. Tell what you did to correct this.
(d) List things in your home that can be used to put out fires.
5. Make a rough drawing of the sleeping part of your home. Show which persons sleep where. Then explain:
(a) A home fire-escape plan that you have talked over with your whole family.
(b) What you would do if alone and a small fire started in your house.
(c) How to turn in an alarm in your town.
(d) What to do if you smell smoke at night.
(e) How to save a person whose clothes are on fire.
(f) How to save yourself and your family in case of fire.
(g) What extra care is needed during the winter holidays.

6. Do the following:

(a) Visit a fire station nearest your home. Identify the equipment there. Describe what each piece does. Include equipment used for electrical, chemical, and oil fires.

(b) Explain what fire hazards are a problem in your neighborhood. Tell what is being done about them.

7. Do the following:

(a) Tell how to set up a camp so it is safe from fire.

(b) Describe the fire equipment you need before lighting a fire in a camp.

(c) Have your unit leader state that you have properly put out a campfire. Describe where and how you did this.

(d) Tell how forest fires start. Explain what is done to prevent them. Tell how you can help.

(e) Tell what to do if fire breaks out on a camping trip.

(f) Explain how a grass or brush fire can be fought with improvised equipment.

First Aid

1. Earn the First Aid skill award. Show you know the skills by doing any of them asked by your counselor.

2. Do the following:

(a) Describe the signs of a broken bone. Tell first aid rules for handling fractures, including compound fractures.

(b) On a person lying down, and using improvised materials, show the first aid for any two of the following fractures as asked for: forearm, upper arm, wrist, collarbone, upper leg, lower leg, crushed foot, spine.

3. Do the following:

(a) Explain what should be done for severe bleeding.

(b) Tell when the use of a tourniquet may be justified.

(c) Show how to stop bleeding from a severe cut of the lower leg and wrist.

4. Do the following:

(a) Tell the dangers of moving a seriously injured person.

(b) If a sick or injured person must be moved, tell how you would decide what way to do it.

(c) Show alone, and again with help, two carries for moving an injured person.

(d) Improvise a stretcher. With helpers under your direction, move a presumably unconscious person.

5. Show the proper way to put on an adhesive bandage. Show how to put on a large gauze compress held in place with tape. Show how to put a dressing on the eye with a cravat.

6. Show the proper way to put a roller bandage on the ankle and foot, the wrist and hand, the forearm, and a finger.

7. Do the following:

(a) Tell the causes and proper first aid for unconsciousness.

(b) Tell what first aid you would give a person with an epileptic convulsion.

(c) Tell what to do for the following:

Heatstroke

Heat exhaustion
Frostbite
Boils and pimples
Bruises
Stomachache
Choking on food
Arm and leg cramps

8. Make a list of things you should have in a home first aid kit, first aid equipment for an automobile, or a patrol first aid kit.

9. Help in teaching the First Aid skill award to two or more persons.

First Aid to Animals

4-H FFA

1. Prepare and explain a plan for the management of a farm animal. Cover a month. Show what must be done to prevent illness, blemishes, and defects.

2. Tell the symptoms and explain how to care for the following:

Horses
(a) Lameness
(b) Exhaustion from overheating
(c) Distemper
Cows
(d) Milk fever
(e) Prussic acid poisoning
Sheep
(f) Foot-and-mouth disease
(g) Anthrax

Hogs
(h) Cholera
Dogs
(i) Distemper
(j) Rabies

3. Tell what you would do for:
(a) Wire cuts
(b) Choking
(c) Colic
(d) Bloat
(e) When a horse falls in a stall or on the highway
(f) Cruelty to or neglect of domestic animals

4. Show on an animal how to treat:
(a) A broken bone
(b) A sprain
(c) Serious bleeding
(d) An open sore

5. Do ONE of the following:
(a) Help care for a hurt or sick animal for at least 4 days.
(b) Work with local groups to help animals.
(c) Work with local groups in preventing an infectious disease to which farm animals are subject.

Fish and Wildlife Management

1. Describe the history of fish and wildlife conservation in America. Tell the development of the profession of fisheries management and wildlife management. Define fish and wildlife management. Give examples and dates of main legislation in this history. Explain why past fish and wildlife management has been concerned mainly with game animals.

2. Describe five different relationships between man and fish and wildlife. Use both good and bad examples.

3. Describe the four methods used in fish and wildlife management to maintain or increase numbers. Give an example of each for your state.

4. Name three local plants useful as wildlife food. Name three others useful as cover for wildlife.

5. Tell which agencies are responsible for fish and wildlife management in your state. Tell the difference between their authorities and responsibilities. Describe opportunities for a career in one of these. Explain how hunting, fishing, and trapping laws are set in your state.

6. Do ONE:

(a) Pick two 5-acre plots of different wildlife habitats. Get help from your counselor in this. Describe in writing the vegetation. List the wildlife and their numbers seen in two 3-hour visits to each plot. Explain the differences you saw. Suggest ways changes could be made to help the wildlife. Tell what would happen if the numbers of one kind of animal doubled or tripled.

(b) Visit a wildlife refuge or management area or managed fishing waters. Interview the resident manager. Write at least 500 words on what is being done to improve the area for fish and wildlife.

(c) Visit a game farm or fish hatchery. Interview the resident manager. Write a report of at least 500 words on the place of game farm birds or hatchery fish in conservation.

(d) Go out 2 days with a commercial fisherman. Describe his catch. Tell methods used. Write about the importance of such fish to the world's economy and health.

(e) Work with your counselor on the following study. Study for 6 weeks the kinds of wildlife within several blocks of your home. List those good for your neighborhood. Also list those that are bad. Explain why you have put each on your lists. Suggest plans for increasing the good wildlife in your neighborhood. Tell what groups might help to do this.

(f) Attend a camp for a week or more where conservation is a major part of the program. Write about how you will use the things learned.

7. Do ONE of the following:

(a) Plan and carry out a project that will improve a water or land area for fish or wildlife. Work with your counselor or a fish and wildlife manager.

(b) Organize and run a neighborhood campaign to clean up places that harbor rats or other harmful wildlife

Fishing

1. Catch three different kinds of fish by any legal, sportsmanlike method. Identify them. (One of the fish must be taken on an artificial lure.) Clean for cooking.

2. Point out the different parts of a fly, casting, saltwater, or spinning rod. Name them. Point out the main parts of a fly, casting, saltwater, or spinning reel; OR show how to take care of your fishing tackle; OR tell where the chief kinds of fish are likely to be found where you live, at different times of year, different times of day, in different kinds of weather.
3. Catch and identify three kinds of live bait.
4. Give the open seasons on game fish where you live. Explain how and why they are protected by law. Tell what fish conservationists are doing to make better fishing for you.

groups. This is a total of 12.
Grasses—Do THREE.

1. Show samples of five kinds of perennial grasses. Explain their uses for feed and soil conservation.

2. Show how to prepare a seedbed for a lawn, pasture, or meadow.

3. Show:
(a) Samples of three annual grasses used both for hay and pastures.
(b) Samples of three large seed grasses. Explain the use of each.

4. Make a blotter, plate, or ragdoll seed tester. Show how to use in testing seeds for vitality.

5. Do the following:
(a) Show six of the most important grasses found where you live. Identify and explain the use of each.
(b) Explain the difference between "bunchgrasses" and "sodforming grasses" and their uses.

Legumes—Do THREE including Nos. 1 or 3.

1. Show samples and name the five most important legume crops grown where you live.

2. Name three small and three large seed legumes. Explain use of these for seed, soil conservation, cash crop, and for keeping soil moisture.

3. Show how to fertilize, lime, prepare seedbed, seed, and manage a crop of legumes grown where you live.

4. Explain:
(a) How legumes may be used to build soil fertility and control erosion.
(b) How legumes deplete the soil.

Forage Crops

4-H FFA

Meet THREE requirements as shown in each of the following

5. Explain:

(a) What is meant by inoculation of legumes.

(b) How this is done. Tell why it is important.

Pastures—any THREE including Nos. 3 or 5.

1. Explain the best way to improve an old pasture. Tell how to manage and keep pasture fertility where you live.

2. Explain under what conditions grasses, legumes, and hayfields may be used for pastures.

3. Collect five poisonous or undesirable grasses and weeds which can harm pastures or be poisonous to livestock.

4. Explain from what you have seen how cows, horses, and sheep are different in the way they graze.

5. Prepare an exhibit of at least five pasture grasses, showing whole plant with stem, leaf, flower, and seed.

Hay Crops—Do THREE.

1. Explain how grasses such as legumes and grain crops may be used for hay or feed for livestock and wild game.

2. Tell how to store hay crops safely in barns, stacks, sheds, and in bales. Explain how to prevent hay-barn fires.

3. Mount and show five kinds of properly cured hay crops. Explain the qualities of "succulent" or "well-cured" hay.

4. Show samples of two kinds of hay crops best suited to different livestock.

5. Show how to run one hay-making machine and use one hand tool. Name five tools and machines used for haymaking where you live. Explain what each does.

Forestry

4-H FFA

1. Point out 15 different species of trees or wild shrubs in the field and tell their names and chief uses. (If fewer than 15 kinds grow locally, identify and tell the uses of those that may be found.)

2. Do ONE of the following:

(a) Collect leaves or winter twigs of 15 forest trees or shrubs; mount them in a notebook, writing the name of each, where it grows in the United States, and the chief uses.

(b) Obtain wood samples of 10 different trees and tell some of the uses of each kind of wood.

3. Do the following:

(a) Describe the value of forests in protecting soil and building fertility, regulating the flow of water, wildlife management, and as recreational areas. Tell from what watershed or other source your community obtains its water.

(b) Describe briefly the part that forest products play in our everyday life.

4. Do ONE of the following:

(a) Make a diameter tape or Biltmore stick. Show how to determine the height and diameter of trees. Estimate the board-foot volume of three trees selected by the counselor.

(b) Find and examine several stumps or logs that have variations in the rate of growth as shown by rings and discuss reasons for these variations.

5. Describe what is meant by forest management.

6. Working with your counselor or a forester, plan and carry out a forestry project that meets a need such as tree planting, seed collecting, range improvement, or forest wildlife management.

7. Do the following:

(a) Describe the damage to forests and watersheds, resulting from fire, insects, tree diseases, overgrazing, and unwise cutting practices. Tell what is being done to reduce this damage.

(b) Tell what to do if a fire is discovered in woodlands.

(c) Take part in a forest-fire prevention campaign or build a fire lane of at least 100 yards at a location designated by a local fire warden, forester, or counselor.

8. Do ONE of the following:

(a) Take a field trip to a logging operation or to a wood-using industrial plant and write a 500-word report telling what the raw material is, where it comes from, how the finished product is made, how products are used, and how waste materials are disposed of.

(b) Visit a managed public or private forest area or watershed with its supervisor and write a 500-word report on how the area is managed to grow repeated crops of lumber, to protect the watershed, to support repeated crops of wildlife, or to provide other services and benefits.

Fruit and Nut Growing

4-H FFA

1. Do the following:
(a) Point out on a map of the United States the chief regions where 10 different kinds or varieties of fruits and/or nuts are grown.
(b) List the kinds and varieties of fruits and nuts that can be grown economically where you live.
2. Pick a good place for a fruit or nut orchard, vineyard, or berry patch. Make a plan for planting it.
3. Take full care of fruit or nut trees, grapevines, or berry plants through a crop season or for 1 year. Keep accurate records of costs, observations, and yield; or help take care of a fruit or nut orchard or vineyard of 1 acre or more through a full crop season.

419

4. Prune a tree, vine, or bush properly. Explain why pruning was needed.

5. Describe three of the insect pests most harmful to fruit or nut crops where you live. Name two diseases most harmful. Explain how you would control each without hurting wildlife or destroying useful insects.

6. Do ONE of the following:

(a) Plant five fruit or nut trees to improve your home grounds, Scout camp, or other good place in years to come.

(b) Bud or graft a fruit or nut tree successfully with some better variety.

(c) Pick or gather your fruit or nut crop (No. 3). Grade and prepare it for market. Figure out its market value where you live.

(d) Show your crop at a fair; or visit a fair. Compare samples of your crop with those shown.

(e) Help preserve some of your crop for sale or home use.

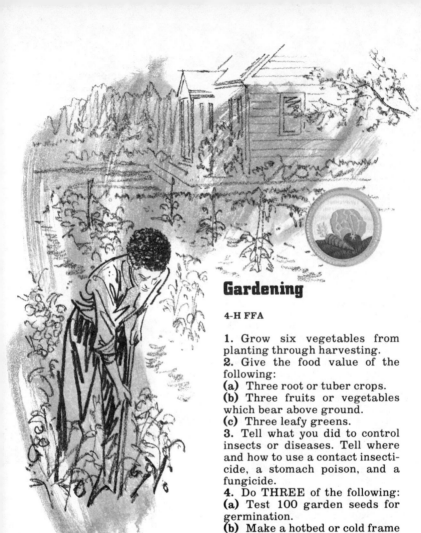

Gardening

4-H FFA

1. Grow six vegetables from planting through harvesting.
2. Give the food value of the following:
(a) Three root or tuber crops.
(b) Three fruits or vegetables which bear above ground.
(c) Three leafy greens.
3. Tell what you did to control insects or diseases. Tell where and how to use a contact insecticide, a stomach poison, and a fungicide.
4. Do THREE of the following:
(a) Test 100 garden seeds for germination.
(b) Make a hotbed or cold frame and grow plants in the same.
(c) Clean, grade, bunch, or pack any three vegetables for market.
(d) Show one of the vegetables you have grown at a harvest festival or fair.
(e) Make a storage bin or pit for home use.
(f) Store part of the crop grown. Describe the process.
(g) Carry out a project approved by the counselor.

421

Genealogy

1. Tell where the word "genealogy" comes from. Tell what it means.
2. Give the history of genealogy in one of the following:
(a) Ancient world
(b) Medieval world
(c) Modern world
3. Name three societies that further genealogical study.
4. Name two lineage societies.
5. Give the three key genealogical study questions. Tell about them.
6. Name five ways to get genealogical information.
7. Prepare a five-generation pedigree chart.
8. Do ONE:
(a) Prepare family group records for each of the couples on your pedigree chart through the first three generations.
(b) Prepare a history of your life to date. Include pictures and a family group record.
(c) Prepare a history of the life of one of the people on your pedigree chart. Include pictures and a family group record.

9. Do ONE:
(a) Visit a genealogical library, public records office, or archives depository. Write about the visit.
(b) Copy the gravestone inscriptions of the surnames of one of the people on your pedigree chart.
(c) Get from a public records office (county, state, or federal) two documents showing proof of things on your pedigree chart.

General Science

1. Do TWO of the following:
(a) Chart the motion of the Moon and one planet during 4 hours. Relate this to a point on the horizon.
(b) Chart the position and appearance of the Moon on the days or nights you can see it for 28 days.

(c) Chart the positions of three constellations and the North Star during 4 hours. Relate to a point on the horizon.

(d) Watch and report on an eclipse of the Moon, a meteor shower, or similar astronomical event.

2. Describe your findings after checking TWO of the following:

(a) The erosion during a month's time of one of the following: A stream's banks. A tract of land from which the vegetation has been removed recently.

(b) An exposure of a rock stratum or strata. This could be at a road cut, an excavation, or at a natural canyon or river gorge.

(c) The appearance of three different kinds of clouds in the sky.

(d) The environmental conditions which come before and during three different kinds of precipitation.

(e) The changes in the looks of three different kinds of rocks or minerals after being freshly broken and the newly exposed surfaces allowed to weather for a month.

3. Describe what you learned after watching TWO of the following:

(a) The germination of three different kinds of seeds.

(b) The metamorphosis of an insect.

(c) The parts of one flower before and after pollination, and some time before the seeds are ripe.

(d) The buds of five kinds of trees while dormant and after partial opening, either natural or forced.

4. Build models or show the basic scientific principles or ideas that are applied in FIVE of the following:

(a) Using lenses to make a telescope or compound microscope.

(b) Making a dry cell or other kind of electrical "battery."

(c) Extracting a metal from its ore.

(d) Getting crystals from a solution of a substance.

(e) Lifting something too heavy to lift directly.

(f) Making a magnet that can be "turned on and off."

(g) Using materials that are more dense than water to build something that will float.

(h) Shaping an airplane wing so it will lift a plane.

(i) Changing back and forth motion to rotary motion.

(j) Generating carbon dioxide so that some kinds of baked foods will "rise."

5. Design, carry out, and report on or show FIVE experiments that will:

(a) Show the change in volume of salt water above and below freezing temperature.

(b) Show that the composition of the air in a bottle has changed when a bottle is placed over a burning candle until the candle goes out.

(c) Show what happens when new seedlings are badly crowded in a pot of soil.

(d) Show the effects of rusting tendency on an iron nail placed in a jar of water when different metals are wrapped around the nail.

(e) Find out how the strength of an electromagnet is changed by the number of turns of wire and the current.

(f) Show the effect of available water on the root development of seedlings.

(g) Compare the orientation of a plant grown in complete darkness with one grown in light.

Geology

1. Do ONE of the following:
(a) Make a collection of different ores, rock-forming minerals, and fossils. Give name and use (or age) of each. (minimum, 20 specimens.)
(b) Make a collection of different sedimentary, igneous, and metamorphic rocks. Name the important minerals found in each. Tell what use can be made of these rocks. (minimum, 10 specimens.)

2. Do ONE of the following:
(a) Visit a mine or quarry; oil or gas field; a gravel, clay, sand, or shell pit; or other like operation. Explain the deposit. Tell how the product is removed, transported, sold, and used. What safety precautions are used?
(b) Visit your water system. Describe the source, quality, and amount of water needed for your town. Give its relation to your geology.
3. Get a topographic map of your home area. Study it. Explain the important geological features shown on it. (If you can't get a local map, study one of another place that you know. Air photos may be used instead of a topographic map.)
4. Do ONE of the following:
(a) Prepare a report including maps or drawings of the geological features on or below the surface of an area that you know.
(b) Describe how the soil was formed where you live. Tell the kinds of rock from which it came.
(c) Describe the earth materials used in your home or a public building. Tell where they came from. List those which you use every day. Tell where they came from.
ALTERNATIVE: In place of Nos. 4a or 4c, the counselor may make up a project of like merit. It must make use of some of the interesting geological features where you live.

Hog Production

4-H FFA

1. Explain how important hog production is nationally and in your own state. Describe the type of hog in greatest demand by the consumer. Make a rough drawing showing the main cuts of pork.

2. Raise or help raise hogs. Give four rules for success from your own experience. Outline good management in breeding methods. Tell care needed to be sure of healthy litters, with minimum loss before weaning. Give labor-saving methods.

3. Write at least 200 words on sanitation, food, water, shade, and pasture. Explain why grains alone are not an adequate food. Outline in writing the proper feeding from the breeding time through weaning of a litter of pigs. Discuss fattening and growth.

4. Describe two breeds of hog with which you are personally familiar. Name at least two other breeds. Visit a farm where hog raising is a major project; or visit a packing plant or stockyard. Describe your visit.

5. Describe symptoms of two hog diseases and two parasites. Tell what you should do if you find these. Explain how roundworm infestation can be prevented.

6. Tell how to prepare and show a hog for exhibit.

Hiking

1. Explain and show, where possible, the main points of good hiking practices.

2. Make a written plan for a 10-mile hike. Include map routes, a clothing and equipment list, and a list of things for a trail lunch.

3. Take five hikes of 10 continuous miles each, on 5 days.

4. Take a hike of 20 continuous miles in 1 day.

5. Within a month of the last hike and after taking all six hikes, make a short report of each of the six hikes. Give dates, routes covered, weather, and any interesting things you saw.

425

Home Repairs

Do **14** of the following:

1. Know where your main electric switch is. Replace a fuse.
2. Waterproof a basement wall.
3. Repair or put in curtain rods. Hang curtains.
4. Build or fix a stair or porch handrail.
5. Repair furniture.
6. Repair window screen or screen door.
7. Repair sagging door or gate.
8. Repair a picture frame.
9. Clean out a sink trap.
10. Repair a sash cord.
11. Put in a new faucet washer.
12. Repair a break in a cement walk, drive, garage floor, or in an asphalt surface.
13. Repair a fence.
14. Recondition a garden tool.
15. Repair an electric cord, plug, or lamp socket.
16. Replace a broken pane of glass.
17. Mend china.
18. Paint or varnish a piece of furniture, door, or part of the trim on a house. Clean brush afterward.
19. Repair a leaky hose.
20. Calk cracks or joints open to the weather.
21. Put in fixtures for storing equipment or tools.
22. Paint a wall or ceiling. Clean brush afterward.
23. Lay linoleum or asphalt tile or fix a worn place.
24. Solder.
25. Put in new cords in a Venetian blind.
26. Build a workbench.

Horsemanship

1. Name 15 main parts of a horse.

2. Name four leading breeds of horses. Explain what each breed is noted for.

3. Show the care of saddle and bridle. Name the main parts of the saddle and bridle.

4. Show how to groom, pick out feet, and care for a horse after riding.

5. Describe the symptoms of colic. Describe four other horse diseases.

6. Name three main defects of feet and legs. Explain how to detect.

7. Describe the right way to feed the horse that you use for this test. Explain why the amount and kind of feed will be changed according to the work and the kind of horse he is.

8. Show how to lead a horse from a stall, corral, or field and saddle and bridle properly.

9. On level ground, continuously do the following movements. Do them correctly, at ease, and in sympathy with the horse:

(a) Mount.

(b) Walk horse in a straight line for 60 feet.

(c) Make a half circle of not over 16 feet in radius at walk.

(d) Trot in a straight line for at least 60 feet.

(e) Make a half circle of not over 20 feet in radius at trot.

(f) Canter in a circle 20 feet in radius on proper lead.

(g) Change direction. Either reverse at canter and change leads or come down to a walk, reverse, and take up canter on proper lead.

(h) Halt straight.

(i) Back up straight four paces.

(j) Halt and dismount.

10. Show how to safely approach and remove a horse from a stall in a fire.

Indian Lore

1. Give the history of one Indian tribe, group, or nation. This should be one that lives or has lived near your home. Visit it, if possible. Tell about the following: dwellings, food preparation, dress, religious beliefs, kind of life, language, war, means of getting around, where the members, if any, now live and how they now live.

2. Do TWO of the following:

(a) Make a full authentic Indian costume.

(b) Make and decorate authentically three Indian articles approved by your counselor.

(c) Make an authentic model of an Indian dwelling used by any Indian tribe, group, or nation.

(d) Visit a museum to see Indian artifacts. Talk about them with your counselor. Identify at least 10 artifacts by shape, size, and use.

3. Do ONE of the following:

(a) Learn three Indian games. Teach and lead one game with a Scout group.

(b) Learn and show Indian-style cooking. Cook three things.

(c) Show the Indian way of hunting, fishing, or trapping.

4. Do ONE of the following:

(a) Take part in an Indian show in which dances and songs, based on authentic Indian themes, are used.

(b) Sing two Indian songs in Indian dialect. Explain their meaning.

(c) Plan and take part in an Indian campfire ceremony based on an Indian theme.

(d) Learn in Indian dialect at least 25 common terms and their meaning.

(e) Show 25 signs in Indian sign language. Include those that will help you ask for water, food, and where the path or road leads.

(f) Learn in English an Indian story of at least 300 words, or any number of shorter ones adding up to 300 words. Tell the story at a Scout meeting or campfire.

(g) Write or tell about eight things adopted by the white man from the Indian.

(h) Learn 25 Indian place names. Tell their origin and meaning.

(i) Name five well-known Indian chiefs. Give their tribes. Describe their relationship to history.

Insect Life

1. Tell how insects are different from all other animals. Show the differences between insects, spiders, and centipedes.
2. Point out and name the main parts of an insect.
3. Collect and mount 50 different species. Include six orders and 18 families of insects. Label each with common and scientific names where possible.
4. Point out the things that distinguish each of the families and orders in your collection.
5. Show your collection.
6. Compare the life histories of a butterfly and a grasshopper. Tell how they are different.
7. Raise a butterfly or moth from a caterpillar.
8. Tell things that make social insects different from solitary insects.
9. Collect and watch an ant colony or a beehive. Tell what you saw.
10. From your collection, identify:
(a) Four species of insects helpful to man. Tell how they are helpful.
(b) Six species of insects harmful to man. Tell how they can be controlled.
11. Tell how insects fit in the food chains of other insects, fish, birds, and mammals.

Journalism

1. Write stories good enough for publication of any THREE of the following. Show that you know the principles of good news or magazine writing.
(a) A news story
(b) A Scout story
(c) A sports story
(d) An editorial
(e) A feature
(f) A review of a play, movie, or television show.
2. Do FIVE of the following:
(a) Prepare a script for a 5-minute radio or television newscast.
(b) Write good heads for the three stories covered in No. 1. Follow a standard head schedule but use different type style and size. Show face, type size, and count for each.
(c) Take and show a picture to illustrate any one of the stories covered in No. 1. Write a caption for the picture.

(d) Show at least 15 of the proofreader's or copyreader's marks. Correct a proof or copyread a manuscript. Use as many of these marks as needed.
(e) Explain the following terms: font, pica, face, machine-set type, handset, galley proof, half-tone, electrotype, mat, copy, flush left, beat, copy desk, streamer, plagiarism, libel, and copyright.
(f) Prepare a dummy of a four-page newspaper or magazine. Include several different-size advertisements.
(g) Visit a newspaper or magazine office. After the visit, explain how a newspaper or magazine is prepared for publication. Explain the different departments and executives and what they do. Explain the importance of the deadline.
(h) Describe how a wire service works. Tell how a syndicate is different from a wire service.
(i) Look into and tell about jobs in journalism.

Landscape Architecture

1. Describe the work of the following: Landscape architect, landscape contractor, nurseryman, and gardener.

2. Make a drawing, (1/8 inch equals 1 foot) of your home grounds. Show all buildings such as the house, garage, and barn. (NOTE: If this is not possible, make a drawing of friend's yard.)

(a) Make a plan for these grounds. Change walks, drives, walls, fences, and plantings as you wish.

(b) Show flow lines for drainage of surface water.

3. On a tracing of the drawing, prepare a planting plan. Have at least two kinds each of deciduous and evergreen trees and shrubs.

4. Name 10 shrubs, 10 trees, 5 ground covers, 5 perennials, and 5 annuals good for planting in your town. Describe their growth habits and soil and climate needs.

(a) Tell the difference between evergreen and deciduous plants.

(b) Describe the difference between broadleaf and coniferous evergreen plants. Name one of each.

(c) Tell the difference between perennials and annuals.

5. Show how to read topographic maps. Explain the importance of a good drainage plan.

6. Visit a well-landscaped yard, park, or building. Describe how the landscape architect has helped it.

Leatherwork

1. Collect samples of five different kinds of leather. Tell the chief characteristics and best uses of each.
2. Make an article of leather which uses:
(a) Transfer of a pattern.
(b) Cutting leather.
(c) Decoration by one or more of the following: tooling, embossing, stamping, carving, or burning.
(d) Punching holes.
(e) Lacing.
3. Show that you take proper care of your shoes and other leather things.
4. Do TWO of the following:
(a) Learn how to tan, cure, and finish leather.
(b) Tan or cure the skin of a small animal.
(c) Show proper care of leather goods. Make small repairs on something made of leather.
(d) Sole and heel a pair of shoes or boots. Keep a record of costs and time spent.
(e) Plait or braid an article of leather or leather substitute. Make a terminal Turk's head.
(f) Find out what jobs there are in leather industries. Choose one job in which you are interested. Report on the qualifications you must have for the job. Tell what the working conditions are.

Lifesaving

1. Before doing the following requirements:
(a) Earn Swimming merit badge.
(b) Swim 440 yards.
2. Spend 6 hours practicing lifesaving skills.
3. Explain:
(a) The Safe Swim Defense.
(b) The order of methods to be followed in lifesaving.
4. Show reaching rescues using such things as arms, legs, branches, sticks, towels, shirts, paddles, and poles.
5. Show rescues using things that can be thrown such as lines, ring buoys, and free-floating supports such as boat cushions.
6. Show the use of floating devices such as boats, canoes, and boards in making rescues.

7. With a helper and a subject, show a line rescue both as line tender and as rescuer. Use a 50-foot length of line. If you have one, use of a torpedo buoy on a surf line should also be shown.

8. Show twice that you can take off street clothes,* except underwear or swim trunks, in 20 seconds or less. Explain the importance of taking off clothes before trying a swimming rescue.

9. Make a leaping or running entry into the water. Show the correct approach to a drowning person who is in the following positions: Back to you, face to you with head above and also below water.

10. Keeping a struggling person in sight, enter the water feetfirst by jumping or running.

(a) Swim 30 feet. Make the correct approach. Tow the subject 30 feet to shore with a cross-chest tow.

(b) Swim 30 feet. Make the correct approach. Tow the subject 30 feet to shore with a wrist tow.

In each case put the subject on a deck or shore. Use the proper lift to carry him from the water.

11. Show in deep water your defense against grasps by blocking, turning, and placing the subject in position for towing to shore.

12. Swim 30 feet, make the correct approach to a tired swimmer. Move him 30 feet to safety using:

(a) Foot push.

(b) Underarm swim-along.

(c) Tired swimmer's push (subject on back).

13. Make four surface dives in 6 to 8 feet of water. Bring up different things three times.

Bring up a 10-pound weight once.

14. Show search techniques:

(a) As a part of a "lost bather's drill" team.

(b) As a lone diver using a mask, fins, and a snorkel (not scuba).

15. Take off clothes in the water. Show how street clothes* can be blown up to help hold you up. Use your shirt and pants. Then swim 100 yards.

16. Explain artificial respiration. Show you know how to give rescue breathing (mouth-to-mouth or mouth-to-nose) and manually (chest-pressure arm-lift or back-pressure arm-lift).

---

*Street clothes means low shoes, socks, underwear (or trunks), pants, belt, long-sleeved shirt, and jacket or sweater or sweat shirt.

Machinery

1. Explain the proper way to use the following hand tools: screwdriver, ball peen hammer, file, calipers, hacksaw, rule, combination square. Tell how to use these kinds of wrenches: open end, adjustable, monkey, pipe, box, and socket. Show the use of any eight of the above tools.

2. Put together or build wooden or metal models of these: lever, inclined plane, screw, wedge, wheel and axle, block and tackle, and gears.

3. Make a drawing showing how each of the following works: diesel engine, steam turbine, four-cycle gasoline engine. Explain how the power in a shop or factory is transmitted to the machines.

4. Make a drawing showing how a drill press and metal-working lathe are made. Explain three operations that can be performed on each.

5. Make a metal object from a plan or blueprint. Use a machine lathe and a drill press.

6. Visit a machine shop, trade school, or factory. Note the benchwork, power equipment, machine tools, and safety devices to protect workers. Describe your visit. If no such shop is available, make a chart or outline showing five mechanical occupations. List the work and training needed for each.

Mammals

1. Explain the meaning of "animal," "invertebrate," "vertebrate," and "mammal." Name three characteristics that distinguish mammals from all other animals.

2. Explain how the animal kingdom is classified. Explain where mammals fit in the classification of animals. Classify three mammals from phylum through species.

3. Do ONE of the following:
(a) Spend 3 hours in each of two different kinds of natural habitats or at different elevations. List the different mammal species and individual members that you identified by sight or sign. Tell why all mammals do not live in the same kind of habitat.
(b) Spend 3 hours on each of 5 days on at least a 25-acre area. List the mammal species you identified by sight or sign.

(c) From study and reading, write a simple life history of one nongame mammal that lives in your area. Tell how this mammal lived before its habitat was affected in any way by man. Tell how it reproduces, what it eats, what eats it, and its natural habitat. Describe its dependency upon plants, upon other animals (including man), and how they depend upon it. Tell how it is helpful or harmful to man.

4. Do ONE:

(a) Make study skins of two small, unprotected mammals, such as mice. Tell the uses of study skins and mounted specimens, respectively.

(b) Take good pictures of two kinds of mammals in the wild. Record light conditions, film used, exposure, and other factors, including notes on the activities of the pictured animals.

(c) Write a life history of a native game mammal that lives in your area, covering the points outlined in No. 3c. List sources for this information.

(d) Make and bait a tracking pit. Report what mammals and other animals came to the bait.

(e) Visit a natural history museum. Report on how specimens are prepared and cataloged. Explain the purposes of museums.

(f) Write a report of 500 words on a book (approved by your counselor) about a mammal species.

(g) Trace two possible food chains of carnivorous mammals from soil through four stages to the mammal.

5. Working with your counselor, select and carry out one project that will influence the numbers of one or more mammals.

Masonry

1. Do the following:

(a) Prepare or read correctly plans for a useful masonry structure such as a wall or outdoor fireplace.

(b) Lay it out on the ground. Dig as needed for a foundation. Pour a foundation of solid concrete mixed by yourself.

(c) Prepare mortar correctly.

(d) Build the structure. Use mason's tools correctly.

2. Point out examples of course ashlar, random ashlar, and rubble construction.

3. Do THREE of the following:

(a) Lay a steppingstone or flagstone walk.

(b) Plan and mold in a form something ornamental in concrete.

(c) Make major repairs in a masonry structure.

(d) Build a useful, dry masonry structure, such as an outdoor fireplace.

(e) Plaster or stucco a wall or ceiling.

(f) Visit a rock quarry or a factory where masonry material is made. Report on what happened from beginning to end.

(g) Find out what jobs there are in masonry. Choose one in which you are interested. Report on the qualifications you must have for the job. Tell what the working conditions are.

Metals Engineering

1. Do the following:

(a) Name three metals found by early man. Tell how they were probably discovered. Tell how they were used.

(b) Collect three rocks that contain a different recoverable metal in each. Show them. Tell how the metal in each might be recovered.

(c) Explain what a metal is. List from around your home examples of five different kinds of metals or their alloys.

2. Name four different fields of metallurgy. Describe what two of the fields include.

3. Pick three different industries which require metals and alloys having highly specialized properties. Tell how the properties of that metal made the industry possible.

4. Do ONE of the following:

(a) Show three of the following mechanical properties of metals: strength, elasticity, ductility, hardness, malleability. Use a different material for each demonstration.

(b) Show strengthening of metals by cold working and by heat treatment.

5. Do any TWO of the following:

(a) Collect a sample of alloys from each of the following groups; tell what metals are part of each: carbon steel, stainless steel, cast iron, brass, sol-

der, aluminum alloys, bronze, pewter. Describe the main properties of the alloys. Tell what property is most desirable for each.

(b) Compare the properties of common household materials such as plastics, porcelain, wood, and glass with the properties of metallic alloys like steel and brass.

(c) Explain what is meant by corrosion and protective coatings. Put in a glass of strong salt water four pieces of steel, three of which have been protected from corrosion by: (1) galvanizing or coating with zinc, (2) painting, (3) tin plating. Put a scratch that cuts through the coating on each. After a few days write a brief report on what took place and why.

(d) Pick a metal article commonly used around the home. Find out what metal or alloy is used in making it. Tell the main steps in making it.

Metalwork

1. Use tin cans to make two useful things that need cutting, bending, and edging.

2. Use metal 20 gauge or thicker. Make two or more useful things from the metal. Etch a design. Hollow or otherwise shape a part. Join two pieces of metal with solder or rivets. Stamp a pattern with stamps you have made yourself.

436

Model Design and Building

1. Create your own design for one of the following passenger-carrying vehicles:
(a) Land
(b) Air or space
(c) Water
   Use a scale of 1 inch equals 1 foot. Show from side, top, rear, and front.
2. Build and paint a model from your plan. (No kits.)
3. Show that your finished project is:
(a) Creative.
(b) Original and practical in its ideas.
(c) Craftsmanlike in the building.

Motorboating

1. Before doing other requirements, swim 100 yards as follows: 75 yards with any strokes. Then 25 yards on your back using an easy resting stroke. Then rest by floating as still as you can for 1 minute.
2. Show you know safety laws for motorboating:

(a) Have a permit to run a motorboat, if needed.
(b) Explain laws affecting pleasure boating in your area.
(c) Show that before going in a boat you know about any features or hazards of the body of water to be cruised.
(d) Promise that you will live up to the Scout Boating Code. Explain the meaning of each point.
(e) Explain and show, as many as possible, the rules of the road. Describe aids to navigation used where you cruise.
(f) Examine the condition of the following safety gear: Lifesaving device for each person on board. Fire extinguisher. Lights. Oars or paddles. Tool kit. Extra shear pins and spark plugs. Horn, whistle, or other sound signals. Compass. Anchor and line. Safety chain (for outboard motor). First aid kit. Bilge pump or similar device that can be used for bailing.
(g) Explain and show correct use of this gear.
3. Show you know how to run a motorboat by doing the following the right way:
(a) Get in a boat.
(b) Fuel and check motor before starting.
(c) Start motor and get under way from a dock or beach.
(d) Run a straight course for a quarter mile. Make right angle turns to left or right. Make a U turn.
(e) Stop boat. Drop anchor. Raise it. Get under way.
(f) Come alongside a dock. Tie up or beach.
4. Show how to:
(a) Tie up or take boat from water.
(b) Store gear.
(c) Prepare motor for the winter.

437

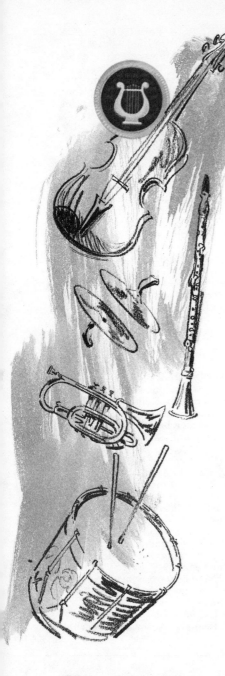

Music

1. Sing or play a simple song or hymn picked by your counselor. Read all the signs and terms of the score. Use good technique, phrasing, tone, dynamics, and rhythm.

2. Name the four general groups of musical instruments. Tell how you get tones from one of each group.

3. Do TWO of the following:

(a) Go to a classical or semi-classical musical performance; or listen to 3 hours of such programs on radio, television, or records. Report what you heard. Tell who wrote them. Tell who the artists were. Name the conductors. Know the story of any program music or opera you heard. Talk over how you feel about the music.

(b) Outline the development of music in the United States. Show that you know the lives and works of five of this country's better known composers and musical artists.

(c) Serve for 6 months as a member of a school, church, Scout unit, or other town musical organization; or take part as a soloist in public six times.

4. Do ONE of the following:

(a) Teach three songs to a group of people. Lead them in singing the songs. Use proper hand motions.

(b) Compose and write the score for a piece of music of 12 measures or more.

(c) Make a primitive musical instrument. Learn to play on it.

(d) Catalog your own or your family collection of 12 or more records. Show how to handle and store records.

Nature

1. Name three ways in which plants are important to animals.
2. Name three ways in which animals are important to plants.
3. Explain the term "food chain." Give an example of a four-step land food chain and a four-step water food chain.
4. Do all of the requirements in FIVE of the following fields:

Birds
(a) In the field, identify eight species of birds.
(b) Make and set out a birdhouse; OR a feeding station; OR a birdbath. List what birds used it during a period of 1 month.

Mammals
(a) In the field, identify three species of wild mammals.
(b) Make plaster casts of the tracks of a wild mammal.

Reptiles or Amphibians
(a) Show that you can recognize the poisonous snakes in your area. Identify in the field three species of reptiles or amphibians.
(b) Recognize one specie of toad or frog by voice; OR identify one reptile or amphibian by eggs, den, burrow, or other signs.

Insects or Spiders
(a) Collect, mount, and label 10 species of insects or spiders.
(b) Hatch an insect from the pupa or cocoon; OR hatch adults from nymphs; OR keep larvae until they form pupae or cocoons; OR keep a colony of ants or bees through one season.

Fish
(a) Catch and identify two species of fish.
(b) Collect four kinds of animal food eaten by fish in the wild.

Mollusks and Crustaceans
(a) Identify five species of mollusks and crustaceans.
(b) Collect, mount, and label six shells.

Plants
(a) In the field, identify 15 species of wild plants.
(b) Collect and label seeds of six plants; OR the leaves of 12 plants.

Soils and Rocks
(a) Collect and identify soils found in different layers of a soil profile.
(b) Collect and identify five different types of rocks from your area.

5. Do ONE:
(a) Raise tadpoles from eggs; OR raise adults from tadpoles;

OR keep an adult reptile or amphibian so it stays healthy for 1 month.

(b) Develop a simple aquarium with fish and plant life. Keep it so they stay healthy for 1 month.

(c) Develop an aquarium. Keep in it two species of mollusks or crustaceans so they stay healthy for 1 month.

(d) Build a terrarium with three species of plants. Keep it so the plants stay healthy for 1 month.

(e) Grow seeds for 1 month in two kinds of soil. Describe difference in rate of growth.

Oceanography

1. Name five branches of ocean-ography. Describe at least five ways that man is becoming more dependent upon knowing about the oceans.

2. Describe the effects of the oceans. Include the effect of currents on the weather and climate. Point out how air and ocean currents are alike and different.

3. Tell how ocean waves are described. Point out the differences between the storm surge, tsunami, tidal wave, and tidal bore. Tell the difference between sea, swell, and surf. Explain how breakers are formed.

4. Draw a cross section of underwater topography. Show what is meant by:

(a) Continental shelf.
(b) Continental slope.
(c) Abyssal plains.
  Name and put on your drawing the following: seamount, guyot, deep, rift valley, canyon, and trench. Compare the depths in the oceans with the heights of mountains.

5. List the main salts, gases, and foods in sea water. Describe the importance of these to life in the sea. What is meant by Dittmar's principal? Why is it important?

6. Tell the meaning of phyto-plankton, zooplankton, nekton, and benthos.
  Describe the importance of phytoplankton as a main producer of living things. Tell the place and importance of plankton in the food chain.

7. Do ONE of the following:
(a)* Make a plankton net. Tow the net by a dock, wade with it, hold it in a current, or tow it from a rowboat. Do this for about 20 minutes. Save the sample. Examine it under a microscope or high-power glass.

———————————

*May be done in lakes or streams.

Identify the three most common types of plankton in the sample.

(b) Make a series of models (clay or plaster and wood) of a volcanic island. Show the growth of an atoll from a fringing reef through a barrier reef. Describe the Darwinian theory of coral reef formation.

(c)* Measure the water temperature 1 foot below the surface of a body of water four times daily (8 a.m., 12 m., 4 and 8 p.m.) for 6 straight days. Measure the air temperature. Note the cloud cover and roughness of the water. Show your findings on a graph. Tell how the water temperature changes with air temperature.

(d) Make a model showing the inshore sediment movement by littoral currents, tidal movement, and wave action. Include such things as high and low waterlines, low tide terrace, cusps, beach scarp, and berm. Show how the offshore bars are built up and torn down.

(e) Make a wave generator. Show reflection and refraction of waves. Show how groins, jetties, and breakwaters affect these patterns.

8. Do ONE of the following:

(a) Write a 500-word report on any good book about oceanography. (Before reading have your counselor approve it.)

(b) Visit one of the following. Write a 500-word report about your visit. (1) an oceanographic research ship or (2) an oceanographic institute.

(c) Explain to your troop in a 5-minute prepared speech "Why Oceanography Is Important" or "Jobs in Oceanography." (Before making it, show your speech outline to your counselor.)

---

*May be done in lakes or streams.

442

Painting

1. Do the following:
(a) Explain three ways paint can improve a surface.
(b) Explain the chief uses of oil, water, and rubber-base paints. Tell the use of enamel, shellac, varnish, and lacquer. Tell why each is best for these uses.
2. Prepare and paint any two of the following items or similar ones approved by your counselor. Use proper fillers, priming coats, covering coats, and finishing coats as needed:
An outside surface
An inside surface
A piece of furniture
A concrete wall
A boat or canoe
A floor
A porch rail or fence
A lawn mower
3. Prepare an old painted surface, that has holes in it and uneven surfaces, to receive and hold a new coat of paint.
4. Add colors to a white paint base to make paints of two predetermined colors that harmonize. With these, paint one of the following in two colors: model plane, birdhouse, dollhouse, picture frame, or similar useful item.
5. Show the right way to use, clean, and store painting equipment.

Personal Fitness

If meeting Nos. 1 and 5 are against the Scout's religious convictions, they will not have to be done if the boy's parents and proper church officials state in writing that:
(a) To do so would be against religious convictions.
(b) The parents accept full responsibility for anything that might happen because of such exemption. They release the Boy Scouts of America from any responsibility.
1. Before you try to meet any other tests, have your physician give you a thorough health examination. He is to use the Scout medical examination form. Describe the examination. Tell what questions you asked about your health. Tell what recommendations your doctor made. Report what you have done about them.

2. Explain what physical and mental health means to you, including:

(a) Reasons for being fit.

(b) Normal differences in rate of growth and development.

(c) What it means to be mentally healthy. Discuss three healthy personality traits.

3. Show you know health facts by answering questions asked on the following:

(a) Basic foods needed in the daily diet of a person of your age.

(b) Cleanliness of the hands, food, and dishes and the control of illness.

(c) Bad effects of tobacco and alcohol, and the use and abuse of drugs.

(d) The illnesses against which you may be immunized or otherwise protected.

4. Present a list of your health habits including:

(a) Number of hours of sleep.

(b) Care of your skin, hands, fingernails, toenails.

(c) Care of your eyes.

(d) Care of your ears.

5. Have an examination made by your dentist. Get a statement saying that your teeth have been checked and cared for. Tell how you care for your teeth.

6. Carry out daily for 4 weeks six exercises for all-round physical development. Use those that strengthen your arms, shoulders, chest, abdomen, back, legs, and one for endurance. Pick three activities from No. 7. Test yourself at the beginning and weekly during the 4 weeks. Show the record of your test. This is to be completed before starting No. 7.

7. Fitness Tests: Earn a minimum of 200 points. These 200 points must come from not more than 5 events. Only one alternate, A or B, is allowed in each event.

EVENT 1 *Swimming* (50 point maximum)

A. 20-yard speed swim—5 points for each second faster than 25 seconds

B. Distance swim—50 points for swimming 1 mile, 25 points for swimming ½ mile

EVENT 2 *Arm Strength* (50 point maximum)

A. Pull-ups—10 points for each pull-up

B. Push-ups—2 points for each push-up

EVENT 3 *Abdominal Power* (50 point maximum)

A. Bent-knee sit-ups—1 point for each sit-up

EVENT 4 *Speed Running* (50 point maximum)

A. 50-yard dash—2 points for each 1/10 of a second faster than 9 seconds.

B. 40-yard shuttle run—2 points for each 1/10 of a second faster than 12 seconds

EVENT 5 *Endurance Running or Walking* (50 point maximum)

A. 600-yard run-walk—1 point for each second faster than 2 minutes 50 seconds

B. Mile walk—10 points for each minute faster than 18 minutes

EVENT 6 *Jumping* (50 point maximum)

A. Standing long jump—5 points for each inch over 5 feet

B. Vertical jump and reach—5 points for each inch over 9 inches

EVENT 7 *Body Coordination* (50 point maximum)

A. Basketball throw—2 points for each foot over 50 feet

B. Softball throw—1 point for each foot over 100 feet

8. Show that you are reasonably good in one team or one individual sport.

Personal Management

1. Talk over with parents or guardian how family funds are spent to meet day-to-day and long-term needs. Tell how you can help with the family budget.

2. Make a budget for yourself for 90 days. Keep a record of income and expenses for that period. Review it and report.

3. Help to pick and buy family groceries for 1 month. Make a report of what you learned.

4. Explain the possible use, advantages, and risks in using $100 in each of the following ways. Tell how it might help you and others.

(a) Hide it in a mattress.

(b) Put it into a savings account at a bank or savings and loan association. (Explain the difference.)

(c) Buy a bicycle.

(d) Open a checking account.

(e) Buy a U.S. Savings Bond.

(f) Buy a power mower or paint sprayer.

(g) Invest in a mutual fund.

(h) Start a life insurance policy.

(i) Buy fishing gear.

(j) Buy common stock.

5. Talk about things you would like to do within the next 90 days. Tell how you plan to get these done. After 90 days, tell what you did. Tell how you did them.

6. Tell how important credit and installment buying are to our economy and the individual and the family. Visit an officer of a bank or credit department of a store. Find out and tell what you must do to establish a good "credit rating." Tell what it means to you now and in the future.

7. Check out jobs or career opportunities through interviews or reading. Tell what the "next step" would be to prepare yourself for one of these careers.

Pets

*1. Present evidence that you have cared for a pet for 4 months. Get approval before you start.

2. Write in 200 words or more about the care, feeding, and housing of your pet. Tell some interesting facts about it. Tell why you have this kind of pet. Give local laws, if any, relating to the pet you keep.

3. Show that you have read a book or pamphlet, approved by your counselor, about your kind of pet.

4. Do any ONE of the following:
(a) Show your pet in some pet show.
(b) Start a friend raising a pet like yours. Advise him. Help him get a good start.
(c) Breed your pet. Show the offspring.
(d) Train a pet in three or more tricks or special abilities.

---

*Work done for other merit badges cannot be used for this requirement.

Photography

1. Tell what makes a good picture. Show your understanding of these as you take pictures for No. 2.

2. Do EITHER a or b.
(a) Take 10 good black-and-white or color pictures. Do the following:
(1) Take from three to five of these pictures indoors with flash.
(2) Take at least 5 of the 10 pictures so they tell a story.
(3) Show your pictures to your counselor in an organized way.
(b) Make planning cards and take 50 feet of movie film. Do the following:
(1) Edit your film so you have at least 25 feet of quality movies that tell a story.
(2) Show your edited film to your counselor.

3. Make a pinhole camera. Explain how it works. Obtain one finished print taken with your pinhole camera. Compare it with a print of the same scene which you took with a regular camera. Explain the differences.

4. Explain how photographic film is processed. Tell how black-and-white prints are made.

5. Explain common photographic terms such as lens, shutter, viewfinder, camera angle, exposure, negative, transparency, f-number, and planning card.

6. Describe jobs in photography.

Pigeon Raising

4-H FFA

1. Do the following:
(a) House and care for two pair of pigeons for 3 months.
(b) Keep a record of cost of birds, feed, equipment, and other things. Record income received from sale of squabs or birds for this same time.
(c) Keep records of eggs laid, squabs hatched, sickness, and deaths for this same time.
2. Take a picture or make a drawing of your loft and flypen.
3. List the four main requirements for successful pigeon raising.
4. If you live in city or town, give its laws about keeping pigeons.
5. Describe two breeds of utility pigeons used for squabbing. Describe two fancy breeds used for exhibiting. Describe two breeds used for flying (racing or high flying).
6. Do ONE of the following:
(a) Pick, dress, and cook one squab you raised. Visit a squab farm. Write a 300-word report on it.
(b) Enter one pigeon you own in a pigeon show. Visit a show. Write a 300-word report on it.
(c) Enter one pigeon you own in a pigeon race. Visit a racing loft or racing club meeting. Write a 300-word report on it.

Pioneering

1. Hand coil a length of rope.
2. Describe the following:
(a) Kinds of rope.
(b) Care of rope.
(c) Weakening effect of knots.
3. Tie 10 knots and hitches. Explain how to use them in pioneering.
4. Make a short, end, and eye splice.
5. Build a machine to make rope. Using twine or cord, make a 6-foot rope ½ inch or more in diameter. Whip the ends.
6. Make and show one device for moving heavy logs or rocks. Use rope and natural materials. OR use rope to build a conveyor cable system for hauling materials over a ravine or up a steep hillside.
7. Build ONE of the following: log bridge, signal tower, monkey bridge, shelter, or raft.* Take down after use and inspection. Follow an approved design. Use square, diagonal, and shear lashings.

---

*This may be done in a camp pioneering area using camp poles. Live trees should never be cut without permission of the property owners. Help from another Scout may be used.

Pottery

1. Explain the properties and ingredients of a good clay body for pottery.

2. Make two drawings of pottery forms. These are to be on paper at least 8½ x 11 inches. One must be a recognized pottery type. The other must be of your own design.

3. Explain the meaning of the following pottery terms: bat, wedging, throwing, leather dry, bone dry, green ware, bisque, terra cotta, grog, slip, earthenware, stoneware, porcelain, pyrometric cone, glaze.

4. Do THREE of the following. Each is to be painted, glazed, or otherwise decorated by you:

(a) Make a flat tray or dish.

(b) Make a box, using the slab method.

(c) Make a vase or jar, using the coil method.

(d) Make four different tiles of your own design.

(e) Make a human or animal figurine or decorative design.

(f) Throw a simple vase on a potter's wheel.

(g) Make a pottery form. Help to fire it.

5. Make a rough drawing of a potter's wheel. Tell how it works.

6. Do ONE of the following:

(a) Explain the scope of the ceramic industry in the United States. Tell some of the things made, other than craft pottery.

(b) Visit a pottery, brickyard, ceramic plant, trade school, or workshop. Take notes on how pottery is made. Describe your visit.

Plumbing

1. Do the following:

(a) Make a drawing and explain the way the hot- and cold-water supply system in your home or that of a neighbor works. Tell how you would make it safe from freezing.

(b) Make a drawing and explain the drainage system of the plumbing in a house. Show and explain the use of drains and vents.

2. Show how to use five important plumber's tools.

3. Identify and describe the use of each of the following: washer, cap nut, float, force cup, half-and-half solder, flux, elbow, tee, nipple, coupling, plug, union, trap, drainpipe, water meter.

4. Tell what kinds of pipe are most often used in a plumbing system. Tell why.

5. Cut, thread, and connect two pieces of galvanized pipe.

6. Using a gas torch under supervision, solder three copper tube connections. Include one tee, two straight pieces, and one coupling.

7. Do the following:

(a) Replace a washer in a faucet.

(b) Clean out a sink or lavatory trap.

8. Make a list of five important local health regulations related to plumbing.

Poultry Keeping

4-H FFA

Do ONE of the following groups:
Raising Pullets
1. Raise 20 or more chicks (straight run or pullet) for 5 months.
2. Keep records on all management practices. Include amount of feed, deaths, medicine, and vaccinations.
3. Tell how to spot three common poultry diseases. Tell how you keep your pullets from getting these.
4. Make one piece of poultry keeping equipment. Use it.
5. Describe the brooding house in which you raised your chicks. Explain how you gave them proper sanitation and ventilation.

Flock Management
1. Take care of a flock (your own or a neighbor's) of 10 or more birds for 6 months. They should be at least 5 months old at the start.
2. Keep daily egg production records. Keep records on amount of feed and deaths.
3. Tell how to spot three common poultry diseases. Tell how you keep your birds from getting these. Explain culling.
4. Make one piece of poultry keeping equipment. Use it.
5. Candle, grade, and pack 2 dozen eggs for market.

Poultry Meat Production
1. Raise 20 or more birds to market age.
2. Keep records of amount of feed, deaths, and weight gains.
3. Write a report on the management of your birds.
4. Make one piece of poultry keeping equipment. Use it.
5. Kill and dress two birds for market.

Printing

Do EITHER No. 1, 2, or 3.
1. Using *letterpress:*
(a) Set a paragraph by hand.
(b) Read and mark proof correctly.
(c) Set type from copy for display card or handbill.
(d) Run 100 copies of the same job on a 10 x 15 or smaller job press. Show the correct way to ink, set gauge pins, use makeready, feed accurately, and wash up press.
2. Using *silk-screen:*
(a) Make a stencil screen and base.
(b) Print at least 50 copies of a poster, greeting card, or other material.
3. Using *offset:*
   Make a finished piece of publicity. The size is to be set by the equipment used. It can be a newspaper, poster, etc.

Public Health

1. Explain the difference between infectious and chronic disease.

2. Explain how people catch the following diseases. Describe how they are spread: typhoid fever, poliomyelitis, hookworm, Rocky Mountain spotted fever, tetanus, rabies, tuberculosis, yellow fever.

3. Do the following:

(a) Explain the meaning of "immunization."

(b) Name three diseases against which a baby should be immunized.

(c) Name two diseases against which you should be immunized.

4. Name two diseases that can be caught from drinking unpasteurized milk.

5. Do the following:

(a) Describe the health aspects of preparing and handling food.

(b) Explain how dishes and utensils should be washed.

6. Show two ways to make water safe to drink.

7. Do the following:

(a) Explain how flies may be controlled. Tell how their breeding places can be destroyed.

(b) Get rid of garbage and rubbish from a camp or home. Tell how this helps control flies.

(c) Prepare a drawing of a home sewage system. Tell how it should be located and built to keep from polluting wells and springs.

8. Do the following:

(a) Describe the health dangers from air and water pollution.

(b) Describe health dangers from cigarette smoking.

9. Explain the reason for the camp arrival medical screening.

10. Visit your city, county, or state health department. Prepare an outline of its various services.

Public Speaking

1. Do the following:

(a) Prepare a written speech of 750 words. (1) Give the main idea or topic of the speech in one complete sentence. (2) Tell the kind of audience for whom it was prepared. (3) Describe your purpose. Tell what main idea you want the audience to remember about your speech.

(b) Show the following: (1) The ideas list you used in preparing your outline. (2) The outline. (3) The final text.
(c) Give this speech before an audience.
2. Give a 10-minute speech (on a subject other than used in No. 1). Use a visual or audio aid.
3. Give an impromptu talk of at least 2 minutes, either as part of a group discussion or before your counselor. Use a subject interesting to you but for which you do not have time to prepare.
4. Read aloud a selection of 500 words you have never seen.
5. Show you know parliamentary procedure by leading a discussion or meeting according to accepted rules of order; or answer questions on the rules of order.

Pulp and Paper

1. Tell the history of papermaking. Describe the part paper products play in our culture and economy.

2. List the trees which are the major source of papermaking fibers.
(a) Tell what other uses are made of the trees and of the forest land owned by the pulp and paper industry.
(b) Describe ways the industry plants, grows, and harvests trees.
3. Describe two ways of getting fibers from wood.
(a) What are the major differences?
(b) Why are some pulps bleached? Describe this process.

4. Describe how paper is made. Make a sheet of paper by hand using the process described.

5. What is coated paper, and why is it coated? Describe the major uses for different kinds of coated paper. In what other ways are papers changed by chemical or mechanical means to make new uses possible?

6. Make a list of 15 pulp or paper products in your home. Show samples of 10 such products.

7. Do ONE:
(a) Visit a pulp mill. Describe how wood is converted into cellulose fibers.
(b) Visit a paper mill and get a sample of the paper. Describe the process used for making this paper. Tell how it will be used.
(c) Visit a container plant or box plant. Describe how the product was made.
(d) Visit a printer or newspaper plant to learn how paper is used. Describe the visit. Explain why particular types of paper were used.
8. Describe six of the major jobs in the pulp and paper industry.

451

Rabbit Raising

4-H FFA

1. House a litter of rabbits, from mating until marketing time for the litter.
2. Explain the use of your breed. Tell about one used for meat, one for fur, and one for wool.
3. Keep a breeding record, a feeding schedule, and a financial record.

Radio

1. Learn the safety precautions for working with radio gear.
2. Do the following:
(a) Show correct way to solder radio wiring.
(b) Show how to stop heat damage during soldering.
(c) Explain why rosin-core solder is used.
3. Do the following:
(a) Draw 10 schematic symbols often used in radio diagrams.
(b) Explain what each of the parts represented by the symbols does.
4. Build from parts or from a kit at least one piece of radio gear using a vacuum tube, transistor, or diode. (Include selenium, germanium, or silicon rectifiers.) Show that the wiring is safe, correctly soldered, and neat. (Crystal radios, buzzer-type code sets, and continuity testers are not acceptable.)
5. Show you can send and receive the Morse code by ear for at least 1 minute at a rate of at least five words (25 letters) per minute without any mistakes. (Holders of unexpired amateur licenses of any class are exempt.)
6. Do the following:
(a) Name and explain five "Q" signals. Give five abbreviations used by radio operators.

(b) Explain how amateur radio operators prepare to handle emergency messages during disasters.

7. Check out jobs in radio. Talk about these with your counselor. Tell what job might interest you. Tell what training you need to prepare for it.

Railroading

1. Do TWO of the following:

(a) Know the name, scale, and track gauge for four model railroad gauges. Show the right way to clean and oil model train equipment.

(b) Draw to scale, the layout of your own model railroad; or one that could be built in your home. Have a point-to-point or loop road with different routings. Include a turnaround, a terminal, a yard, and a siding.

(c) Alone or with others, build a model railroad layout. Lay track with ties, ballast, and scenery. Make connections from power supply to track and accessories.

(d) Make a scale model of a locomotive (with or without power), or make two cars. (Kits may be used.)

(e) Draw scale plans and build two accessories.

2. Do the following:

(a) Explain how real electric and diesel locomotives develop power.

(b) Identify by model or picture six different kinds of railroad cars used to carry people or products.

(c) Show arm or lantern signals used by trainmen. Pick one kind of semaphore or light signal system. Tell what its different signals mean. Explain the meaning of five whistle signals. Describe an emergency way to signal a train to stop.

3. Do ONE of the following:

(a) Name four departments of a railroad company. Describe what each does.

(b) Name and explain 10 jobs in railroading. Tell which job interests you most. Tell why.

4. Explain six rules of safety to use aboard trains; on platforms; at crossings; and around bridges, yards, and tunnels.

5. Do the following:

(a) Make a written plan for a trip by rail to a city 500 miles from your home. Get train information from the Amtrak agent at the railroad terminal or the Amtrak ticket office. List time you leave and arrive, the number of the train, and the kind of service you want.

(b) Name the railroads that serve your town. Explain how to arrange for the shipment of a carload of freight to a city 500 miles from your home.

6. Do ONE of the following:

(a) Plan and take a rail trip of at least 25 miles. Buy your own ticket. Read the timetables and footnotes correctly.

(b) Identify 10 different railroads by the symbols on freight cars.

7. Outline the major steps in the growth of railroads in the United States. Discuss the importance of the railroads to daily life.

Reading

1. Read 12 books during the year. Not more than 3 of these can be from school assignments. The 12 books shall be from at least three of the following classifications: fiction, adventure, Scouting, biography, poetry, the arts, or books on hobbies. Present a list of books read and who wrote them.

2. Tell where in your town or county you may borrow, rent, or buy books. Show a library card or tell how you got the books read in No. 1.

3. Tell how you became interested in your favorite hobby. Tell how reading helped to make your hobby worthwhile. Make a list of books, pamphlets, and magazines for someone just starting this hobby.

4. List the books you own.

5. Report on newspapers or news magazines you read.

6. Subscribe to or read regularly a magazine for the preceding 6 months. Report other magazines read.

7. Find and deliver books and magazines to some shut-in or sick person or help someone find books on his hobby or give service to your school or public library or do some similar service.

NOTE: Books and magazines must be approved by counselor.

Reptile Study

1. Know approximately the number of species and general distribution of reptiles and amphibians in the United States.

2. Make sketches from your own observations, showing markings and color patterns of seven reptiles and three amphibians found in the United States. Record the habits and habitats of each of these species.

3. Describe the main differences between (a) alligators and crocodiles, (b) toads and frogs, (c) salamanders and lizards, and (d) snakes and lizards.

4. List 10 reptiles or amphibians useful to man. Tell how they take in food. List food habits of each species. If there are laws in your state for their protection, tell why each is protected.

5. Describe how reptiles and amphibians reproduce themselves.

6. From observation, describe how snakes move forward. Describe the functions of the muscles, ribs, and belly plates.

7. Describe in detail six poisonous snakes and the one poisonous lizard found in the United States. Describe their habits. Demonstrate first aid treatment for snakebite.

8. Maintain one or more reptiles or amphibians for at least

a month. Record the food accepted, methods employed in eating, changes in coloration, shedding of skins, and general habits; OR keep the eggs of a reptile from the time of laying until hatching; OR keep the eggs of an amphibian from the time of laying until the transformation of the tadpoles or (salamander) larvae.

9. Do ONE of the following:

(a) Identify at night three kinds of toads or frogs by their voices. Imitate the song of each for your counselor. Stalk each with a flashlight and discover how each sings and from where.

(b) Take a recognizable photograph of a live turtle, snake, and amphibian.

(c) Give a brief talk to a small group on the subject of reptiles and amphibians. Use three living specimens or 20 pictures you have collected.

10. Give 10 superstitions about reptiles and amphibians and a correct explanation in each case.

Note: The Scout must use nonpoisonous reptiles only in fulfilling requirements 8 and 9.

Rifle and Shotgun Shooting

1. Do the following:

(a) Explain the meaning of each point in the Shooter's Safety Code. Agree to live up to it.

(b) Write 200 words on "My Responsibility as a Shooter."

(c) Explain the main points of the laws for owning and using guns in your town.

(d) Explain how guns are related to wildlife conservation.

(e) Explain the main points of the hunting laws in your state. Tell the kinds of game which may be hunted. Give any special laws on the use of guns.

(f) Explain how a good sportsman acts when handling guns.

2. Do the following:

(a) Describe two main differences between the rifle and the shotgun. Explain how these differences affect their use in the field.

(b) Draw and explain proper sight alignment and a proper sight picture with the rifle and the shotgun. Explain how these differences affect their use in the field.

(c) Explain the principles of good rifle shooting positions. Show three positions. Explain and show the differences between a good rifle shooting position and a good shotgun shooting position.

(d) Explain and show the right use of the trigger in rifle shooting. Explain and show the right use of the trigger in shotgun shooting.

(e) Explain and show shotgun swing. Explain why "follow-through" is so important.

3. Do the following:

(a) Explain the general principles of safe handling of guns and ammunition.

(b) Explain the safety precautions for guns having fixed or detachable magazines. Tell the special precautions for tubular magazines.

(c) Show how to check for safety at least THREE of the following. Explain how to check the others. (1) Rifle or shotgun—a) semiautomatic action; b) pump action; c) break-open or hinge action; d) bolt action; e) lever action. (2) Handguns—a) semiautomatic; b) revolver. (3) Muzzle loader of any kind. (4) Gas, pneumatic, or air gun.

(d) Show the following: (1) Safe carrying of a gun when alone or with other hunters. (2) Proper relationship of hunters when loading and unloading guns. (3) Safe handling of a gun when taking it out of and putting it in a car. (4) Safe gun handling when crossing a fence.

(e) Explain what is meant by "safe zone of fire."

(f) Explain the principles of safe storage of guns and ammunition at home.

(g) Explain what you would do if a friend visiting your home asked to see your target rifle.

(h) Explain the care needed to keep a gun in good and safe working condition.

4. Meet the standards shown in either "Option A—Rifle Shooting" or "Option B—Shotgun Shooting."

OPTION A—RIFLE SHOOTING

(a) *Score required.* Make a total score of at least 380 points out of a possible 600 on a total of 12 targets. Include the following: (1) Four targets from the prone position, each scoring at least 35 points out of a possible 50; (2) Four targets from the kneeling position, each scoring at least 25 points out of a possible 50; (3) Four targets from the standing position, each scoring at least 20 points out of a possible 50.

Note: You will have to make more than the minimum score on some targets to make the required total of 380 points.

(b) *Specifications.* Qualification may be fired on any one of the following courses of fire: (1) The 50-Foot Course—fired with the .22-caliber rim-fire rifle using the .22 cartridge. Use 50-foot A1, A2, A4, A5, A16, or A17 targets. (2) The 25-Foot Course—shot with any air gun or gas gun having a rifled barrel. Use 25-foot A18 or A19 targets. (3) The 15-Foot Course—shot with any smoothbore air or gas gun using BB's. Use 15-foot A45 or A46 targets.

Range distance: Measured from firing line to face of target.

Number of shots: Five shots per target.

Sights: Any not using glass.

Targets: Official BSA, NRA, or those issued by the director of Civilian Marksmanship.

Sling: The sling may be used only with the arm and hand supporting the barrel.

OPTION B—SHOTGUN SHOOTING

(a) *Score required.* Break at least 13 clay birds out of a possible 25 in each of five separate 25-bird events.

(b) *Specifications.* (1) The .22 Caliber Shotgun Course—fired with .22-caliber smoothbore gun, using .22 rim-fire shot cartridges. Targets must be of the Mo-Skeet-O type, about 2 inches across. Targets may be thrown from a hand or foot trap. (2) The Large Caliber Shotgun Course—fired with a standard shotgun of .410 gauge or larger. Targets shall be of the standard type, about 4½ inches across. Targets may be thrown from a hand or a foot trap. Standard skeet or trap courses may be used.

Rowing

1. Before doing other requirements, swim 100 yards as follows: 75 yards with any strokes. Then 25 yards on your back using an easy resting stroke. Then rest by floating as still as you can for 1 minute.

2. Do the following correctly:

(a) Launch and land a rowboat from and to shore.

(b) Bring a rowboat alongside a dock. Help a passenger into it. Row 50 feet, stop, pivot, and come back to the dock. Help the passenger from the boat.

(c) Tie a rowboat to a dock using: (1) A clove hitch. (2) Round turn and two half hitches. (3) A bowline. (4) A hitching tie or mooring hitch.

3. Do the following with another person in the stern:

(a) Row in a straight line for a quarter mile. Stop, make a pivot turn, and return to the starting point. If a quarter-mile straight course is not available, shorter courses may be used. Row back and forth in a straight line until a quarter mile has been covered.

(b) Backwater in a straight line 200 yards. Make a turn under way still backing water. Return to the starting point.

(c) Change places with your passenger. Show sculling in good form for 25 yards. Turn under way, and return to starting point.

4. Alone, or with one other person who is a swimmer, tip over a rowboat. Turn it right side up, get in, and paddle 10 yards with your hands or an oar. Tell why you should stay with a swamped boat.

5. Alone in a rowboat push off from shore or dock. Row 25 yards to a swimmer. Turn the boat so that the swimmer may hold onto the stern. Tow him to shore.

6. Show and explain the proper use of anchors for rowboats.

7. Describe the following:

(a) Dory, dory skiff, dinghy, punt, pram.

(b) Four common boatbuilding materials. Give some good and bad points of each.

(c) Two of the following rowlocks: Tholepin, box rowlock, ring rowlock, open top rowlock. Tell why pin-type rowlocks are not recommended.

8. Explain the advantages of feathering oars while rowing. Answer the following questions:

(a) How would you handle a rowboat if caught in a storm?

(b) How would you figure the number of pounds that might be carried under normal conditions in any given boat under oars?

(c) How would you properly fit out a rowboat, maintain and care for it during the boating season? How would you prepare and store it for winter season?

Safety

1. Prepare a safety notebook. Include: (a) Newspaper and other stories showing main kinds of accidents, (b) similar materials showing five causes of accidents, (c) the approximate yearly loss for main kinds of accidents in terms of deaths, injuries, and cost in dollars, (d) how a serious fire or accident involving you or your parents can change your life, (e) how safe practices and safety devices make your life easier and more pleasurable.

2. At three appropriate and safe locations spend 3 hours observing and listing safe and unsafe practices by (a) motor vehicle drivers, (b) pedestrians, (c) bicycle riders, (d) passengers (car, bus, train, or plane). Show this list to your counselor.

3. Do the following:
(a) Using a safety checklist, approved by your counselor, make an inspection of your home. Explain the hazards found, why they are hazards, and how they can be corrected.
(b) Review your family's plan of escape in case of fire in your home.

4. Sketch your troop meeting place (or another public building where people gather) and show exits. Are they adequate? Show which exit you would use in an emergency. Explain what should be done in a panic.

5. Make two safety checklists, one each for school and recreation. Include 10 points on each.
6. Make a plan for an accident prevention program for the following outdoor situations: (a) camping and hiking, (b) storm and wind, (c) water activities. Each plan should include an analysis of possible hazards, proposed action to correct the hazards, and reasons for the correction you propose.
7. Do ONE of the following:
(a) Report on a safety project that you helped to plan or took part in.
(b) Go with a company representative on a safety inspection tour of his company's premises (plant, or other place where people work). Make a report.
(c) Join a building or fire inspector on an inspection tour of a public building. Make a report.
(d) Plan a farm safety project to correct unsafe conditions and equipment hazards.
8. Tell how you contribute to the safety of yourself, your family, and your community.

Salesmanship

1. Explain the responsibilities of a salesman, how he serves his customers, and how he helps the economy grow.

2. Do ONE of the following (including the keeping of records): (a) Help your unit raise funds through sales either of merchan-

dise or of tickets to a Scout event such as a circus or show, accounting for more than your proportionate share of the sales.

(b) Earn money for yourself through retail selling, such as in a store.

3. Explain the value to a salesman of the following points, with regard to the item he is selling:

(a) Properly researching the market for the potential salability of the item.

(b) Proper training in sales, particularly concerning the item he wants to sell.

(c) If possible, visiting the plant that produces the item and seeing the manufacturing process.

(d) Continuing the follow-up with accounts after their primary purchase.

4. Develop and present to your counselor a sales program for a territory and product assigned by the counselor.

5. Assume you have the proper background and traits for a sales job that appeals to you. Prepare a written statement of your qualifications and experience that you could send to a prospective employer.

6. Interview a salesman and a retailer who buys from salesmen, using the questions provided in this merit badge pamphlet. Submit your answers to your counselor.

7. Make a sales presentation of a product assigned by your counselor of a reasonable value.

8. Investigate and report on career opportunities in sales. List high school courses most helpful in beginning such preparation.

Scholarship

1. Do ONE of the following:
(a) Show that you have had an average grade of 82 (B) or above for one term or semester.
(b) Show that for one term or semester you have improved your school grades over the previous period.
2. Do the following:
(a) Make a list of educational places where you live (other than schools). Visit one. Report on how you used the place for self-education.
(b) Interview two people other than teachers or school people. Find out the following: Where were they educated? What were they trained in? How did this help prepare them for the life they now live? Find out how each continues to educate himself. Write a report of your findings.
3. Get a note from the principal of your school* that during the past year your behavior, leadership, and service have been better than average.
4. Show that you have taken part in a school extracurricular activity.
5. Write an essay of 400 words on "How School Training Will Be of Value to Me in the Future."

---

*Or from another school person named by the principal.

459

5. Show and explain four of the different grades of wool from sheep.
6. Explain the uses of wool.
7. Make a set of pictures of at least five sheep breeds. Show samples of wool produced by each.

Sculpture

1. Model in clay or plasteline or carve in wood, soft stone, soap, or other soft material the following:
(a) A full-size human head.
(b) A small scale model of a group of animals or people in action.
2. Do the following:
(a) Make a plaster mold of a fruit or vegetable.
(b) In this mold make a copy of the fruit or vegetable.

Sheep Farming

4-H FFA

1. Explain the different uses of sheep.
2. From stock seen, name and explain characteristics of four leading breeds of sheep. Explain which is your favorite and why.
3. Give the origin and history of one breed of sheep.
4. Visit a meat market. Get information for making a drawing of a sheep. Mark off the meat grade sections of the animal.

Signaling

1. Make an electric buzzer, wireless, blinker, or other signaling device.
2. Send and receive in the International Morse Code, by sound device, a complete message of not less than 35 words, at a rate of not less than 35 letters per minute.
3. Show you can send and receive a message in the International Morse Code by wigwag and by light signaling device at the rate of not less than 20 letters per minute.
4. Send and receive by semaphore code at the rate of not less than 30 letters per minute.
5. Know when, where, and how the Morse and semaphore codes can be used to best advantage.
6. Tell about other codes and methods of signaling in common use.

Skiing

1. Do the following:

(a) Give the meaning of the Skier's Safety Code. Explain how you use it.

(b) Present yourself properly equipped and clothed for skiing. Show how to adjust your gear. Describe two kinds of ski bindings (including one release type). Talk over their merits.

(c) Show four exercises that help make a person fit for skiing.

(d) Make a list of the first aid equipment, food, other gear, and clothing you would carry in your pockets and pack on a day ski trip.

2. Do the basic and standard tests of the United States Ski Association listed:

(a) Walk on skis on the level. Use a one-step and a gliding step. Use your skis properly.

(b) Show a kick turn to the left and right on the level.

(c) Show side step up hill (about 15 degrees). Using the forward side step, go up a hill of 100 feet. Use a kick turn between traverses.

(d) Herringbone 50 feet up a 10-degree hill.

(e) Show straight running in a downhill position for 50 feet or more on a 10-degree hill.

(f) Show braking speed for 50 feet on a 10-degree hill. Show a double stem from a standing start, slowing down and speeding up while remaining in the double-stem position. End at named spot.

(g) Show four linked snowplow turns.

(h) Show four linked stem turns on a hill of 15 degrees or more.

(i) Go straight down a hill of 15 to 25 degrees. Show side-slipping, first in one direction and then the other. Link such slipping with turns.

(j) Show right- and left-stop christiania and four linked christiania turns on a hill of 15 degrees or more.

3. Do ONE of the following:

(a) Run a slalom course without faltering or a fall. The course will cause you to mix turns with parallel running. The course will be simple. The gates will allow smooth running. There will be 10 or 12 turns in a drop of about 150 feet.

(b) Make a cross-country ski run of 4 miles in 1 hour. This is to be over country of different kinds of terrain. There shall be travel on the level as well as up and down.

(c) Make four jumps on an official junior ski jumping hill. Show good form. Get good distance.

4. Describe the program and services of the United States Ski Association and the National Ski Patrol. Tell how they affect your skiing activities.

461

Small-Boat Sailing

1. Before doing other requirements, swim 100 yards as follows: 75 yards with any strokes. Then 25 yards on your back using an easy resting stroke. Then rest by floating as still as you can for 1 minute.

2. Describe the following:

(a) Sailing dinghy, catboat, yawl, sloop, ketch, schooner, cutter, and catamaran.

(b) Lateen, Marconi, leg-o-mutton, spritsail, standing lug, and sliding gunter.

(c) Jibs, spinnaker, mainsail, staysail, foresail, mizzen, and jigger.

3. Draw a Marconi-rigged and a gaff-rigged boat. Show in each drawing the following:

(a) The names of the sails and spars.

(b) The names of the sides and corners of all the sails.

(c) The names of the main parts of each. Explain their use.

4. Tell the general reason for the centerboard, keel and dagger board, bilgeboard, and leeboard. Tell their differences.

5. Describe how you would care for and maintain a sailboat and its gear throughout the year.

6. Do the following:

(a) Show how to tie the square or reef knot, clove hitch, bowline, figure-eight, sheet bend, slipknot, mooring hitch, and round turn with two half hitches. Tell the use of each.

(b) Show how to secure sheets so they don't jam. Properly coil and hang sheets or halyards.

(c) Make the following splices: long, short, and eye.

(d) Describe whipping, worming, parceling, and serving.

(e) Show how to throw a line. Show how to belay.

(f) Describe the kinds of fibers used in rope. Tell the advantages of each.

7. Know the sailing rules of the road. Include the following:

(a) Government rules of the road compared with the yacht racing rules in your locality.

(b) Rules about night lights on sailboats.

(c) How a sailboat legally becomes a motorboat.

(d) When a sailboat must keep clear of a motorboat.

8. List the safety gear and safety rules that are needed on a sailboat when under way.

9. Describe the safety procedures to use in the following: helping others, bad weather, running aground.

10. Explain the safety rules to use in the following: capsize, man overboard, picking up a tow.

11. Explain: center of effort, irons (in irons), luffing, apparent wind, loose-footed, wing and wing, and one design.

12. With the help of another person, show you can sail a boat properly by doing the following. Use proper safety.

(a) Get under way from a mooring or dock.

(b) Set the sails.

(c) Beat, reach, and run.

(d) Jibe.

(e) Reef.

(f) Anchor.

(g) Land at a mooring or dock.

(h) Furl or stow the sails.

13. Give a short history of the America's Cup.

Small Grains

4-H FFA

1. Show on a map of the United States where the following crops are grown in volume: rye, oats, barley, wheat, rice, flax, corn, soybeans, sorghum.

2. Run a germination test of 100 seeds each for two of the above crops raised where you live. Tell how you would treat these seeds to control disease.

3. Make a drawing of a field on which grain is to be grown. Show how you would control erosion. Describe crop rotation, strip farming, and contour farming.

4. Show in an outdoor seedbed or large box filled with soil how to prepare a seedbed. Plant two small grains native to where you live.

5. Explain steps farmers take to protect crops from disease and insects. Tell how they protect stored crops from rodents.

6. Make an exhibit of three or more grain crops. Show it at a school, fair, or Scout show. Include root systems, stems, leaves, and seeds.

7. Do THREE of the following:

(a) Collect, bottle, and label seeds of three grains grown where you live. Mark the variety and where grown. Show the number of days from planting to harvest.

(b) Do a soil conservation project. Describe how it was done. Give the results.

(c) Explain how you would prepare the field for two grains grown where you live. Give dates and methods of planting. Tell the amount of seed per acre. Describe "certified" seed.

(d) Help to harvest a crop of grain. Describe a combine and how it works.

(e) Visit a grain elevator, a seed sales plant, or a grain marketing center. Take notes. Write about what you learned.

(f) Visit a grocery store. List the grain products sold. Describe how one of these products is made.

(g) Prepare and serve a hot cereal food at home or camp. Describe protein and other food ingredients in cereal and grain products. Tell how they contribute to health.

2. Do the following:
(a) Define soil erosion.
(b) Tell why it is important. Tell how it affects *you*.
(c) Name three kinds of soil erosion. Describe each.
(d) Take pictures or draw two kinds of soil erosion.

3. Do the following:
(a) Tell what is meant by conservation practices.
(b) Describe the effect of three kinds of erosion-control practices.
(c) Take pictures or draw three kinds of erosion-control practices.

4. Do the following:
(a) Explain what a watershed is.
(b) Outline the smallest watershed that you can find on a contour map.
(c) Then outline on your map, as far as possible, the next larger watershed which also has the smallest in it.
(d) Explain what a river basin is. Tell why all people living in it should be concerned about land and water use in it.

5. Do the following:
(a) Make a drawing to show the water cycle.
(b) Show by demonstration at least two of the following actions of water in relation to soil: percolation, capillary action, precipitation, evaporation, transpiration.
(c) Explain how removal of vegetation will affect the way water runs off a watershed.
(d) Tell how uses of forest, range, and farm land affect usable water supply.
(e) Explain how industrial use affects water supply.

6. Do the following:
(a) Tell what is meant by water pollution.

Soil and Water Conservation

1. Do the following:
(a) Tell what soil is. Tell how it is formed.
(b) Describe three kinds of soil. Tell how they are different.
(c) Name the three main plant nutrients in fertile soil. Tell how they can be put back when used up.

(b) Describe ways water is polluted in rivers or streams. Explain what pollution does to fish and wildlife, boating, and swimming. Tell what it does to water for homes, farms, and factories.

(c) Tell what is meant by "primary water treatment," "secondary waste treatment," and "biochemical oxygen demand."

(d) Making a drawing showing the principles of complete waste treatment.

7. Do TWO of the following:

(a) Make a trip to one of the following places. Write a report of more than 500 words about the conservation practices you saw. (1) An agricultural experiment. (2) A managed forest or woodlot, range, or pasture. (3) A wildlife refuge or a fish or game management area. (4) A conservation-managed farm or ranch. (5) A managed watershed. (6) A waste treatment plant. (7) A public drinking water treatment plant. (8) Industry water use installation. (9) Desalinization plant.

(b) Plant 100 trees, bushes, and/or vines for a good purpose.

(c) Seed 1/5 acre for a good conservation purpose.

(d) Study a soil survey report. Describe the things in it. On tracing paper over any of the soil maps, outline an area with three or more different kinds of soil. List each kind of soil by full name and map symbol.

(e) Make a list of places in your neighborhood, camps, school ground, or park having erosion, sedimentation, or pollution problems. Describe how through individual or group action these could be corrected.

(f) Carry out any other soil and water conservation project approved in advance.

Space Exploration

1. Write a report on the history of space exploration. This is to be at least 500 words.

2. Do the following:

(a) Name from pictures five U.S. space launch vehicles. Do the same for seven U.S. unmanned spacecraft.

(b) Describe the reason for two U.S. space probes. Give the reason for two satellites. Give the main kinds of instruments in each.

(c) Name and describe the missions of at least three U.S. manned spacecraft.

3. Explain in writing, space problems. Tell how they have been solved. Do this for five of the following: radiation, meteoroids, weightlessness, food, sanitation, clothing, acceleration, deceleration, reentry, breathing, and communication.

4. Plan and build a model of a space launch vehicle. Use it to show how it would put a spacecraft in orbit. Show how a space probe might be launched from such spacecraft. Explain how a satellite stays in orbit.

5. Do ONE of the following:

(a) Describe six exercises that you might use to prepare yourself for space exploration. Explain what they do.

(b) Visit a space laboratory or space rocket launch facility. Report on your visit.

(c) Give a 5-minute talk on the values of space exploration at a troop meeting.

Sports

1. Explain sportsmanship. Tell why it is important. Give several examples of good sportsmanship in sports. Relate at least one of these to everyday citizenship off the sports field.

2. Take part for one full season as a member of an organized team in ONE of the following team sports:

Baseball	Rugby
Basketball	Soccer
Field Hockey	Softball
Football	Team Handball
Hockey	Volleyball
Lacrosse	

3.

(a) Take part for two months on a competitive basis in ONE of the following individual sports:

Bait or Fly Casting

Bowling	Judo
Cross Country	Orienteering
Diving	Paddle Ball
Fencing	Roller Skating
Golf	Swimming
Gymnastics	Table Tennis
Handball	Tennis
Horseshoes	Track and Field
Ice Skating	Wrestling

(b) OR earn ONE of the following merit badges:

Archery	Rifle and
Canoeing	Shotgun Shooting
Cycling	Rowing
Fishing	Skiing
Hiking	Small-Boat
Horsemanship	Sailing
Motorboating	Swimming
	Water Skiing

4. Make a set of training rules for the sports you picked. Tell why these rules are important. Follow these rules. Design exercises for these sports. Keep a record of how you do in these sports for one season. Show how you have improved.

5. Show proper techniques in your two picked sports.

6. Explain the attributes of a good team leader and a good team player.

7. Draw diagrams of the playing areas for your two sports.

8. Explain the rules and etiquette for your two sports. List the equipment needed. Describe the protective equipment. Tell why it is needed. Tell what it does.

Stamp Collecting

1. Show the use of the *Standard Postage Stamp Catalog;* or show the use of a special catalog for your collection in No. 6. Find at least five items picked by the counselor.

2. Explain the meaning of good condition of a stamp. Show one stamp that fully meets this term.

3. Show you can do the following:

(a) Use a perforation gauge to figure the perforation measurement. Do this on a stamp picked by your counselor.

(b) Use a magnifying glass. Study design and condition.

(c) Use the waterwork detector. Show how it may help identify a stamp.

(d) Use tongs and hinges. Mount a stamp in an album.

4. Show stamps to illustrate the following: perforation, imperforate, roulette, cancellation, cover, mint stamp, coil stamp, overprint, surcharge, engraving, and printing process other than engraving.

5. Show one stamp in each of the following classifications. Explain the purpose of each: regular postage, commemorative, semipostal, airmail, postage due, envelope, special delivery, precancel, and revenue.

6. Mount and show in an album ONE of the following:

(a) A collection of 750 or more different stamps from at least 30 countries.

(b) A collection of 150 or more different stamps from a single country or closely related countries.

(c) A collection of 75 or more different stamps on some special subject.

(d) A collection of 200 or more different special items. Use things as precanceled stamps, postage meters, revenue stamps, covers, and postal stationery.

Surveying

1. Do ONE of the following:

(a) From a point, measure by tape a range line north 330 feet and south 330 feet. Using the same point, measure a base line east 330 feet and west 330 feet. From one or more stations along the range or base line, take compass readings of trees, shrubs, and rocks. Pace the distance.

(b) Find and mark the corners of a lot described as follows: From a beginning point go (1) south 83 degrees 30 minutes east, 78 feet. Then go (2) north 35 degrees 30 minutes east, 86 feet. Then go (3) north 64 degrees west, 47 feet. Next go (4) north 89 degrees 30 minutes west, 51.2 feet. Then go

467

(5) south 22 degrees 30 minutes west, 88.9 feet to the beginning point. Your error of closure must not be more than 5 feet. From the corners, take compass readings of trees, shrubs, and rocks. Pace the distance.

2. From the field notes gathered for No. 1, draw a map to scale. Submit a neatly drawn copy.

3. Use the beginning point as a bench mark with an assumed elevation of 100 feet to determine the height of four other points.

4. Without crossing a distance of 300 to 3,000 feet, find its length, then tape the distance. Your answer must be within 5 percent.

5. Find the height of a point that can be checked by raising or lowering a tape. Your answer must be within 5 percent of the taped measurement.

6. Discuss the development and importance of surveying.

Swimming

1. Review swimming safety precautions in the Swimming skill award. Explain how swimming should be run safely for a group.

2. Swim 150 yards. Use the following strokes in good form: Sidestroke for 50 yards. Elementary backstroke for 50 yards. Any of the following strokes for the last 50 yards: overarm side, trudgen, trudgen crawl, American crawl, back crawl, or breast.

3. Surface dive headfirst into 6 feet of water and bring up an object from the bottom. Repeat using feetfirst method.

4. Show a plain front dive from a low board. Show a headfirst dive from a dock. Show a racing start.

5. In water 6 feet or more deep, while dressed in cotton shirt and cotton pants:

(a) Inflate shirt. Show you can float using it.

(b) Remove pants. Use them to float motionless for 1 minute.

6. Show the following elementary rescue methods:

(a) Rescue a person needing help within reach. Use either an arm or leg "reach" or a nearby object.

(b) Take off clothes on shore. Enter water feetfirst. Carry shirt in teeth or hand. Swim 30 feet. Swing one end of shirt to the hands of presumably drowning person. Tow him to shore.

7. Show survival swimming ability by doing the following:

(a) Enter water without sound. Swim silently for 50 feet. Go under quietly and swim three strokes under water before quietly coming up. Leave the water without sound.

(b) Float face up for 1 minute in a resting position, as nearly motionless as possible.

(c) Show floating face down in a relaxed position ("drownproofing"). Use minimum movement of arms and legs to raise head for breathing. Keep afloat this way for 10 minutes or longer.

Textile

1. Talk over how textiles are important to man.
2. Do ONE of the following:
(a) Visit a textile plant or school. Report on what you saw.
(b) Explain the main steps in making a fiber into cloth. Name the machines used in each step. Tell what each machine does.
(c) Describe four ways of adding color to textiles.
3. Do ONE of the following:
(a) Get one sample in each of the three major classes of woven fabrics: (1) clothing, (2) home use, (3) industrial.
(b) Get one sample of knit or double-knit fabric. Compare these to those that were woven.
4. Do TWO of the following:
(a) Show one good way to test fibers for recognition.
(b) Waterproof a piece of cloth.
(c) Weave a piece of a cloth. Use a simple loom that you have made yourself.
(d) Define 10 of the following terms: fiber, filament, yarn, tufting, nonwoven, tricot, plastic, Jacquard, full fashioned, Greige goods, bleaching, finishing, mercerization, screen printing, roller printing, durable press, sanforizing, preshrunk, water repellent, and fire retarded.
5. Get small samples of two of the following natural fibers: cotton, wool, asbestos, silk, or linen. Get two of the following classes of man-made fibers: rayon, nylon, polyester, glass fiber, and acrylic. Tell how two of these are different. Give the advantages of each.
6. Talk over or make a written report on jobs in five main branches of the textile industry.

Theater

1. See or read three full-length plays. These can be from the stage, movies, or TV. Write a review of each. Comment on the story, acting, and staging.
2. Write a one-act play. It must take 8 minutes or more to put on. It must have a main character, conflict, and a climax.
3. Do THREE of the following:
(a) Act a major part in a full-length play; or act a part in three one-act plays.
(b) Direct a play. Cast, rehearse, and stage it. The play must be 10 or more minutes long.
(c) Design the setting for a play. Make a model of it.
(d) Design the costumes for five characters in one play set in a time before 1900.
(e) Show skill in stage make-up. Make up yourself or a friend as an old man or woman, an Indian, a clown, or a monster as directed.
(f) Help with the building of scenery for one full-length or two one-act plays.
(g) Design the lighting for a play; or handle the lighting for a play under guidance.
4. Pantomime any ONE of the following picked by your counselor.
(a) You have come into a large room. It is full of pictures, furniture, other things of interest.
(b) As you are getting on a bus, your books fall into a puddle. By the time you pick them up, the bus has driven off.

(c) You have failed a school test. You are talking with your teacher. He does not buy your story.

(d) You are at camp with a new Scout. You try to help him pass a cooking test. He learns very slowly.

(e) You are at a banquet. The meat is good. You don't like the vegetable. The dessert is ice cream.

5. Explain the following: proscenium, central or arena staging, spotlight, floodlight, flies, highlight, lowlight, scene paint, stage brace, cleat, stage crew, batten, foyer.

6. Do two short entertainment features that you could give either alone or with others for a troop meeting or campfire.

Design to be determined

Truck Transportation

1. List the major truck lines serving your town.

2. Tell the importance of trucks in providing freight service to towns served by no other means. Name some towns in your area served only by trucks.

3. Describe how trucks fit in with other forms of transportation.

4. Describe the difference between the gasoline engine and the diesel engine that power trucks. List the advantages of each.

5. Visit a truck terminal and do the following:

(a) Check the use of communications facilities. What means are used? How does a dispatcher control over-the-road trucks? How does he control local trucks?

(b) Find out from the maintenance department the following: How many miles are engines run between overhauls? How do they get better tire life? How are breakdowns prevented? What maintenance work is done by the company? What work is done outside the company?

(c) Talk with a professional truck driver about safety. List five safe-driving rules he follows.

6. Outline the general organization of a truck company. Describe what each department does.

7. Do the following:

(a) List five jobs with trucking companies. Describe each.

(b) Talk with the safety director or driver supervisor about the requirements for becoming a professional truck driver.

8. Name five government agencies that regulate trucking. Tell what they regulate.

9. List six different kinds of trucks. Tell the service each gives.

10. Assume that you are going to ship 100 pounds from your town to another by truck. Explain in writing how you would handle this shipment from your town to a place 500 miles away. Tell when the things are needed. List what truck lines are used. Tell how it is insured for damage. Tell when the shipment must be made if it is to arrive on time.

11. Define the following terms: A.P.U., bill of lading, blue label, common carrier, containerization, ETA, log book, fifth wheel, OS&D, LTL.

Water Skiing

1. Do the following:
(a) Before doing other requirements, swim 100 yards as follows: 75 yards with any strokes. Then 25 yards on your back using an easy resting stroke. Then rest by floating as still as you can for 1 minute.
(b) Spend 6 hours in practice of the skills.

2. Know the Water Skier's Safety Code. Promise that you will live up to it. Follow it in all water work for this badge. Know the safety precautions that must be used by the boat operator in pulling skiers.

3. Show the following water-skier signals to safety observer in boat: in gear, start, faster, slower, speed required, speed OK, turns, whip off, jump, stop, back to dock, cut motor, skier in water. Help others to ski by acting as the safety observer in the boat.

4. Show you can adjust binders to fit. Put on skis in knee-deep water.

5. Make a shallow-water start on two skis without help.

6. Show you can fall properly in avoiding an obstacle. Drop handle and coast to a stop without loss of balance.

7. Show you can recover skis that have come off during a fall. Put skis on in deep water. Make a deep-water start on two skis without help.

8. Show you can cross both wakes and return to center of wake without falling. Repeat three times.

9. On two skis, jump off the wake. Lift both skis clear of the water.

10. During a demonstration run, lift one ski clear of the water for 2 seconds. Then do the same with the other ski. Show that you are steady and comfortable on skis at all times.

11. Ski on one ski for 30 seconds. Show reasonable control.

471

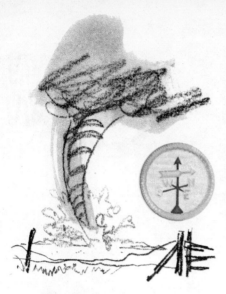

Weather

1. Find out about the climate where you live. Tell how it influences business, farming, clothing, transportation, housing, and recreation.

2. Do the following:

(a) Tell what meteorology is. Visit a weather station. Explain how observations are taken. Describe the following instruments: wind vane, anemometer, barometer, thermometer, hygrometer, rain gauge.

(b) Tell how radar, satellites, and electronics are used in weather forecasting.

(c) List your radio and television stations. Show the times they broadcast weather forecasts. Tell how weather warnings are given.

(d) Read a weather map. Describe the meaning of the symbols used.

3. Do the following:

(a) Draw a cross section of the atmosphere. Show its three main layers.

(b) Describe hurricanes, tornadoes, cyclones, squall lines, and blizzards. Tell the differences between them.

(c) Estimate the wind speed and direction by seeing how these affect trees, flags, etc.

4. Do the following:

(a) Make a drawing showing the water cycle.

(b) Identify types of clouds. Tell the differences between them.

(c) Tell the difference between drizzle, rain, freezing rain, sleet, hail, and snow.

5. Do the following:

(a) Make a simple wind vane, rain gauge, anemometer, hygrometer, and nephoscope.

(b) Make a daily weather chart for a month showing: (1) Dew or frost in the morning. (2) Wind direction, temperature, kinds of clouds, and precipitation at the same time each day.

(c) On the chart, list the weather forecasts from radio or television at the same time each day. List how the weather really turned out. Count the times forecast and what really happened were the same.

Wood Carving

1. Give the qualities of wood that are useful for carving. Tell why you chose the wood used in Nos. 4 and 5.

2. Do the following:
(a) Describe five wood-carving tools. Tell their use.
(b) Describe several kinds of sharpening stones. Tell how they are used.
(c) Show how to sharpen a pocketknife and other tools used in wood carving. Use a sharpening stone and a "slipstick" that you have made.
3. Show the safety principles for using a pocketknife and wood-carving tools.
4. Plan and carve in the round a simple object. Prepare it for finish.
5. Plan and carve in low relief a design on some simple object. Prepare it for finish.

Woodwork

1. Do the following:
(a) Describe how timber is grown, harvested, and milled. Tell how lumber is cured, seasoned, graded, and sized.
(b) Collect and label blocks of six kinds of wood useful in woodworking. Describe the chief qualities of each. Give the best uses of each.
2. Do the following:
(a) Show proper care and use of all working tools and equipment which you own or use at home or school.

(b) Sharpen correctly the cutting edges of two tools.
3. Make something useful of wood. Use a saw, plane, hammer, and brace and bit to make it. Cut parts from lumber which you have measured and squared from working drawings.
4. Do the following:
(a) Make a working drawing of a carpentry project. List the material needed.
(b) Make it. Report on time spent and cost of things used.
5. Do any TWO of the following:
(a) Make working drawings of some things needing—(1) Beveled or rounded edges or curved or incised cutting. (2) Miter, dowel, or mortise and tenon joints. Make it.
(b) Make something for which you have to turn duplicate parts on a lathe.
(c) Make cabinet, box, or something else with a door or lid fastened with inset hinges.
(d) Help make and repair wooden toys for needy children; or help carry out a carpentry service project.
(e) Make a scale model of a house or barn.
(f) Talk with a cabinetmaker or carpenter. Find out the job opportunities and conditions, needed training, apprenticeship, work hours, pay rates, and union organization for woodworking craftsmen where you live.

INDEX

A

Ad Altare Dei, **360-61**
Advancement, **23**, **68-91**
Age to join, inside cover
Aids to Scouting, **369-70**
Ailanthus, **282**
Air
  mattress, **235**; pollution, **312**
Alamo, The, **118**
Alcohol use, **336**
Alder, **286**
Algae, **284**
Allergic reactions, **139**
Alpha Omega, **360-61**
Alpha Phi Omega, **362**
Aluminum foil meal, **273**
American crawl, **350**
Animal bites, **142**
Animals, **282-96**
Ankle bandage, **137**
Announcements, **183**
Ant, **282**
Apple
  baked, **271**; tree, **296**
Application, Scout, inside cover
Aquarium, **300**
Aquatic food chain, **277**
Ararat, **360-61**
Arrowhead plant, **288**
Arterial bleeding, **126-28**
Artificial respiration, **130-31**
Aspen, **294**
Assistant
  patrol leader, **21**; senior patrol leader, **26**
Awards (earning), **68-91**
Ax
  care, **254-55**; parts, **254**; safety, **255-56**; sharpening, **254**

B

Baby-sitting, **161**

Backstroke, **352**
Baden-Powell, **368-72**
Badge
  meaning, **58**, **86**; parts, **86**; placement, **59**
Badger, **296**
Balanced menu, **248**
Bandages, **146**
Barbiturates, **339**
Barnacle, **284**
Basic foods, **249**
Bass, **286**
Bear, **294**
Beard, **370**, **373**
Beaufort scale, **298**
Beaver, **286**
Becoming a Scout, inside cover, **32-67**
Bedroll, **220**, **234**
Beech, **292**
Beginner swimming, **347**
Bell, Alexander, **115**
Belt loop, **71**, **92-93**
Be Prepared, **12**, **52-55**, **121**
Bindweed, **282**
Birch, **292**
Birchbark Rolls, **373**
Bird feeders, **304**
Birds, **282-96**
Birdseed lunch, **198**
Birthday, Scouting, **373**
Biscuit cup, **269**
Biscuits, **268**
Bites, **138-42**
Bittern, **288**
Blackberry, **296**
Black widow, **139**
Blankets, **234**
Bleeding, **126-28**
Blisters, **135-36**
Bluebird, **296**
Bluefish, **284**
Blue-green algae, **284**
Bobcat, **294**
Bobwhite, **296**
Boer War, **370**
Boone, Daniel, **115**
Bowline, **226**
Bow saw, **253**
Boyce, William, **372**
Boys' Life, **16-17**

B-P, **368-72**
Brave, **48**
Breadstuff, **268-69**
Breaking camp, **244-45**
Bronze Palm, **91**
Brown recluse spider, **139**
Brownsea Island, **371**
Buddy plan, **347**
Budget items, **160**
Bugler, **27**
Bullhead, **286**
Burns, **134-35**

C

Cactus, **290**
Cactus wren, **290**
Camp
  breaking, **244-45**; cleanup, **240-43**; clothing, **221**; council, **30**; plan, **216**; summer, **30**
Camping
  equipment, **218-19**; patrol, **22**; troop, **8-9**
Camping skill award, **214-45**
Camporee, **28-29**
Campsite selection, **230**
Canoe bases, **359**
Cattails, **288**
Cedar, **282**
Celery, wild, **288**
Centipede, **282**, **290**
Cereal, **270**
Charcoal, **237**, **259**
Cheerful, **46**
Chemical burns, **134**
Chickadee, **292**
Chief
  Scout, **373**; Scout Executive, **373**
Child care, **161**
Chili, **272**
Chimney swift, **282**
Chipmunk, **292**
Chlorophyll, **314**
Chopping block, **257**
Chowder, **273**
Citizenship rights and responsibilities, **110-11**

474

Jellyfish float, **349**
Joining, inside cover, **32-67**
Jones, John Paul, **119**
Jump-reach, **327**
Junior assistant Scout-master, **26**

K

Kabob, **266**
Kelp, **284**
Key, Francis, **108-9**
Kind, **44**
Kindling, **259**
King, Martin Luther, **115, 119**
Kingfisher, **286**
Kitchen, camp, **261**
Knife, **252-53**
Knot of badge, **86**
Knots, **225-29**

L

Lakes, **286-87**
Land food chain, **276**
Lark bunting, **296**
Latrine, **195, 201, 233**
Law, Scout, **32, 38-51**
Leadership Corps, **27**
Lean-to fire, **259**
Lee, Robert E., **115**
Legal problems, **157**
Letter writing, **184**
Liberty Bell, **117**
Librarian, **27**
Lichens, **296**
Life requirements, **90**
Lifesaving, **354-55**
Lightning, **194**
Limpets, **284**
Lincoln, **114, 119**
Litter, **63**
    bag, **243**; prevention, **320**
Lizard, **290**
Local council, **28**
Lockjaw, **145**
Locust, **282**
Lodgepole pine, **294**

London fog, **372**
Loon, **286**
Lost, **195**
Loyal, **40**
LSD, **338**
Lunch, hike, **198**

M

Macaroni and cheese, **272**
Mackerel, **284**
Mafeking, **370**
Magnetic North, **209-10**
Maine Wilderness Area, **359**
Map
    and compass, **213**; hike, **210**; orientation, **212**; scale, **208**; symbols, **211**; use, **208, 212-13**
Maple, **282, 288, 292**
Maps, **208, 211**
Marijuana, **337-38**
Marshes, **288-89**
Masturbation, **334**
Mayfly, **286**
Meadowlark, **296**
Meaning of badge, **86**
Meat, **266-67**
Medal of Merit, **367**
Medical tag, **123**
Menu planning, **250**
Merit badge
    application, **73**; counselor, **10-11, 73**; idea, **10-11**; pamphlet, **73**; plan, **72-73**
Merit badge requirements, **374-473**
Mesquite, **290**
Mile Swim, **364**
Milk production, **317**
Mink, **288**
Minuteman, **118**
Moon shell, **284**
Morphine, **339**
Mosquito, **282**
Moss, **282**
Moth, **282**
Motto, Scout, **12, 52-53**
Mount Rushmore, **114**

Mouse
    house, **282**; white-footed, **292**; deer, **284**
Mulberry, **282**
Multiflora rose, **296**
Muskrat, **288**
Mussels, **284**

N

Narcotics, **339**
National
    anthem, **102, 108-9**; Eagle Scout Association, **363**; emblem, **86**; high adventure bases, **358-59**; jamborees, **363**; office, inside cover; Scout Commissioner, **373**
Natural resources, **67**
Nature
    communities, **279**; identification, **282-96**; scavenger hike, **203**; signs, **280-81**
Ner Tamid, **360-61**
News sources, **188**
Newt, **286**
Nighthawk, **282**
Night hikes, **194**
Nonswimmer, **347**
Northern Wisconsin Canoe Base, **359**
Norway rat, **282**
Nosebleed, **144**
Nutcracker, **294**

O

Oath, Scout, **12, 32, 34-37**
Oatmeal, **270**
Obedient, **45**
Ocean, **284-85**
Ocotillo, **290**
Old
    Glory, **97**; Ironsides, **117**
Opium, **339**
Order of the Arrow, **362**

480